DATE

BOOKS BY MORTON M. HUNT

HER INFINITE VARIETY
The American Woman as Lover, Mate, and Rival

MENTAL HOSPITAL

THE NATURAL HISTORY OF LOVE

HER

INFINITE

VARIETY

THE AMERICAN WOMAN AS

LOVER, MATE AND RIVAL

by MORTON M. HUNT

HARPER & ROW · PUBLISHERS

NEW YORK AND EVANSTON

Grateful acknowledgment is hereby made to the following publishers and persons for permission to reprint the materials specified:

Howard Allen, Inc.: miscellaneous excerpts from case materials appearing in Dating, Mating, and Marriage by Jessie Bernard, Helen E. Buchanan, and William M. Smith, Jr., copyright © Howard Allen, Inc., Publishers, 1958;

Doubleday & Company, Inc.: lines from Archy and Mehitabel by Don Marquis, copyright 1927 by Doubleday & Company, Inc.;

Holt, Rinehart and Winston, Inc.: miscellaneous excerpts from case materials appearing in Premarital Dating Behavior by Winston Ehrmann, copyright © 1959 by Holt, Rinehart and Winston, Inc.;

Chappell & Co., Inc.: lines from "A Hymn to Him" (from My Fair Lady), copyright © 1956 by Alan Jay Lerner and Frederick Loewe, Chappell & Co., Inc., New York, N. Y., publisher and owner of allied rights throughout the world.

THIS BAEDEKER

TO A FAR COUNTRY

IS FOR JEFFREY

CONTENTS

The innate abilities and potentialities of men and women have changed but little through the ages. However, man's concept of woman and woman's concept of herself have varied a good deal from culture to culture and even within given cultures.

Throughout history, women have demonstrated amazing versatility and vitality in fulfilling the roles expected of them. This has been accomplished in conjunction with their continuing basic biological function of bearing children, which has been unaltered by science, technology, or culture. In some societies and in certain pioneer communities, women have succeeded in carrying the burden of providing economic necessities. In patriarchal societies they have been dutiful and undemanding helpmeets. In societies with matriarchal institutions they have been recognized as scholars, political leaders, queens, priestesses, and goddesses. It cannot be overlooked that even in cultures where women could not assert themselves directly, their influence has been of vital significance.

In the United States today our women face the conflicting demands of diverse value systems. The impact of a patriarchal culture some six thousand years old is still apparent. The Christians, who took over this inheritance from the Jews and the later Greeks, accepted ideals and established institutions which suppressed women's opportunities. This was effected through laws which deprived them of independence, and through religious teaching which emphasized their subservience to men. Even today many psychologists attempt to restate the patriarchal creed of dichotomy between men and women, in labeling men active and intellectual, women passive and emotional.

In conflict with this, the ideal of our democracy is that each individual has the opportunity to develop to the limits of his or her innate capacity. This concept has enabled women today to participate more and more in productive enterprises and in professional and public life. It has also inspired them to share their experiences as women in a joint effort with men to achieve the ideals of both. There is abundant evidence that, despite the lingering influence of patriarchal values, women are attaining their goals. And whether one wishes to reverse this trend or not is hardly the point, for to do so in contemporary America, in the face of our economic system and of increasing technological facilitation of living, is both unrealistic and backward looking.

It is with this historical perspective, and with a recognition of these conflicting cultural values, that the modern, educated, and privileged American woman, of whom Morton Hunt writes, must be explored and understood. Mr. Hunt's book is not only of essential significance to women, but equally to men. To read it is like opening a window to a strong, refreshing breeze.

Drawing freely upon history, psychology, and sociology—and bringing them all to life with a profusion of human details and intimate documents—Mr. Hunt has written a book about modern woman that begins where the others have left off. He persuades the reader that there is nothing innately wrong with modern women, and that their difficulties exist in the conflicts produced by the continuation of outworn cultural values in a progressive modern democracy. He tells us that women are not the opposites of men, but are beings of equal worth. He decries the return of women solely to the home, and finds their best chance of success and fulfillment in modern life lies in the combining of the roles of mate, mother, and independent member of society. By happy circumstance, he argues, this at the same time suits modern man the best.

In my travels I have seen that women are able to attain a degree of contentment under a multiplicity of family conditions, and I have found no scientific evidence which can lead us to conclude that women are necessarily happier, better or worse mates and mothers, following one rigid prescription for life under all sorts of external circumstances. But as a clinician who has worked for thirty years in America with thousands of women and men troubled about their marriages and themselves, my observations make me want to emphasize that woman's potential contribution to her culture as a human being of worth is fortified and given scope when her family and community support and encourage her endeavors, but is dampened and disappointed by criticism and condemnation.

Perhaps it is because Mr. Hunt has put into delightfully acceptable form many of these undocumented thoughts, and because our respective work has led us both to believe in the strengths and potentialities of women, that I find it so congenial a task to write this foreword.

—EMILY H. MUDD, *M.S.W., Ph.D., Sc.D.*
Director of Marriage Council of Philadelphia, Inc.
Professor of Family Study in Psychiatry
School of Medicine, University of Pennsylvania

This book is an attempt to describe certain chronic problems and dissatisfactions in the life of that female who, if one ignores queens and such, may be the luckiest of her species in history—the modern middle-class American woman. Her good fortune and her dissatisfactions alike arise from the fact that contemporary life offers her, and indeed almost forces upon her, a multiplicity of roles and a bewildering variety of desires and purposes. I have tried to see her entire and also anatomized, role by role; in so doing, I hope I have shown the kinds of adaptations she is currently making to her manifold needs and opportunities, and indicated the direction in which she is evolving—a direction I view less glumly than many of her intemperate and choleric critics.

Because woman's life is motivated more by her relationship to man than by any other single factor, I have concerned myself chiefly with married women, and dealt only fleetingly with spinsters, widows, and divorcees. Similarly, because the many-sided woman is a type found primarily among the better-educated and middle-to-upper income groups, I have made no systematic effort to deal with the lives of less-educated and lower-income women. Judging, however, by what we have seen of the downward diffusion of cultural ideals in the past half century, that which is true today of the women I am writing about will be true of a very much larger segment of American womanhood in another generation or two. The many-sided woman of today is distinctly in the minority, but she is the model for American womanhood of the future.

The argument of this book rests on a foundation of the facts and

findings existing in hundreds of studies made by scholars and behavioral scientists. But rather than impede the reader's way with a
tangled underbrush of footnotes, I have indicated my sources at the
end of the book, where those who disagree with or question various
statements can find the origins of the evidence.

In addition to these scientific and generally published sources, I
have drawn many of my illustrative materials and direct statements
by women from three bodies of nonscientific and unpublished
sources. First, I constructed a questionnaire and sent it to several
hundred women, almost all of them married and many of them college-educated. This did not constitute a true random sample, according to the protocols of social science, but an analysis made for
me by a graduate sociologist indicates that in fact it did turn out to
be a quite fair sampling of the kind of women the book deals with,
including reasonable proportions of each major ethnic, religious,
and occupational segment of upper-middle-class society. Nevertheless, I have rarely made generalizations based on this sample alone,
but used the questionnaire replies chiefly as illustrations of the findings more rigorously arrived at by psychologists and sociologists.

Second, I had access to a vast mass of manuscripts or extracts of
manuscripts sent to *Redbook* by its readers. In the fall of 1960 the
editors of that magazine announced that they would pay for pub-
lishable articles by young mothers telling about their problems or
significant experiences. Within the first year, some ten thousand
manuscripts had come in from all sorts of women discussing many
aspects of their lives; and though this mass of material too is not a
scientific sample, it is an extraordinarily rich source of confidences,
experiences, and attitudes, all expressed in the words of women
themselves rather than those of an interpreter of women.

Third, for the past six years, while writing *The Natural History
of Love* and the present book, I have kept notes on my voluminous
correspondence with hundreds of strangers, acquaintances, and
friends on the very subjects I deal with here. I have had only to
mention the subjects I was studying to have information and misin-
formation thrust upon me by people ranging from directors of men-

tal hospitals to those ultimate oracles of wisdom, New York City cab drivers. These files are not the basis of any theory, nor should they be, but they have furnished some of the flesh for the bare bones of theory derived from sound but less entertaining sources.

More people deserve my thanks than I can name. I am grateful to all the women who replied so candidly and sincerely to my questionnaire; I wish I could personally thank each of them here, but I promised them anonymity and must thank them *en masse*. I am also deeply grateful to Mr. Robert Stein, Editor of *Redbook*, for granting me access to the file of manuscripts from his readers. A number of people gave me assistance in the form of consultation or the loan of research materials. They include Mrs. Opal D. David, formerly of the American Council on Education, Dr. Harold Feldman of Cornell University, Dr. H. David Kirk of McGill University, Professor Mirra Komarovsky of Barnard College, Dr. Emily H. Mudd of the Marriage Council of Philadelphia, and Dr. Ruth Hill Useem of Michigan State University; also, Miss Caroline Bird, Dr. Samuel Deitcher, Mrs. Henry S. Drinker, Miss Helen M. Hacker, Dr. Florence Kluckhohn, and Mr. Tom Mahoney; and many others who, I hope, will forgive me for not listing them here. I owe an obvious and immense debt to certain other people whom I did not consult, but whose ideas I have freely availed myself of; they include, most notably, Drs. Margaret Mead, Robert O. Blood, Robert F. Winch, Karl Menninger, and Robert K. Merton. Among federal bureaus, I owe special thanks to the Bureau of the Census, the Women's Bureau, and the Children's Bureau, all of which have been most cooperative and helpful.

Among the people who have read this book in manuscript and offered guidance of various sorts were Dr. Mudd; Dr. Louis Ormont, psychoanalyst and instructor in the Department of Home and Family Life of Teachers College, Columbia University; and Mr. Robert L. Heilbroner, gifted writer, friend, and unsparing critic. The research assistants who at one time or another helped verify and correct the data were Mrs. Cynthia Epstein, Mr. Alan Fuchs, Mrs.

Linda Moses, and Miss Betsy Wallace. Miss Violet Serwin was once again my uncomplaining and marvelously accurate amanuensis.

Authors almost always pay respectful thanks to their wives for having been long-suffering and patient. Mine has been neither, but I owe her my sincerest thanks for another reason: there is no way to understand women as effective as trying to understand just one of them, a project on which I have thus far spent sixteen years. I like to think there is wisdom in the old saying that "He who knows one woman knows all women; he who knows all women knows no woman."

What makes men write books about women? Some diligent mole of a scholar ought to burrow through the 14,700 books on women—almost all of them by men—in the New York Public Library, and add his scrap to human knowledge by compiling their motives in several scores of Figs., Tabs., and Apps. Lacking any such study to go by, I imagine that some men write about women because, like St. Jerome, they hate them and enjoy castigating them on the pretext of improving their character; some because, like Casanova, they love women but have got to that sad age where they can relish them only in loquacious retrospect; and most because, whether hating or loving them or both, they wish they could understand how any creature seemingly of the same species as themselves could be so peculiarly different.

My own motive is in part the latter. The female first began to seem bewildering to me when I was ten years old. That year, I was shifted from one classroom to another in mid-term, and in my new room, two seats forward on the row to my right, there was a vision of delight named Esther Morris, whose tilted little nose, saucy expression, and long brown hair instantly mesmerized me. She kept glancing back at me from time to time and giggling, which I took to indicate disdain; after a few days, however, she opened a copybook during class and let me see for a moment something she had written in block letters. It took me three days of short peeks before I was able to read the message, which looked like this:

READ	AND	THAT	AND
UP	YOU	I	YOU
AND	WILL	LOVE	LOVE
DOWN	SEE	YOU	ME

"Bliss was it then to be alive," if I may borrow Wordsworth for such a context. I recall a number of recess periods during which we chased each other around the schoolyard or hung by our knees on the monkey bars side by side, in the full flush of Young Love. Then on Saturday, thinking to increase the measure of my joy, I went to her house and rang the bell. Someone brusquely told me she wasn't in, but I had seen her peeping out from behind an upstairs curtain. In school on Monday she ignored me, and I whispered desperately to her until, perfidiously, she stood up and told the teacher I was pestering her. Esther, ah, Esther, what did I do wrong? Where did I fail? I was only ten, but woman had already become a puzzle; and like many another man, I have been trying to understand her ever since.

Yet I have grounds more relative than this. Several years ago, while writing a history of love, I was struck by the curious paradox of modern American woman: she has almost everything that thoughtful and intelligent women have wanted and lacked for many centuries, yet there are many indications that she is not really content with herself or her place in contemporary life. The emancipated middle-class American woman—free to train her mind and use it, free to move about unchaperoned in her society, free to marry for personal joy, free even to accept or refuse her mate's passion at night —is more nearly a complete human being than any Western woman, save a handful of queens, viragos, and salonières, since the days of the Roman Empire. Yet far from being completed and fulfilled by all this, it appears that she is often unsure of what to do with her freedoms, distracted and intimidated by her many opportunities, fearful that she may lose her femininity if she experiments too far with them, and fretful, bored, and discontented when she limits herself to safe, traditional ways. In brief, she is afraid to be all the things she can be, and dissatisfied to be only some of them.

All this is true, to be sure, only of some modern women, not all. Opinions as to the frequency of discontent differ, but Margaret Mead conservatively estimates that over one-quarter of the women in the United States are "definitely disturbed" about their lot as women, the proportion being greater among those very middle-class pace setters who are the most favored and emancipated. If one were to include lesser levels of disturbance of which women are not clearly or consciously aware, the figures would be far higher.

But what troubles them in this earthly female's paradise? Many things—most of which cluster about the several bewilderingly different roles a woman can now play in life, and the conflicts among them. She can be primarily a seductress, but that grates against her functions as a loving mother or an efficient businesswoman; she can be a community worker or a careerist, but either of these takes her away from her home and her children; any and all of these roles, furthermore, seem to get in the way of her being her husband's lover, let alone his companion—both of which functions are, in turn, somewhat inconsistent with being his housekeeper. Is she a person, her own person, at all, or merely an ill-assorted aggregate of satisfactions of other people's needs? And which kind of person, whether her own or theirs, should she choose to be, and why?

In a medieval French barony, a frontier American settlement, or an Inca village, there were specified sets of activities and duties which a girl anticipated and grew into; whatever the hardships or shortcomings in these several patterns, each of them was at least unambiguous. Woman's chief problem was how to play her part well; modern woman has the prior and additional problem of which part or parts to choose, and how to combine them without disaster or else give up some of them without bitterness. "Somehow we must *find* ourselves," bravely proclaims a young woman writing to me from Wharton, Texas, "we must learn our personal abilities and limitations, proceed carefully through the maze of things to be done, picking the few that genuinely fulfill us"—but she does not know what they are. Anne Lindbergh's *Gift from the Sea* was one of the great best-sellers of the 1950's because it poetically pleaded that woman's life was too complicated, and needed pruning and the rediscovery of its essentials; but she, too, gave no answers.

In more formal sociological language, Dr. Florence R. Kluckhohn of Harvard University writes, "Women give every evidence of being extremely ambivalent and confused about their roles as women, their expectations for themselves, and their responsibilities to others." *What to be* is a problem that men do not face and women in the past never knew; it troubles modern women to a degree their husbands rarely realize, even after living with them for years. An old friend of mine learned from me of my intention to write a book on this subject, and with kindly concern tried to dissuade me. "No doubt some women can't cope with the conflicting demands made upon them," he wrote, "and can't solve the problem of evolving a means of fulfilling themselves, but I feel they are a small minority and require individual professional care." Then, apparently, he showed the letter to his wife, for he added in a chastened marginal note, "Seems I should have asked my spouse. She says the 'small minority' is 100 percent, and furthermore *she* hasn't found a solution and doesn't know anyone who has."

Woman's confusion is no trivial matter. Some pessimists have held that her present freedoms and conflicts are responsible for a host of social ailments: alcoholism and neurosis in herself, waning potency in her husband, delinquency in her children, and such other assorted ills as ulcers, divorce, teen-age immorality, and suburban conformity. More fairly, the eminent sociologist Talcott Parsons has written that "the feminine role is a conspicuous focus of the strains inherent in our social structure." The health of society, of the family, and of woman all interact upon each other; woman is not wholly or largely to blame for present social problems, but she is an integral part of whatever has produced them.

The very forces that make women fearful of using their intellectual abilities, for instance, have also prevented them from serving their society well and relieving some of its problems. The shortage of physicians is an example: three-quarters of Russian doctors are women, as against a little over 6 percent of American doctors. Russian women have fewer of the amenities of life, but they are serving their society better, perhaps as a result. Ironically, though, American woman's decision to limit herself to domesticity hurts her more than anyone else, by virtually ending her purposeful life at about forty-five, when she still has thirty years to spend—decades which are a slow shriveling rather than a harvest time. The paradox of American woman that I stated a moment ago can be restated thus: out of her very satisfactions she makes her dissatisfactions, and out of her disregard of society's needs there sooner or later comes her failure to meet her own needs.

The strains and maladaptations of modern woman's life are all implicit in one question she never quite answers. Each child, as he grows up, asks himself, "Who, or what, am I?," but modern woman never really finds out. If she is not sure who she is, plenty of people have been ready to tell her who she ought to be. She is urged by some to preserve her figure, by others to improve her mind, and by still others to be fertile and earthy. She is told to quit envying men and competing with them, and to get back into the kitchen and nursery, but Hollywood actresses, lady novelists, women delegates to the United Nations, and female fashion buyers are held up to her as examples of successful women. She can choose her medicine from a wide-ranging pharmacopeia: Simone de Beauvoir's polemic *The Second Sex* assures her that women will never know genuine happiness until the system of marriage is done away with and every woman is fully independent of the male; psychoanalyst Marynia Farnham proclaims in *Modern Woman: The Lost Sex* that she will only find real peace and happiness by returning to sewing, baking, fertility, and dependency, forgoing all the delusive pleasures of emancipation; and hundreds of others offer solutions over the whole intervening range.

All of the more extreme answers offered are, to tell the truth, simple rather than difficult; they narrow down, define, crystallize, specialize. And because they are simple and clearcut, they have a great surface appeal. But my thesis is that in the long run they tend to be maladaptive and disappointing. The hundreds of research studies I read, the thousand-odd statements I collected from American women, the file cabinet I filled with notes and documents showing the effects on their lives, and the lives of those around them, of divers modes of adjustment, have led me to think that there is a better answer, though surely not a simple one. Quite briefly, it is this: under the conditions of modern life, the only choice that will lastingly satisfy a growing number of middle-class women is the conscious effort to play many roles and perform many functions harmoniously, the mature decision in favor of the complicated life and of full development.

I hope to show that this complex answer not only serves woman best, but those around her as well: when she is not intent only on being seductive, she can make the best lover for modern man; when she is not totally concerned with being a homemaker and mother, she can do each thing better than a woman obsessed by the effort; and when she is not fiercely bent on competing with man, she is able to gain her competitive ends without blocking the way to all the others.

This general doctrine is far from being a simple, clear-cut panacea for all of woman's ills. Rather, it is a highly flexible approach, and fittingly so; women vary greatly, and so do the men they marry, the friends they acquire, the children they bear, and the towns they live in. There is no universal prescription for woman's happiness in what follows; but I hope that there do appear numerous ways to minimize conflicts and increase satisfactions, and that from them the intelligent woman can assemble the pattern that best fits her own personality and background, her marriage and social milieu.

If a single, simple plan for achieving the happy life made sense, I would be delighted to set it forth, but I do not believe that such a thing exists. Despite all the proselytizers and partisans in history, the good life has never proven to be attainable by only one route; and though multi-role answers for woman's problems are neither simple nor easy, I comfort myself with a notion that philosophers as unlike as Cicero and Spinoza have espoused: noble ends are almost always difficult to achieve.

PART ONE

WHAT IS

A WOMAN?

CHAPTER ONE

THE MANY FACES

OF WOMAN

1 THE ETERNAL FEMININE

"There is no new thing under the sun," observed the author of Ecclesiastes when our civilization was twenty-two centuries younger than it now is, and even earlier Thucydides had written that many things "have happened, and always will happen, as long as the nature of mankind remains the same." Over the intervening centuries the idea that human nature never changes has been popular with men. No doubt it is a handy point of view for the dominant and successful.

A special case of the general viewpoint is the belief of men that the feminine personality has an immutable timeless configuration—*das Ewig-Weibliche,* as Goethe called it. Bits and scraps of evidence, gathered from far shores and distant centuries, are often offered in support of the doctrine of the sameness and invariance of woman's nature. The face of a mother grieving for a newly dead child, it may be pointed out, will tell much the same tale whether she is a Berlin *Hausfrau* or the wife of a Congolese tribesman. A whore in Hong Kong is apt to have a strong family resemblance to a whore in Covington, Kentucky, or even to one in a Roman comedy of 150 B.C. A little joke made by some unknown calligrapher centuries ago may seem in its way to prove the point: in the ideographs used by the Japanese, a scribble that remotely resembles a human figure signifies "woman," but a cluster of three of them is the symbol for "noisy." Or consider a gently spoofing poem in which two well-to-do women meet on a gala day. The first one starts by complaining about the terrible traffic; the second tells what she dislikes about her house and its location; both voice complaints about their husbands, discuss the stupidity of housemaids, and bemoan the high cost of new fabrics; finally they rush off to the festival somewhat late, distractedly shouting orders to the household help. The poem, entitled "Adoniazusae," was written by Theocritus in the third century B.C.

But such odds and ends of "proof" are not enough; men all too easily see and collect such bits of evidence to bolster their opinions, while walking blindly past those that contradict them. Without this propensity they would long since have had to admit that "human nature," despite a fundamental substructure of some sort, has varied immensely over the centuries and assumed widely differing forms in different societies. Certainly it must be so with woman's nature, or how could men have held so many contradictory notions about her, all with such utter conviction? On the one hand they have believed that women boss them around (Cato the Elder: "We Romans command all men, and our women command us"), and, on the other hand, that women are feeble, and are bossed around by man:

> Women are born to thraldom and penance,
> And to ben under mannes governance.   *(Chaucer)*

Woman is the finest product of Nature (Milton: "O fairest of Creation, last and best of all God's works!"), but she is a hopeless mess (Plautus: "There's no such thing as picking out the best woman; one is worse than another"). She ennobles and transforms man:

> O woman! lovely woman! Nature made thee
> To temper man: we had been brutes without you.   *(Otway)*

yet she is the sinful cause of his brutish condition (Clement of Alexandria: "She was created as a helpmate for her husband, yet brought only ruin upon him"). According to two learned inquisitors of the fifteenth century, she is endlessly lustful (*Malleus Maleficarum:* "A woman is more carnal than a man. . . . Carnal lust is insatiable in women"), although a widely read nineteenth-century gynecology textbook by the American physician Dr. William Acton later assured the world that normal women are quite free of sexual appetite, any statement to the contrary being nothing but a "vile aspersion" on their character.

Where shall one find the truth in this mass of contradictions? The very question implies that there is *a* truth, a single correct picture of the character of woman. This is just what has often been taken for granted—but it is an absolute prerequisite to any useful thinking about modern woman to be certain whether this is so or not, and to ascertain what factors in her make-up limit the extent to which she can vary her life without harm. Nature produced dinosaurs in the swampy Mesozoic era, but when the swamps dried up their doom was inevitable. If woman, too, has a fixed nature which can thrive only under prescribed conditions, then she had better abjure all others—to be specific, she should forgo most of the appealing possibilities in her modern life as being inappropriate for her nature, and potentially disastrous to herself and her society.

Sage maxims, poetic phrases, and cutting epigrams will not help us settle this question: as we have seen, many men have spoken wisely about women, and contradicted each other at every point. Let us then start with objective data; let us look at some of the actual evidence. And, first of all, the evidence of history.

2 THE GOOD WIFE AND THE LADY

Nearly everyone admits that women in remote cultures often act very different from women in our own, but even within the confines of Western civilization the past three thousand years of history have produced a broad spectrum of dissimilar styles of womanhood. Women—at least, those of the dominant class, who have been the cultural ideals—have assumed such radically different forms that a taxonomist from some other planet might be hard put to know whether to assign them all to the same genus, let alone species.

It is highly instructive, for instance, to contrast the ideal of the woman in Old Testament times with that of woman in the medieval French aristocracy. The ancient Hebrew woman was above all a chaste, thrifty, hardworking mother and homebody, who never dreamed of pampering her body for beauty's sake, indulging in flirtations, pursuing cultural interests, or finding outlet for her creative urge. She hardly needed such distractions; her life, as set forth ten centuries before Christ (perhaps by Solomon himself) in Proverbs 31, was full enough:

> She seeketh wool, and flax, and worketh willingly with her hands. She is like the merchants' ships; she bringeth her food from afar. She riseth also while it is yet night, and giveth meat to her household, and a portion to her maidens. She considereth a field, and buyeth it: with the fruit of her hands she planteth a vineyard. . . . She layeth her hands to the spindle, and her hands hold the distaff. . . . She maketh herself coverings of tapestry; her clothing is silk and purple. . . . She maketh fine linen, and selleth it; and delivereth girdles unto the merchant. . . . Favour is deceitful, and beauty is vain: but a woman that feareth the Lord, she shall be praised.

How many women kept to this demanding schedule one cannot be sure, but the combination of fertile wife, skilled artisan, hard worker, and prudent household manager was the ideal and goal of Hebrew womanhood. One finds it, too, in many a later frontier or agrarian society, and even among the thrifty, hard-working bourgeoisie of recent centuries—wherever, in fact, it was more valuable for a woman to be productive than to be inspiring or delectable.

Yet in other situations woman's nature was conceived of quite otherwise. Mundane and productive work were not always her métier; she was made of finer stuff, and had nobler purposes. The medieval lady of noble blood, for instance, toiled not, neither did she spin, but applied herself to the perfecting of her intricate clothing and toilette; to manipulating her trailing sleeves and towering headdress with grace; to practicing rhetorical conversations about manners, chivalry, and love; and to conducting idyllic love affairs via all the complications of intermediaries, secret messages, and occasional trysts under difficult circumstances. She was able to run her household, too, through servants, and may even have practiced complete stewardship of the estate when her husband was off to war, but this was not seen as any part of her basic charm or fundamental femininity and almost nothing is said about it in the literature of the period.

The nature of woman was not that of a good and faithful worker, but of a beautiful, semi-angelic inspiration, and a vision of purity and divinity in bodily and desirable form. Inspired by love of his lady, the knight strove to improve his character, serve God and liege lord faithfully, and fight in the lists valiantly; as a reward for all this he was granted "favors," beginning with the kiss and sometimes ending, after long service, with her whole person. One should add, of course, that none of this applied to the lady's husband, who could possess her any time he wanted, and no nonsense about it. But no inspiration either; he found *his* incentives and ideal in the form of some other lord's wife, which seems only fair. Meanwhile, no one said a word about either's rising while it was yet night, planting vineyards, or laying her hands to the spindle.

It thus seems that the dissimilar circumstances in which the Good Wife of Proverbs and the medieval lady lived caused them to develop, with facility, into radically different kinds of women, and caused their men to hold radically different views of the essential, timeless "female nature." Evidently this immutable female nature is mutable after all, among the potent forces shaping it being the state of economic development of a social order and the amount of leisure available to its ruling class. Man's theory and woman's practice of female nature are greatly affected by the presence of servants or slaves, the level of productivity, the assurance of income or tribute, and the like. Woman will be what she has to be; she will not be what she needn't be. If women must labor fourteen hours a day to insure the survival and comfort of her family, she becomes the kind of woman who finds it natural to do so; if she need do no productive work, her personality evolves in other directions, which she finds normal and inevitable.

Even more important, any pattern may be inappropriate and hurtful if attempted in the wrong surroundings. The Good Wife would have seemed addled and a disgrace to her husband in a French baronial castle of the twelfth century, while in ancient Israel the courtly medieval lady would probably have been thrown out of the window, like Jezebel.

In the wealthy and complacent first century in Rome, the Emperor Augustus yearned to reform morals and to restore woman to her proper nature; to please him, his wife Livia spun wool and wove cloth. But almost no other patrician women followed her lead, for it was as artificial and useless as the milking of cows by the court ladies at Le Petit Trianon. It may even have been damaging: Augustus insisted that his daughter Julia likewise spin and weave, much to her distaste, and as soon as she married and escaped her home, she revengefully flung herself into dissipation, ending in compulsive promiscuity, for which her father had to exile her to a remote barren island. The story may have a moral: if you would reform woman, first try to understand her; and if you would understand her, first lay aside all your assumptions about her fundamental nature.

3 "A SORT OF NATURAL DEFICIENCY"

A perennial question about woman's nature is whether it is actually different in kind from man's, or simply a lesser and inferior version of it. The classic Greek answer was that man's nature was the basic design, and woman's not a different one but merely an incomplete and inadequate copy, all her distinctiveness consisting of imperfection. "We must look upon the female character as being a sort of natural deficiency," said Aristotle impartially and without malice. Applying this to the problem of reproduction, he even held that the woman contributes to the new fetus only corporeal matter; soul comes from the man. The philosopher was stating in theoretical terms the everyday attitude of the Greek upper-class man, who often treated his wife as an uneducated and not very bright servant, kept her in strict household seclusion, and in consequence found her unworthy of his thoughts or his leisure time. These he lavished instead on male friends, and when he brought them home for dinner, his wife and daughters stayed discreetly hidden in the women's quarters. When he was emotionally drawn toward any woman (rather than to a boy), it was to some high-grade courtesan, trained in singing and playing, in the arts of entertaining, and in the use of bright wit and scintillating talk—in fact he could fall in love with her precisely because she was not typical of her sex.

This general view of woman fitted well with the ideas of the later Hebrews and the early Christians as to woman's inferior mental and moral equipment. Was not Eve a sort of afterthought of God, and a mere by-product of Adam's body? Was it not her feeble moral character and her stupidity of judgment that caused the Fall? "And Adam was not deceived, but the woman being deceived was in the transgression" (I Timothy 2:14); no wonder the Lord commanded her be ruled by her husband, and Paul said he would not suffer her to teach —her judgment simply could not be trusted. The Christian ascetics and misogynists even came to identify her seemingly incomplete groin with this overall inferiority; her sexual organs became not only the source of the Fall, but the contemptible symbol of her whole character. *Mulier speciosa templum oedificatum super cloacam,* said the clerics, following Boethius—Woman is a temple built upon a sewer.

Even when in kindlier times men ceased to see moral inferiority in woman, they believed that intellectually she was far beneath man, and women themselves usually agreed. Sir Thomas More, who educated his daughters more liberally than did most other Renaissance English lords, one day found one of his daughters in tears over a Latin version of the New Testament, of which she was making a concordance. Gently he took the work away from her and told her that such strenuous mental efforts were not meant for women; she meekly, almost thankfully, agreed.

One can find any number of similar scenes in the recorded social history of the West. Scores of generations of women have chattered to each other after dinner of children, clothes, food, and love affairs, while their men discoursed of metaphysics, natural history, finance, and diplomacy. Monasteries turned out hundreds of textual commentaries, chronicles, translations, and theological studies, while nunneries produced prayers and some kindly deeds. The New England Puritans prized their women highly, but Governor John

Winthrop, musing in 1645 about the insanity of the wife of Connecticut's Governor Hopkins, typically surmised that it had come
from her exertions at reading and writing. "If she had attended her
household affairs and such things as belong to women," he wrote,
"and not gone out of her way and calling to meddle in such things
as are proper for men, whose minds are stronger, etc., she had kept
her wits." As totally dissimilar a man as the elegant Lord Chesterfield felt almost exactly the same way: "Women are only children of
a larger growth," he wrote to his son; "they have an entertaining
tattle, and sometimes wit, but for solid, reasoning good sense, I
never in my life knew one that had it." Any number of women have
concurred and played the part expected of them, the terms of which
were ideally set forth by Tennyson:

> Her faith is fixt and cannot move,
>   She darkly feels him great and wise,
>   She dwells on him with faithful eyes,
> "I cannot understand; I love."

Yet in sharp contradiction to all this, any good historian can provide a long list of names of women who have used their minds just as
if they were complete and wholly formed human beings. Despite
Aristotle's low opinion of woman's intellect, there were a number of
women among the active Pythagorean philosophers of Greek times,
and at least twenty-eight of their names are known to history. (Aristotle may not have been impressed; he had no great opinion of
Pythagorean thought to begin with.) Other schools, too, had their
female adherents and luminaries. Epicurus lived in amicable retreat
with his beloved Leontion, a brainy courtesan who wrote critiques of
other philosophers, and Socrates himself stated (perhaps not altogether seriously) that his elegant theory of love and its relationship
to abstract ideas had been given him by Diotima, a priestess at
Mantineia.

But more to the point than these scattered examples are the
periods of history when, for complex reasons, a whole class in society
would believe that women were intellectually and spiritually on a
level with men, and when women accordingly used their gifts with-

out apology or embarrassment. In Rome of the first and second centuries, for instance, the life of upper-class woman was not all gluttony, games, and adultery with Nubian slaves. Roman women—some of whom, at least, were virtuous—also read books and wrote letters, studied philosophy, went to the theater, dabbled in finance, banded together on occasion to demand tax reforms, and at dinner chatted wittily and even learnedly about poetry, mythology, history, rhetoric, and religion—all without losing their wits like poor Goodie Hopkins of Connecticut.

During the Italian Renaissance women again flourished intellectually. Well-to-do merchants and noblemen found it attractive when a woman could read Greek and Latin, quote from the classic philosophers and playwrights, and gather humanists and poets in her palazzo to make a heady atmosphere of thought and creativity. Some Renaissance women became serious scholars, others took up astronomy and the sciences, and some actually received doctorates in the universities.

These may have been exceptional women, but they reflected the cultural assumptions about womankind. One authority on the Renaissance, Jacob Burckhardt, summarized the situation thus: "[Renaissance] woman was regarded as in a position of perfect equality with man. One should not allow one's self to be deceived by the cunning and in part malicious researches respecting the presumptive inferiority of the beautiful sex. . . . The education of the woman of rank, just as well as that of the man, sought the development of a well-rounded personality in every respect."

In France and England during the Age of Reason, woman had another brief efflorescence of intellectuality as the salonière, that patroness of thought and learning whose drawing room was a meeting place for the literati, and whose role was not only that of hostess, but of moderator and participant in the discussions. This was a type of woman much admired by the more liberal spirits of the time; indeed, it almost seems that woman's sex appeal was not diminished but enhanced by her intellectuality in that era. Ninon de l'Enclos and Madame du Deffand are the prime cases in point. Ninon supported herself as a high-level courtesan, choosing her current lover (taste-fully having only one at a time) from among the gentlemen in her salon, who included such men as Saint-Evremond, Boileau, and La Rochefoucauld. Yet she was not only a patron of bold thinkers, but one herself, whose ideas had a considerable impact in the upper echelons of her society; King Louis XIV himself was wont to ask his agents, a bit apprehensively, "What is Ninon saying now?" She long remained extremely attractive to men and is said to have begun her last love affair when nearly sixty. Madame du Deffand, whose salon a century later was just as splendidly crammed with the illustrious, had a long love life capped by a tempestuous platonic romance with Horace Walpole that began when she was seventy and concluded only with her death eighteen years later. Intellectuality as a specific prescription for feminine appeal has been somewhat out of vogue ever since Romanticism introduced the image of the lovable bird brain—but how many bird brains have still captured men's hearts at three score and ten years of age? To be fair, the use of the intellect does not automatically produce sex appeal; but it is undeniable that at certain times in the past men have believed that woman is a com-plete human being in her mind and spirit, and that it is right—and attractive—for her to act accordingly. And so she has, and liked it very well.

4 MODERN WOMAN AND THE LEFTOVERS OF HISTORY

In much the same way, one could rummage around in the past and pull out other pairs of strikingly contrasting models of womanhood. Christian tradition, for instance, has almost always held women to be lacking in the gifts and graces necessary to act as a religious leader, let alone be God or a part of the Trinity; but the Egyptians, the Thracians, the Babylonians, Greeks, Norse, and Romans all wor-shiped goddesses who ruled over certain areas of their lives, and in most of these cultures women served as priestesses alongside male priests. Again, Western society has long supposed woman to be unfit for the exercise of command, or of the military arts; but in *Woman as Force in History* Mary Beard has offered an extraordinary collection of examples to prove that women have, from time to time, been excellent administrators, oligarchs, and generals.

None of this, to be sure, proves that woman is identical with man, but it certainly seems to prove that women are not identical with other women. The evidence of history is clear enough: woman has worn many a different face, with soul to match. In her character there may be certain unalterable components, but when seen in the long perspective of history they appear the lesser part of her. History does not give us the passport to woman's mystery, but it does show us that men's theories about her timeless nature are good only when issued (if then); yesterday and tomorrow they are not valid at all.

Is it a part of the female nature to faint at embarrassing moments? Certainly—that is, sometimes; can you picture the likes of Lucrezia Borgia or Carry Nation fainting? Is it a part of woman's nature to yearn for motherhood? Of course—but not always; the Roman matrons avoided it by a host of contraceptive methods, the aristocratic ladies of the eighteenth century handed their infants over to wet nurses and servants without a pang of regret, and for seventeen centuries nuns have practiced the ultimate rejection of the maternal ideal while idolizing the most notable mother figure in Western culture. Is woman vain, gossipy, and shrewish; or flighty, gentle, and shy; or foolish, adorable, and lovely? She is each of these sets of things—at least, in eras when she is not modest, secretive, and sweet-natured; or loyal, strong, and courageous; or shrewd, fearsome, and hard-bitten.

But at least in many a bygone time people knew what they thought; whatever their notion, it was coherent and clear. Today we are perplexed and uncertain because we have not one but a whole spectrum of conceptions of woman's nature. Within the memory of any woman in her middle years are the late-Victorian prudery and seclusion of her mother, the aggressiveness of the suffragettes who angered her father, the frivolity of the flappers of the 1920's (she may have been one of them herself), the toughness of female war workers, and the suburban domesticity of the young postwar "to-getherness" housewives.

So rapidly have these patterns succeeded each other in the transition from Victorian society to our present one that a host of self-contradictory or unworkable images of woman is embedded in law and custom. One cultural ideal of the woman is the Hollywood love goddess, but let the attractive young wife try to pattern herself after that ideal and she becomes either the pariah of the neighborhood or, what is far worse, its laughingstock.

A husband may expect his wife to run a whole household without confusion or blunders, while maintaining that women do not have the heads for business; conversely he may entrust any number of important matters to his private secretary, while maintaining at home that he alone can balance the checkbook, choose the right car, or make sense of local politics.

A woman's income is taxed at the same rate as a man's, which would seem to imply equality of economic responsibility, but only twelve states have statutes requiring a wife to support her husband if he is ailing and unable to support himself. Women everywhere in this country vote at the same age as men, and with the same weight per ballot, but only thirty states require a woman to serve on jury duty; seventeen others excuse her from this democratic duty upon her request, on the grounds of her other duties, and Alabama, Mississippi, and South Carolina, with Southern gallantry, exclude her from state juries altogether on the medieval grounds of her "defect of sex."

Music is one of the fields in which women are particularly acceptable, and are thought to have considerable feeling—yet, although there are many women ensemble members and soloists, there is not one notable female orchestra conductor in America today. Cooking, sewing, and tending the sick are activities at which women are supposed to be innately superior, but when jobs involving these skills pay well or carry power, women are deemed inappropriate in them: you cannot imagine a lady chef at Le Pavillon, a female head tailor at Brooks Brothers, or a woman president of the American Medical

Association. Even in the field of infant care, it is Dr. Spock who tells millions of young women what to do; nobody ever asked Mrs. Spock what she thought.

The American woman is, in sum, a set of odds and ends of her own history, worked into the strange fabric of her new contemporary self. She is something of a lover and mistress, something of a housewife and mother, something of a success-oriented emancipated woman; she is a bit of a courtesan, of an intellectual, of the biblical Good Wife, and of a handful of other leftovers of time, all assembled upon the canvas of her present days and ways. She may be man's lover, his mate, or his rival—or something of each, blended and entangled in any one of a score of ways. History has given her the precedent for each of these aspects of her being, but it has never told her how to be all of them at once; this is her problem today, and her continuing quest.

CHAPTER TWO

THE MYTH OF THE

FEMININE CHARACTER

1 "BOUND TO SERVE, LOVE, AND OBEY"

As G.B.S. once observed, we learn from history that we learn nothing from history. The preceding chapter is therefore probably not sufficient to convince most readers of woman's potentialities and variability. The majority of people brush aside such historical facts and cling to the cultural clichés of our own era, which they take to be eternal truths. In this mythology, woman is inherently entrancing but difficult, warm but hypersensitive, frail but stubborn, gifted (in her fashion) but much in need of a wiser, stronger head to rule her, and, though less competent and creative than man, more loving and lovable. Such evidence as we saw in the previous chapter is dismissed as dealing with exceptional individuals or exceptional times.

Believers in these clichés rely not on objective evidence, but on the emotionally convincing trivia of daily life. Do they not see plainly enough every day that females have a special and fundamentally different nature from males? Little girls don't get as dirty or make as much racket as little boys. They screech about snakes and bugs, stick their tongues out at enemies, and throw a ball like an unstrung marionette. Older ones giggle, fuss about their hair, and develop unmistakably regular round handwriting. As for women, they almost never write dirty words or draw obscene sketches on the walls of public toilets, they invariably drop their gloves when getting up, they are unable to grasp the theory involved in parking a car in a tight space, and they are constitutionally incapable of getting their money ready in time or of having anything on hand smaller than a ten-dollar bill.

Above all else, everyone "knows" that man is intellectual and logical, while woman is emotional and—well, "intuitive" is the polite way to put it. But the crotchety Professor Higgins of *My Fair Lady,* wondering, "Why can't a woman be more like a man?" was not inclined to be so tactful:

> Why is thinking something women never do?
> Why is logic never even tried?
> Straightening up their hair is all they ever do.
> Why don't they straighten up the mess that's inside?

And since they can't think, it obviously follows that they can't accomplish anything of merit. Surveys have shown that even intelligent and successful women subscribe to this distressing corollary; as I. A. R. Wylie writes, "For the life of me I cannot think of any sphere of activity in which [woman] is even passably successful, except in the matter of surviving." A youthful woman doctor in California, who gave up her practice to take care of her children—she had seven at the time she replied to my questionnaire*—is an ideal spokesman for the cultural myth:

Woman is tied to earth and things of the heart and hearth, while man's mind is free to soar into the ether. The wail of the baby and the dust on the table keep woman down to terra firma; there is a primordial pull which keeps her close to realities and the clutter and contentment of the home. Men all but burst with creativity and imagination, but no woman ever has it in full degree—the best are but minor poets, minor musicians, minor scientists. Men are the lofty thinkers and the makers of theory; women are the intuitive thinkers who evaluate other people swiftly, and usually accurately.

The net effect of woman's behavioral oddities and these clichés of thought is to justify the age-old patriarchal position, which has never been summed up better than it was by Shakespeare's termagant Kate, after she had been beaten into her senses by a strong man:

> I am asham'd that women are so simple
> To offer war where they should kneel for peace;

---

* See Prefatory Note, page xii.

> Or seek for rule, supremacy, and sway
> When they are bound to serve, love, and obey.
> Why are our bodies soft and weak and smooth,
> Unapt to toil and trouble in the world,
> But that our soft conditions and our hearts
> Should well agree with our external parts?

It is none too easy to make this kind of philosophy mesh with contemporary democratic ideas, but many try. The late Pope Pius XII, in a speech reminiscent of *Animal Farm,* told the fifteenth World Congress of Catholic Women that men and women were "equal in rights and rank" but that the husband was the head of the wife and she must therefore obey him. Many non-Catholics, ranging from ministers to psychiatrists, hold a similar view: Governor Mark Hatfield of Oregon, for instance, recently wrote a magazine article telling how he and his wife, though equals, have kept the "obey" in marriage (his wife, of course, doing the obeying). It is not an easy doctrine to believe in, but one succeeds with trying. As the White Queen told Alice, it only takes practice to be able to believe impossible things; "why, sometimes," she said, "I've believed as many as six impossible things before breakfast."

2 *THE SO-CALLED PSYCHOLOGY OF WOMAN*

This traditional patriarchal position on woman has recently been dusted off and given a new luster by Freudian psychoanalysis—an influence usually thought to be radical rather than conservative, and revolutionary rather than old-fashioned. How does this paradox come to be? The crux of it is the famous Freudian apothegm "Anatomy is destiny," which is taken to mean that woman's biological traits define and control her personality, fatefully and predictably. The major factor in woman's life is her inevitable discovery, as a little girl, that she lacks that fascinating appendage boys have. Freud, who derived his theory from his studies of neurotic patients, held that this awareness causes a severe trauma, which he labeled "penis envy." When she first notices her deficiency, the little girl gets the childish idea that she has been deprived of a penis she once owned; this leads to a sense of imperfection and inferiority; then, as she learns that not only she, but all women, are the same in this respect, "she begins to share the contempt felt by men for a sex which is lesser in so important a respect."

Freud speculated that there are only three possible outcomes of this situation: sexual inhibition and neurosis arising from woman's dislike of her own sexuality; pseudo-masculine distortion of character (aggressiveness, career interests, and the like); or growth into true femininity, with the development of modesty (to conceal her genital deficiency), vanity about her looks by way of compensation for her lack of masculine equipment, and charm (winning people being a kind of substitute for conquering them). The road to femininity is thus paved with acceptance of one's defects, and resignation to one's inferiority; it therefore produces acquiescence, passivity, and a willingness to be dominated, subdued, or even hurt. Still worse, since the girl has no castration fear (being already deprived), she does not develop as much of a self-controlling conscience as do boys; she has no ultimate incentive for developing a strong moral sense, and so can never become a great lawgiver, philosopher, or spiritual leader.

Freud himself offered these opinions with becoming modesty, but a number of orthodox Freudian analysts, writers, and social critics found his psychology of women a convenient hook on which to hang their traditional belief in male superiority and dominance.* Some have even seen it as part of a great Law of Nature: does not the sperm lash about and fight its way to its goal, while the ovum lies dormant, waiting to be found and invaded? Does not the whole animal world exhibit powerful males chasing, biting, subduing, and penetrating their females? Does not the sex act itself consist of the male's attacking, possessing, and symbolically wounding the female

---

* Other psychoanalysts, especially those with cross-cultural perspectives, have not done so, finding Freud's psychology of woman his least satisfactory work; among them have been Ernest Jones, Clara Thompson, Karen Horney, and Abram Kardiner. Currently, many modern psychoanalysts consider that the orthodox Freudian position was valid for his day, but not for modern times.

with a living weapon, and the female's resisting, then yielding, and symbolically permitting herself to be wounded by it? Wilhelm Stekel writes that woman gets her greatest pleasure from the "will to self-subjection"; Helene Deutsch describes intercourse as a "sadistic act of taking possession" by the man and a "masochistic subjugation" by the woman, for whom "the attraction of suffering is incomparably stronger than for men"; and Simone de Beauvoir says of woman's initial experiences of love-making that "the humiliation [the young girl] anticipated is undergone in fact: she is overpowered, forced to compliance, conquered."

These dense and depressing notions find their way, in diluted and cheerier form, into more popular kinds of writing. A recent article in *Good Housekeeping*, for instance, told women how to know if they are truly feminine (Answer: they are if they accept their "altruistic" and "womb-centered" nature, forgo pseudo-masculine aims, and instinctively put husband and children "way before self"). The heroine of the novel and movie *Marjorie Morningstar* scorns domesticity and dreams of a career, but in the end finds that true feminine happiness lies in total conversion to dishes, diapers, mucus, rosebush suckers, and a wholesome dash of religion. A prize novel of 1961 (*Vangel Griffin* by Herbert Lobsenz) has as its hero a young American who rediscovers the meaning of love, and other truths, in bed with a properly submissive Spanish woman; enlightened, he comes home determined to set things right again in America—a job which includes working for the repeal of woman's suffrage. The ideas in such writings may have taken new vitality from Freud, but St. Paul himself would have applauded them as a return to older and better ways.

3 THE WEAKER SEX: A BIOLOGICAL PARADOX

How valid is the cultural cliché and its apotheosis in orthodox psychoanalytic writing? Any good biologist might advise us to disbelieve at the start any alleged law of nature which equates activity with the male and passivity with the female, for it is *not* true that throughout the animal kingdom the female is always weak, inferior, and passive compared to the male. Female spiders, many female in-sects, and most female fish are larger and stronger than the male. In some species, such as one of the crickets, the female actively mounts the male in intercourse, and among some butterflies the male, after copulation, is held and dragged helplessly along by the female in her flight—hardly a lordly or dominating situation. Male birds generally mount and more or less enter the female, but their dominance some-times pertains only to this act: among parakeets, for instance, the females henpeck the males throughout the year except during the breeding and nesting season.

Compared to fish, whose mating is like the mailing of letters by different people in the same box, most land animals do show male dominance and female receptivity during the sex act, but for good reason: if the female won't hold still, the male can't do his job, and the species becomes extinct. Actually, sexual relations among most animal species are a mutual affair, according to the exhaustive study *Patterns of Sexual Behavior* by Professors Clellan Ford and Frank Beach of Yale University. The female, when in heat, approaches or excites the male by her provocative actions just about as often as he approaches or excites her; even more significantly, male animals rarely force their sexual attentions on nonreceptive females, but pur-sue only those in heat, who willingly receive them after some playful skirmishing.

As for the psychological results of physical differences, it is ques-tionable whether they must naturally and inevitably follow the directions of conservative tradition. Some anthropologists and psy-choanalysts have found that in certain cultures with a different ethic and a different type of family life from our own, there is little or no evidence of a female castration complex, no clear-cut male Oedipus complex, and no disparagement of the female genitalia as compared to the male. These "inevitable" consequences of bodily differences may actually be contingent upon the social milieu.

But what of man's general physical superiority? Doesn't it neces-sarily make woman feel inferior? Man has a larger head, a heavier brow ridge, a bigger frame, more powerful muscles, and heavier knobs on the end of his long bones; these made him feel superior to woman, and rightly so, in any and every age when he was whacking away at beasts and his fellow men with clubs and spears, and even when he was merely felling trees and tilling the soil. But in the conditions of modern mechanized living any psychological deformation these traits cause in either man or woman is merely a leftover. Women have never done as well as men at heavy labor, or in sports, but there is no particular survival value today in superior hoisting or running, as there once was, and such physical differences are no longer a valid justification for the different values traditionally assigned to masculinity and femininity.

The structure of the male did make him actually a very superior being in most of the past, and the protector and ruler of woman. In a highly civilized way of life, however, not only do these differences become irrelevant, but the disconcerting fact emerges that woman is biologically superior to man in a great many ways. Fewer females die in the womb or the birth process; girl babies talk sooner, are toilet-trained sooner, and are generally more advanced in most ways, year after year, until their teens. At all ages, men are far more susceptible to heart disease, the number one killer; over forty, their chance of dying from it is just twice as great as it is for women, and under forty the discrepancy is even greater. This is not a matter of the strain and stress of man's daily life, but of his hormones. Men who have lost the function of their testes through sickness or accident have little tendency toward heart disease, but women well past menopause or women who have had their ovaries removed are like men in their susceptibility to it. Apparently, the presence of female hormones in the blood stream lowers the blood fat level, and so protects the body against heart damage from blood clots; the administration of estrogens is, in fact, one of the most interesting and promising of the new treatments for heart patients.

So too with many another disease or cause of death. Bronchitis, pneumonia, ulcers, anemia, tuberculosis, accidents, and infections are all more lethal to males than to females from birth onward. The National Cancer Institute says that women have twice as good a chance as men of "cure" (survival for five or more years) after operation for lung and certain other cancers. Blindness is one-third more common among boys than girls, stuttering five to ten times more common, and gout, the so-called disease of aristocrats, recognizes man's nobility and makes him ridiculous, while leaving common woman alone. A few diseases do selectively prefer woman, but overall longevity is the final test; according to United Nations data, in nearly every civilized country the female lives longer than the male—about as good an indication of biological superiority as can be imagined.*

Biologically, the female seems to be better and more fully equipped throughout her structure; in every one of the billions of cells of her body she has somewhere between 3 and 6 percent more genetic life-saving apparatus than man. Every cell, beginning with the original fertilized egg, has twenty-three pairs of matching chromosomes (it was thought to be twenty-four until quite recently) ; these are long strings of giant molecules (genes) that run the chemistry of each cell and determine the characteristics of the creature. The female has a complete matching set, but the male has one mismatched pair out of the twenty-three: instead of two large sex chromosomes ("X" chromosomes), he has one "X" plus a tiny "Y," which lacks five hundred to a thousand genes. This makes him more subject to hereditary diseases, for if certain genes in his "X" chromosomes are defective, he has no healthy healthy spares or counterparts to offset them, as does the female. More importantly, his specific shortage of genetic material causes him, as he grows from the single-celled stage, to develop the internal chemistry and the physique of the male—with

---

* The life expectancy for newborn girls is about 6.3 years longer than that for boys in the United States; in England and Wales it is 5.5 years longer; in France 5.7 years longer, etc. It is often argued that woman is a parasite who lives on man, and that he dies sooner because he is worn out by his daily exertions in her behalf. But Father Francis Madigan and Professor Rupert B. Vance of the University of North Carolina recently gathered the life records of some 42,000 Catholic Brothers and Sisters, whose ways of life are practically identical, and free from pressure: the Brothers lived longer than other men—but the Sisters lived longer than other women, and by an even greater margin.

its lesser resistance to environmental diseases and to the wear and tear of time. From the first instant of life to the last, the female is better constructed than the male, penis envy notwithstanding.

Yet even if woman's special chemistry makes her live longer, doesn't it also make her a less vital, less active, psychologically inferior being? The little girl produces more estrogens than the boy, even before puberty, and is less aggressive and noisy; at puberty her hormone production greatly increases, and her character seems to soften still more; as a pregnant woman, saturated in female hormones, she is even more somnolent, self-absorbed, and dependent, and, as a nonpregnant one, before her menstrual periods she is moody, fretful, and likely to back the car into a fireplug.*

But the influence of chemistry has been confounded with environmental and learned factors, and thereby greatly exaggerated. The young bluejeaned hoyden of today and the prim little girl of half a century ago have the same chemistry; their differences in personality must be cultural. Emotional and physical upsets before and during menstruation have a basis in reality, but studies of women with severe menstrual disturbances show the difficulties to be frequently rooted in a learned fear of menstruation or a learned dislike of womanhood. The effect of hormones on the personality is also not nearly as simple as often claimed. Barnyard cocks dominate the hens, but the hens are scrappiest with one another when most fertile, and drop down in the pecking order when not. The female ape comes closest to being dominant when she is sexually most available and desirable to the male. As for the human female, it is when her hormone production decreases after menopause that her bodily and personality functions tend to slow down; in fact, sex hormone treatments (androgens for men, estrogens for women) have been reported to make difficult aged persons less somnolent and cranky, more rational and vigorous, more interested in activities and human interchange. For all the trouble they get us into, our sex

* A report in the *British Medical Journal* in 1960 indicates that 52 percent of serious accidents to women occur within four days, either way, of the onset of menstrual flow.

hormones—female and male alike—are a wellspring of activity, creativity, and intellectual vigor.

Still, isn't it well known that something in women's nature makes them inescapably timid, and full of alarms and fears—of mice, of snakes, of blood? Isn't it true that they easily get hysterical or tearful, and suffer depressions after childbirth, during menopause, and in general at almost any time a man least expects them to? And don't they outnumber the men in mental hospitals throughout the land?

All this *is* well known—and true only in part. Mice, snakes, and blood cause not the least tremor in girl lab assistants or lady doctors. Women outnumber men in mental hospitals because females outlive males, and also because women, not usually being the support of the family, can be committed sooner than men. Women may be more subject to emotional upsets and neuroses than men, but at a sub-critical level. They go through the motions of suicide three times as often as men—but men actually succeed in killing themselves three times as often as women do. In London, during the World War II bombings, nearly 70 percent more cases of emotional shock and psychoneurosis occurred among men than among women, while on the Continent various reports indicate that women suffered nervous breakdowns less often in concentration camps. To the extent that our daily life resembles a blitz or a concentration camp—which, alas, it sometimes seems to do—women are biologically and psychologically better fitted to survive it. The final indignity is the late word on space flights: the first human beings in space were men, but the Martin Company recently reported that in simulated space flights women show better orientation and handling of controls, and studies by the National Aeronautics and Space Administration show that they will probably endure the psychological hazards of space flight better than men. Meanwhile, the Department of Agriculture has already successfully demonstrated parthenogenesis (conception without sperm) in turkeys. It may be that the male will soon cease to be either fit for modern life, or useful in it; hopefully, men who read this book will all be dead before that time comes.

4 THE HEAD ON HER SHOULDERS

Second only to woman's supposedly lesser body, as a cause of psychic inferiority, is her allegedly lesser brain. Woman's failure to invent any major philosophy, important machine, or history-making politic is the grand proof that her mental equipment is second-rate, but almost every day men see trivial—and more convincing—proofs close at hand. A friend of mine tells me that when he explains to his wife something she has asked him about—nuclear fission, say, or off-set printing, or the electoral college—there comes a point midway in his exposition when she says it's all clear to her. "Wait a minute," he says, "I haven't really come to the heart of it yet." "Don't say any more," she replies, "—I understand it now, but if you say even one more word, I'll lose it all." ("She's right, too," he adds. "I've learned to shut up and be content with what she thinks she's understood.")

Even in such mundane intellectual areas as finance, woman is fluttery, vague, and amiably foolish. An Alan Dunn cartoon in *Fortune* shows a lady standing up at a stockholders' meeting and brightly chirruping, "Am I to assume then that stocks are different from bonds?" This is only a joke, but many men will assure you that women really *are* like that. Keith Funston, president of the New York Stock Exchange, once epitomized the woman investor by telling of a broker who examined an elderly lady's portfolio; finding it ideal, he asked how she had picked her stocks, and she replied that she just bought shares of companies that ran two-page full-color ads in her favorite magazine.

A serious challenge to the belief in woman's lesser mentality came several decades ago, when I.Q. tests were first put into wide use and indicated that girls were as intelligent, on the average, as boys. Anti-feminists have ever since pointed out that the I.Q. figures are misleading. The tests contain a number of different kinds of questions—verbal, reasoning, visual, and so on—at some of which girls do better, and at other of which boys excel; when the tests were originally constructed, the proportions of the items were balanced so as to have girls and boys average out equally well. The Intelligence Quotient is not an absolute fact but an artifact, and man is probably smarter than woman after all.

Before one accepts that conclusion, he should ask the real question: how do boys and girls compare on the different types of items? From the age of four on, boys do better than girls at abstract words, arithmetical reasoning, induction, and telling what is wrong about an absurd picture, while girls do better at language items, social questions, and aesthetic problems such as matching shapes. (Similarly, on College Entrance Board exams, senior high school girls do as well as boys in an overall sense, but not subject by subject; they are markedly inferior to the boys in physics and in mathematical aptitude, but notably superior in English composition.) But none of this supports the traditional position on women. For the differences between the average score for boys and average score for girls on the several types of I.Q. test items are not large, and do not show them to be two unlike species of human beings. Boys *average* better in arithmetical reasoning—but that does not mean most boys do better than most girls. The larger part of each group lies in exactly the same range of excellence: most boys are no better than most girls in arithmetical reasoning ability, most girls are no better than most boys in verbal ability, and a minority of each sex is exceptionally excellent or poor, creating minor differences in the overall averages.

From this, the only legitimate conclusion is that there *are* sex-linked differences in some specific intellectual abilities, but that they do not justify a dichotomy of human beings, an either-or classification of mentalities. They amount to a slight, but definite, victory for the team, not for the majority of team members. On College Entrance Board tests, for instance, a breakdown of the 1950 results showed that boys did distinctly better than girls in physics—yet 54 percent of the boys did less well than the top 33 percent of the girls.

Human beings, at least in Western civilization, have always tended to think in terms of paired opposites—positive versus negative, good versus bad, victory versus defeat, active versus passive, male versus female. But male and female are not genuine logical opposites, and cannot properly be said to be *versus* each other. To classify girls in terms of opposition to boys, calling them illogical and boys logical, for instance, is in itself a piece of elementary illogic: it is the error of going from the part to the whole. To state the truth accurately requires at least three propositions:

1. Some men are highly logical, and so are some (but not quite as many) women.
2. Some women are exceedingly illogical, and so are some (but not quite as many) men.
3. Most men and women lie in the same range of innate capacity for logical thought, which is far too little for the good of the human race.

But note the word *innate*. Whatever parity we have in the womb, we are instantly identified in the first bloody, wrinkled minute of life as boy or girl; from that moment on the world starts treating us in ways that accentuate and augment the minor differences that exist. Little boys begin to learn that "using one's head" is manly, and little girls begin to learn that not doing so is womanly, even before the psychologist gets around to testing their abilities. What he measures is not an isolated laboratory product, but a hopeless tangle of heredity and environment—that is, a human being.

Once in a while, though, an experimenter catches a glimpse of the separate components. At Yale University psychologist G. Alexander Milton gave a series of logical problems and puzzles to a group of high school boys and girls, and, like several previous researchers, found that the boys did a good deal better. Milton wondered to what extent this might be because the typical logical problem has a masculine sound to it, and so causes girls to blank out. One of his problems, for instance, said that a certain tramp rolls his own cigarettes from butts he picks up, and that it takes him six butts to make one new cigarette. One day he collects 72 butts and smokes 14 cigarettes. How does he do it? The solution goes as follows: 72 butts make only 12 cigarettes, but these, when smoked, yield 12 more butts, hence 2 more cigarettes: *ergo,* 14 in all. Q.E.D.

Milton rewrote his problems to give them a feminine aura, and tested them on undergraduates at Stanford University. The cigarette problem became one in which a cook cuts out round cookies at so many per cup of batter—and makes more than one could figure by straight multiplying. Yet most girls puzzled it out with ease: about one-third more cookies could be made by reworking the leftover corners of dough, thus yielding the right answer. Milton's tentative conclusion was that girls do better at logical thinking when the content of the problem is feminine, and decidedly worse when the content is classically masculine.

Psychologist Paul C. Berry, summarizing the findings of a number of similar studies, concludes that the available psychological evidence does not show sufficient differences in intelligence, specific aptitudes, or knowledge to account for the difference in problem-solving ability between boys and girls. The only tenable explanation is that the prevalence, in our culture, of the belief in male reasoning and in female intuition shapes the growing child's ideas about himself or herself, and hence the ability to *use* his or her abilities. In sum, women can't think because they think they can't think.

Thus one often hears highly intelligent and well-educated women disparaging themselves and their sex, or at least eloquently defending the traditional position. A beautiful, highly gifted advertising woman who keeps trying to convince herself that her place is at home, depreciates her own abilities thus: "Women are more practical, less imaginative, and are characteristically disinterested in the abstract and speculative. In a word, they are earth-bound, and this is their strength and their weakness. I think these differences are built-in and inevitable." And the following *apologia* comes from an artistic young designer of thirty-four who suffers feelings of acute guilt and panic whenever she is on the brink of achievement, and thereupon quickly finds excuses for dropping her efforts and staying home for a while:

Anything women can do men can do better, except having babies and singing soprano. Men still dominate art, literature, philosophy, medicine, etc., though women have been emancipated long enough to have given them a run for their money. I feel that even if the roles were reversed and men took care of household duties, women would be unable to perform as well in any field as men have.

But the accumulated test data prove her wrong. Woman's intellectual inferiority is not innate, but acquired; it is a way of combatting the fear that braininess may be a stigma, a sign of imperfect femininity, a hindrance to lovableness and marriageability. "A woman, if she have the misfortune to know anything, should conceal it as well as she can," wrote Jane Austen bitingly; that was long ago, but the following facts are contemporary:

—Throughout the United States, almost half of boys but less than a tenth of girls have had more than six semesters of mathematics by the time they graduate from high school. Three-quarters of the boys but only half of the girls have completed three semesters of science. (1955 data.)

—Nine-tenths of high school seniors, according to a survey of New Jersey schools, feel that girls *could* succeed in scientific work even though few try to. At least a third of the seniors recognize that the disapproval of peers and families is a potent restraining force.

—The U.S. Employment Service, using a battery of aptitude tests, found that 6 percent of boys and 4 percent of girls have talent patterns suited to engineering. That is, 40 percent of potential American engineering talent is female; however, less than 1 percent of undergraduates studying engineering are girls.

This is not to say that leading a twofold life of intellectual activity and homemaking would be better than one of homemaking alone; that is another question. But it *is* to say that the traditional belief concerning woman's incapacity for rational work is wrong, and that the "common-sense" evidence alleged to prove it merely mistakes a social adjustment for an irreparable genetic defect. So might a creature from another planet, first seeing women on Fifth Avenue in mid-winter, suppose them to be a species of fur-bearing animal with an unfortunate mutation causing defective legs, which the creatures had quite intelligently overcome by propping themselves up on tiny stilts.

5 FEMININITY—NATURE OR NURTURE?

Like woman's logic, or lack of it, most female traits can be shown to result from the interplay of biological and social influences, the latter having the far greater share in producing differences between men and women. Ninety-five percent of prisoners in our jails are men, but this does not mean that women are only one-nineteenth as criminal by nature as men; much female crime is nonviolent, and so either escapes being reported or being punished by imprisonment. Women are generally agreed to be more intuitive and perceptive than men, but according to Amram Scheinfeld, authority on sex differences, this is chiefly because from early childhood on they must learn to gain their ends not by force or direct action, but by making the most of hints and signs in other people. Women do overdraw their bank accounts three times as often as men, but according to anthropologist Ashley Montagu the ratio is steadily decreasing as they become accustomed to the mechanics of keeping a checkbook. Some women are catty, hypersensitive, artistic, vain, fickle, gushing, and mincing, but some homosexuals, despite a normal masculine hormone output, outdo them in all these qualities.

Everyone knows that women are gossips by nature, but in certain Philippine tribes everyone knows that men are gossips by nature. Women are plainly destined to prepare food for men, who caught it or gathered it or earned it; all the great gourmets, cooks, and gastronomic writers, nevertheless, have been men. Women sigh and cry more easily than men, but bloodthirsty medieval barons could, when in love, outweep most women, and the poetic youths of the Romantic era, alone and palely loitering, could gustily outsigh any maiden. Women adore lacy things, perfume themselves until the air around them is a thin syrup, spend hours curling and fussing over their hair, walk with an affected swish, and talk with a sibilant sing-song —all of which perfectly describes the Restoration rakes in the court of Charles II, who, far from being feminine, were intemperately masculine, assuming it be masculine to gamble, fight, and fornicate like a stud bull.

But even if many traits of femininity are a matter of cultural fashion, is it not still true that certain major experiences in life are reserved for woman alone, and in any society must needs set her radically apart from man in temperament and mentality? Dr. Karl Menninger lists menstruation, pregnancy, parturition, and lactation as the four profound female experiences for which there is no male counterpart. Others, without meaning to be funny, add micturition to the list, on the grounds that the way a boy urinates gives him a sense of power and ability, while the way a girl does so gives her a sense of shame and inferiority. These four great and one lesser life experiences of woman, it is argued, necessarily give her such characteristics as an instinctive capacity for nurturing and tenderness, a concern about individuals and a disinterest in the abstract, and a tendency toward self-depreciation and inferiority feelings. When Margaret Mead first published *Sex and Temperament in Three Primitive Societies*, arguing that masculinity and femininity are in large part culturally determined, and hence subject to great variation, one reviewer wrote, "Margaret, this is a very brilliant book. But do you really know any cultures in which men have the babies?"

The barb seems well aimed, yet it avoids the real issue, which is whether woman's unique experiences must make her radically unlike man in temperament, or merely create tendencies which some societies radically exaggerate and others do not. Dr. Mead reported, for example, that in some remote cultures men are as nurturant as women and fully as inclined to care for the young. The female breast alone fills with milk, but in the human animal this physical change does not automatically trigger off a full complement of maternal instincts or of itself determine a woman's attitude toward baby care. In some cultures, including our own, many women regard breast feeding as disgusting, and child care as a chore; in others women like breast feeding their children to the age of three, and regard child care as the be-all and end-all of life. Again, menstruation almost always causes a certain amount of shame in the female because it is so involuntary, and perhaps therefore reminiscent of childish wetting, but some societies make little of it while others regard it as noxious and loathsome, and make women go off into quarantine once each month, until the flow ceases. So it goes too with the other major female life experiences. They may incline woman toward becoming seductive, tender, and nurturant, but they do not insure her becoming so, nor specify how much so she must be; moreover there is no natural law of compensation that says that in return for developing these traits, she must be helpless at numbers, sharp of tongue, dishonest, devious, and tearful. Woman will never urinate as man does, but neither science nor history shows that this must make her a flibbertigibbet, a clinging vine, or a shrew.

From all the historical and cross-cultural evidence, in fact, it seems that although woman's biology, and her unique biological experiences, contribute a fundamental orientation toward much of life, the greater part of what we (or any other people) call "femininity" is the product of transient social fashions, and of differing circumstances of life. The famous Terman-Miles masculinity-femininity test, in wide use for the past generation, provides striking confirmation of this. Psychologists Terman and Miles made no assumptions as to the causes of femininity or masculinity, and offered no bedrock definitions, but simply set out to see to what extent American men and women differ in their attitudes and preferences concerning foods, animals, jobs, amusements, and a great many other things. They found, not surprisingly, that the sexes do differ. But what do the differences signify? Not primarily innate factors, but environmental ones—for the average score of women in any age group, region, educational level or occupation is unlike that of women in dissimilar circumstances; and the same is true of males.

Men in mechanical occupations, for instance, score far more toward the masculine end of the scale than do men in social, cultural, or spiritual occupations (divinity students get a particularly low masculinity rating, as would anyone who followed the precepts of Christ). Women in mechanical occupations are more masculine—in terms of the test—than women in, say, social work. Students with high grades score more toward the feminine direction than students with low grades. Education, generally speaking, reduces the extremes both of masculinity and of femininity: the average difference between junior-year high-school boys and girls on the M-F scale is 155 points, but between college sophomore men and women this gap decreases to 128, and at higher levels of education the difference is still smaller. Similarly, the average difference between male scores and female scores for the population at large decreases with time and experience; men and women become less masculine and less feminine respectively, year by year, as their experiences wear away at the rigid sex-role definitions they began with in adolescence. "Culture," concluded Drs. Terman and Miles, "tends to make men's minds resemble women's; intelligence and education to make women's minds resemble men's."

Masculinity and femininity thus in large part refer to *acquired* ways of behaving. Indeed they consist of traits some of which can even be deliberately assumed without being inwardly *felt*. Terman and Miles gave the M-F test to one group of college sophomore men and women without telling them what it measured; the students got scores normal for their age and background. Then the psychologists gave it to them again, explaining its purpose, and asking them to accentuate their own tendencies; the women promptly racked up excessively feminine scores and the men excessively masculine ones. Finally, Terman and Miles asked a small group of men and women to answer as much like the opposite sex as they could. The results were genuinely astonishing: "A typical group of males at the most masculine age," reported the psychologists, "are able to earn a mean score more feminine by far than the mean of any female group we have tested; a typical female group can make itself appear far more masculine than any male group we have tested."

The many similar studies made in the twenty-five years since the M-F test was first published have overwhelmingly substantiated the finding that the larger part of what is called masculinity or femininity is influenced and molded by education and experience—and that we ourselves, knowing what is expected of us by others, can assume roughly as much femininity or masculinity as we think appropriate. But of course every woman knows this is so; she is well aware that in talking to her cleaning lady she is not the same woman that she is when meeting her fellow alumnae at the annual reunion on the campus, and that in arguing with the butcher she is not the same woman that she is when, meeting an attractive man at a cocktail party, she "turns it on."

6 SEX AND FEMALE MASOCHISM

And yet, according to some students of woman, education and culture are as nothing compared to the mighty influence of the sexual act itself. The shape and characteristics of the sex organs require that woman allow her privacy to be invaded by the intrusive, probing male. He *does,* she is *done to,* and that makes all the difference. Psychoanalyst Helene Deutsch, author of the weightiest psychological treatise on women extant in English, argues that because woman has no visible erectile organ, she is essentially passive and must await the man in order to discover herself fully. The first such discovery, being painful, endows her sexual role (and her whole personality) with a tendency to enjoy pain and passive suffering: "Woman's entire psychologic preparation for the sexual and reproductive functions is associated with masochistic ideas. . . . [in which] coitus is closely associated with the act of defloration, and defloration with rape and a painful penetration of the body." Woman's whole personality is thus supposed to be colored by passivity, masochism, and dependency on the male.

In a later chapter we will look more closely at the sex life of modern woman; for the moment, let us ask only whether this kind of psychology has any real biological justification, or whether it is another case of mistaking the psychological clothing of an era for the person within. In the animal world it is true that the males of many species bite and scratch the females during sex play and actual copulation. But this is not psychological sadism; it is reflexive activity that has survival value for the species, since the pain inflicted by the male promotes the release of the ripe egg from the ovary of the female in heat.

There is, however, no such connection in human physiology: our mating is not based on heat, or egg ripeness, but is permanent and continuous. We are not *any* animal, but a unique animal; we mate not as others do, seasonally, at random, and out of unthinking glandular compulsion, but year round, by personal preference, and out of sensual, sensuous, and affectional drives.

Professors Ford and Beach reviewed anthropological data on nearly two hundred human societies and found that despite the immense variety of methods and styles of love-making, there *was* a general tendency for mild pain to be a sexual stimulus and a part of love play—but that "all human societies that encourage the infliction of mild pain in connection with intercourse take the attitude that *such behavior should be bilateral or mutual.*" Scratching, biting, hair pulling, and playful attacks of all sorts are not visited only by the male upon the passive, masochistic female, but returned by her in kind.

The nineteenth century was all but unique in requiring its better-class women to lie still and endure the male without overt response; it is a cruel quirk of fate that psychoanalysis, which unveiled so many truths about the human soul for the first time, should in this case have misinterpreted a mere custom for a changeless aspect of female psychology. But there is nothing changeless about it; in just the past two generations, women have moved far away from the Victorian ideal of passivity and humiliation in coitus toward one of activity and mutuality—and correspondingly have been suffering less frigidity and attaining satisfaction more often, according to Kinsey's data, than their mothers and still more than their grandmothers. The traditionalists who argue that female masochism and passivity are natural and healthful are, in effect, recommending a return to femininity as understood in the last century, when the Judeo-Christian tradition of patriarchal family life made its last great stand. It may have been a workable and satisfying system in the remote past—but it is no more suited to today's urban democratic civilization and today's people than are the plowshare, oxcart, and hand forge.

7 · THE DIFFERENCES BETWEEN MAN AND WOMAN

What, then, have we learned about the psychology of woman? Much and little. We have learned much about beliefs that should be junked—symptoms mistaken for causes, customs mistaken for immutable natural laws. We have learned little, though, about woman as a different and special variety of Homo sapiens precisely because, except in a few areas of her life, her inborn psychological potentialities and innate limitations are not radically unlike those of men.

To summarize what we do know: (1) Women differ from men in physical ways which, in more primitive times, made men legitimately the dominant sex, and which, in contemporary life, have only a symbolic and mythic value. In fact, in the milieu of an advanced civilization, woman is distinctly superior to man, biologically speaking. (2) Women differ from men in many psychological ways, which to some extent are the result of inherent and genetic factors, to a larger extent are acquired through the experiences of owning a female body, and in still larger part are acquired through the experiences of living as a female in a society with a given set of ideas about females.

The evidence indicates that of the thing we call "female nature," a relatively lesser part of the final result is due to innate factors, and a relatively greater part to experiential or environmental ones. Even so, the resulting differences are only statistical *tendencies,* exaggerated by the habit of dualistic thinking into artificial *oppositions.* Reviewing the available data, Dr. John E. Anderson of the Institute of Child Development and Welfare at the University of Minnesota says that for almost every psychological trait the difference between the average male and average female score is only about one-tenth as great as the range of differences among men, or among women. "In other words," he concludes, "knowing only the sex of a person, no firm prediction with respect to psychological characteristics can be made."

None of this is to be taken as a plea to eliminate sex differences altogether: a world of neuter people would be unutterably drab, and probably self-liquidating. But if we clearly distinguish between the *inherent and biological* components of femininity and the *acquired and social* ones, we will be better able to understand why modern woman is so often torn by conflicting wishes and needs, and better able to assess the soundness of the various choices or combinations of roles available to her in the modern world.

CHAPTER THREE

THE SEVEN

DISCONNECTED AGES

OF WOMAN

1 THE SEGMENTAL LIFE

"One man in his time plays many parts,/His acts being seven ages," says Jaques in *As You Like It*. Woman plays many parts too, but with a difference: her ages do not grow sensibly and smoothly one out of the other. Her life, if it be like a play, is badly written, disjointed, and lacking in development from act to act. What she is in any one age of her life may not only fail to fit her for the next, but even unfit her for it. This is the third major problem in the life of modern woman, compounding the two we have already discussed—the absence of any guide for choosing among the many roles available to her, and the traditional psychology which misrepresents and thereby molds her very nature.

In a way, of course, woman's life is bound to be more sharply demarcated into discontinuous segments than man's; as Margaret Mead points out, the major physical events of woman's life—the first menstruation, the breaking of the hymen, the first pregnancy and parturition, and menopause—make for distinct boundaries to the periods of her life. In comparison, most of man's ages glide into one another, even his prized virility slowly dwindling away rather than ending at some distinct time as is true of her fertility.

Yet it is not the external separateness of woman's ages that makes for difficulty; rather it is the fact that there is so little internal continuity among her roles from one age to the next, and such great discrepancies between the self of any one phase of her life and that of the next one. In less progressive, but more stable societies, there is little or no choice of roles available to a woman; from childhood on she aims for that one kind of womanhood that will serve her all her life. As a result, she comes to play the part almost effortlessly, as one speaks his mind in his own language without having to think of grammar. Modern woman, in contrast, is always speaking in a foreign language, her mind racing ahead to pick the right endings and get them tacked on in time. Dr. John P. Spiegel, professor of psychiatry at Harvard University Medical School, puts it in these sophisticated terms: "[The] automatic function of role systems has significance for psychological economy of effort. The person is spared the necessity of coming to decisions about most of the acts he performs, because he knows his parts so well. . . . [In contrast,] self-consciousness and self-guarding enter the scene along with role conflict, which sharply raises the number of decisions which have to be made with respect to any sequence of acts." Or to put it in terms of Shakespeare's metaphor: Woman half studies a number of parts, but somehow time and again finds herself on stage, nightmarishly uncertain which of them she is supposed to be playing, and distressingly aware that the lines she summons to mind often do not seem to fit.

2 WHAT ARE LITTLE GIRLS MADE OF?

What are these discontinuities and discrepancies in woman's life? Perhaps the first is the shift from the artificial sexlessness of her babyhood to her confused groping for sexual identity in childhood. Gesell reports that even as late as three and a half years of age girls occasionally propose marriage to their mothers, and boys to their fathers. The concealment of sexual functions in middle-class life and the task sharing of togetherness long keep the child ignorant of its sexual identity. The girl has no idea that her mother menstruates, nor what occurs sexually between father and mother, nor any notion how a baby is born; she furthermore has very little idea which parent is responsible for which duties, since Daddy sometimes takes care of her or cooks, and Mommy either works or goes off now and again on incomprehensible adult business. It is civilized of us to be thus, but it does make growing up more complicated for the girl later on. One does not hear about frigidity, fear of pregnancy, or career-marriage conflict in those simpler worlds in which each little girl, even in her first years, knows something of the chiefly biological roles she will someday play and begins making room for them in her psyche.

In the second age of woman—childhood to puberty—sexual differentiation begins, bringing both clarification and confusion. Parents, still withholding and concealing the biology of womanhood from the child, now begin to supply her with simplified traditional concepts of femininity, assuring her that she is made of sugar and spice and everything nice. But the little girl may not feel as though she is constitutionally different from the boy; she may not see at all why she must be neat, quiet, and good when he is allowed and even encouraged to be messy, noisy, and somewhat naughty.

There is only a very limited physical basis for her supposedly innate girlishness in behavior and play. The chemistry of her body gives her a little less vigor, and its structure gives her more finger dexterity and a little less ease in throwing. But these and other differences are very minor; in classroom and playground the pre-school and kindergarten boy and girl are almost on a par. Dr. Gesell himself, though he held that sex differences in behavior have a constitutional basis which culture merely reinforces, stated when reviewing his life work that "on the whole, boys and girls meet most stages of development in a highly comparable manner."

For this very reason, many little girls, being exposed and attracted as they are to so-called masculine interests, are baffled by the increasing disapproval of their parents. Professor Mirra Komarovsky, a sociologist at Barnard College and an expert on woman's life, reports that a considerable number of normally feminine undergraduate girls can recall having been forcibly molded, against their wishes and inclinations, to the conventional stereotype of the female child. Some girls rather abruptly ran into trouble concerning their evident distaste for the clothes and toys which, by nature, they were supposed to like. As one of Dr. Komarovsky's interviewees recalls:

I started life as a little tomboy but as I grew older Mother got worried about my unladylike ways. She removed my tops, marbles, football, and skates and tried to replace these with dolls, tea sets, and sewing games. . . . She bought me small pocketbooks and lovely little dresses. When despite her efforts she caught me one day trying to climb a tree in the park she became thoroughly exasperated and called me a little "freak."

Some parents, not envisioning a future period when their daughters might need to play a skilled part in our technological society, try to stifle any interests in that direction, and frown on or refuse requests for chemistry sets, electric trains, and the like. "One of my biggest disappointments as a child happened one Christmas," said one girl. "I asked for a set of tools and could hardly wait for Christmas morning. I eagerly opened a package only to find a sewing kit." Such trifling incidents, when sufficiently multiplied, become a potent force in forming—or deforming—the growing personality.

Not only is the girl in this second phase of life being manipulated toward a self for which her first several years did not prepare her, but at the same time she is learning that this self will in many ways be less admirable and important than the self of the boy. It is brought home to her by the unflattering opinions boys early develop about her. By first or second grade they no longer want to play with her, consider her beneath them, and are firmly convinced that as a woman she will be afraid of many things, tire easily, be squeamish, act rather stupidly, and feel sad more often than men. One pompous little patriarch told a psychologist that "women do things like cooking and washing and sewing because that's all they can do." Said another: "In going to adventurous places women are pests—just a lot of bother. They die easily and they are always worried about their petticoats."

Still more unsettling, the girl's parents sometimes praise her for winning a spelling bee and then again scold her for vigorously arguing with her brother or a neighboring boy, sometimes get her up to look her prettiest for a birthday party and then again are cross when she admires herself in the mirror instead of helping with the dishes. The inconsistency is repeated over and over again. Her parents want her to do as well at school as she can, but her indulgent father also teaches her to get what she wants by charm rather than achievement. Her brother gets a bike for having gotten good grades; she gets it for being Daddy's little sweetheart.

Year by year girls and boys alike develop a better opinion of masculine traits and a poorer opinion of feminine ones. Loveableness is clearly not as valuable as manliness; though a girl may get in trouble for being tomboyish, it is nowhere near as dreadful as if her brother were to put on girl's clothing or act like a sissy. A few years ago psychologist Daniel Brown (now an associate professor at the United States Air Force Academy) used a picture-card test on grade-school children to discover the extent of these preferences. Each card showed a vague sexless child figure called "It," plus a pair of alternatives such as, for instance, building tools and cooking utensils. The children were asked what they thought It would prefer; in the freedom of the make-believe situations, 60 to 70 percent of girls in the first to fourth grades said It would choose the building tools. In fifth grade, a majority of girls even thought It would rather be a father than a mother. Thus at the very time when girls are learning to identify themselves with traditional female roles, they are also learning to prefer masculine roles which they think inappropriate for themselves. Thus is conflict built into the foundations of the female character; thus is the future woman made uncertain of her worth, hesitant about her abilities, fearful of trying roles other than those of tradition, and anxious if she succeeds in them.

And the most important role of all in the coming several ages of her life is the one in which she receives the most curious training. This is, of course, her function as man's lover; it is crucial to her future happiness, yet is the role for which, in this long formative period, she gets the least psychological preparation. Among the urban middle class, for instance, most children remain quite vague about the nature of the sexual act until puberty or later, with girls being generally more ignorant than boys. Girls' conceptions of it from the fourth to twelfth year range anywhere from the idyllic (it consists of a kiss, and a resultant transport of feeling) to the mis-impression, gleaned from sounds and perhaps a peep or two, that it is a kind of assault or combat. Even when the accidentally witnessed scene does not cause fright, it may be totally misunderstood by the very young: as the five-year-old girl brightly said to a roomful of Sunday visitors, "Last night I saw Daddy exercising on Mommy."

The difficulty lies not in mere ignorance, but in the disjunction of love and sex during childhood. In the home love is presented as a powerful but "pure" affection; as for the sexual side of the love re-lationship, the parents all but deny before the children that any-thing like that happens between them. Moreover, the instinctive sexual attraction of little boys toward their mothers and little girls toward their fathers is soon perceived by the children themselves to be so unacceptable that they are frightened into the long span of seeming disinterest in sex known to psychoanalysts as the "latency period." Some sexual interest does remain, but whether it takes the form of dirty words, masturbation, peeking, or playing doctor, it is clearly and strongly identified as very bad; modern parents force themselves to handle such episodes in calm tones, but children have keen antenna for the unspoken ultrasonic overtones. These factors apply to boys, but still more so to girls, who are far more closely protected, sternly warned against sexual curiosity or play, and have far less experience, at every age until marriage, of masturbation, exhibitionism, peeking, and all forms of homosexual and hetero-sexual experimentation.

In sum, although the girl will someday have to unite sex and affection in one intense, completely fused emotion, her childhood training says that tender intense affection is good and sexual feeling is bad, and that she may love most only those toward whom she dare not have sexual feelings. When married love was not supposed to be the complex amalgam of things it now is, this may not have mattered quite so much; today, though, it is mightily troublesome. There is no simple solution at hand; very likely, the dissociation of love and sex during childhood, and the consequent difficulties for man and woman, are the necessary cost of the quasi-romantic, monogamous love we so highly prize.

3 THE ADOLESCENT DILEMMA

Reading about primitive peoples is always a pleasure—it makes one feel so superior. For instance, they do such stupid and irrational things to their adolescents: some of them ceremonially file down or knock out front teeth of children reaching puberty, others make the children endure the bites of vicious ants, and still others cut the penis of the boy and amputate the clitoris of the girl. In New Guinea, the Arapesh girl at her first menstrual period is isolated in a special hut for five or six days without food or water, rubbed all over daily with stinging nettles, and for good measure is ordered to thrust a rolled-up nettle leaf into her vulva. It is an occasion she is not likely to forget.

But such behavior often has good justifications, in its own milieu. In the minds of the primitives, as soon as the body of a boy or girl is capable of adult sexual activity and impelled toward it, the rest of the creature ought to assume concomitant rights and duties. When primitive children arrive at puberty, they therefore cease to have the status of children and are at once regarded as young adults. As soon as a boy has undergone his ritual of initiation, he becomes a man among men—a hunter, warrior, arguer in councils, and forni- cator. As for the girl, after her puberty ceremonies she becomes a woman among women—cook, seamstress, childbearer, sex partner. Many anthropologists feel that the harsh puberty ceremonies of the primitives are a way of dramatically awakening the child to the whole new life that now becomes his. Some psychoanalysts look deeper and argue that these "rites of passage" are a way of exacting in advance a penalty for the long-denied pleasures the child is about to enjoy; they are thus a permit for the new roles he now is to play. (Even in our own civilization children arrived suddenly at adulthood, until a few centuries ago: Juliet was only fourteen at the time of her love and death, and even two centuries later Mozart could portray Cherubino hotly pursuing adult women, waxing philosophic about love, and departing for the wars—all while still possessing a peach-soft complexion.)

Our modern way of life, however, is out of phase with our biology. Boys and girls are ready to fall in love, and are physically capable of parenthood, many years before they are sufficiently trained in the skills required of adults in our world. The third of woman's seven ages is thus one in which her roles change—but do so inconsistently and ambiguously, without any clear shift to a new status. The girl has her first menstrual period and her mother says to her, "My darling baby is a woman now"—but the next morning she goes off to school again in her bobby socks, and in the afternoon gets scolded for leaving her room a mess and not doing her homework.

So begins the third age of woman's life: the little girl is an adolescent, no longer latent and asexual, but sexual only in a peculiar make-believe way. Her mother pesters her to cut out sweets and lose weight, takes her to get her hair styled and even permanented, buys her a starter bra for which she has only the hope of a need, arranges parties for her, and worries if she doesn't show enough "interest" in boys; the girl is an overnight wonder, a transformed pumpkin, a Sleeping Beauty suddenly awakened to the knowledge that love is all-important. But she is still in the dark as to what it is. Mother now admits that it has a lot to do with sex, but although she wants her daughter to draw the boys as honey does the bees, she still forbids any real sexual activity. The girl is allowed to understand that it isn't really nasty, as she had previously been told, but merely that it is bad and wrong for teenagers, although somehow it is very good for everyone else.

The exact nature of her roles is therefore still mysterious and unclear. But since the adult world has been keeping secrets from her all these years, she proves her adulthood to herself by having secrets of her own. She starts a diary and is fiercely protective of its harmless, gushing entries. She and her girl friends spend countless hours whispering and giggling in conferences that drive parents all but wild, and comparing notes and opinions endlessly about "drips," "idiots" and "dreamy guys," and swapping information as to which boys try to kiss on the first date, purse their mouths this or that way, smell of peppermint, or have sweaty hands.

Mother, meanwhile, warns her about not letting boys get too familiar with her, but shies away from defining her terms. One year the girl draws her own line at the goodnight kiss; another year at necking and open-mouth kissing; a third year at a little feeling; and so on. Meanwhile, she and Mother still pretend that nothing is changing; they both know better, but cannot talk about it. For the girl is, and is not, a woman; she is play-acting the part of a sexual lover, and is not supposed to be a real one.

This new self of hers seems to have nothing to do with the self she was building during childhood. Boys don't date a girl because she is a tender young mommy, but because she is cute, or pert, or sexy, or a good dancer, or "lots of fun." The things Mother taught her about her own personality don't seem any good now—and even Mother has changed her tune. The girl may actually resent her mother, unconsciously regarding her as a "deceiver" who taught her a kind of femininity that doesn't work in the competition for popularity. Sometimes the resentment is close to conscious: according to a survey of teenagers in *Seventeen* magazine, two-thirds of the girls feel closest to another girl friend or a sister, and only one-tenth feel closest to their mothers.

As if she were not already confused enough, still another role is now thrust upon her which doesn't fit very well. She is sold the idea that every middle-class or upper-class girl ought to go to college and study something "worthwhile." Since motherhood is temporarily out of her thoughts, she is able to imagine herself in other roles—as a writer, an artist, an actress, a doctor. Perhaps the whole wonderful masculine world will make room for her too, and without forcing her to give up or risk the loss of love—after all, are there not always Elizabeth Browning and Madame Curie as models? She tries her hand at a short story, or designs her own Christmas cards, or serves as an apprentice at a summer theater; reads college catalogues and thinks of going to a small, cerebral girls' college where everyone wears leotards, does brilliant work, and discusses Great Issues; and sees herself, afterward, becoming brilliant, creative, famous, and beloved. Yet at the very same time, she learns from her parents, her girl friends, and the boys she dates that despite any encouraging signs to the contrary, she had really better not be too smart or too good at anything. It scares the boys away; it isn't feminine. And though it may be shameful to get poor grades in school, it is far worse to spend a Saturday night at home with a good book.

It is little wonder that female vanity is closely allied to self-contempt in the adolescent girl: she sees so many possibilities—and so many reasons for not trying most of them. Outwardly she is vain, giddy, delighted with her own airs and activities, and immensely superior to her parents (Mother is frequently im*poss*ible, and Dad is just a dear old thing), but this is only on the surface; all through the years of adolescence, according to a study by psychologist Catherine Roff of the Putnam Children's Center in Roxbury, Massachusetts, girls grow less and less satisfied with themselves. Only at the end of their teens, when they achieve momentary glory as prospective brides or find avenues of achievement in college, does their opinion of themselves take a turn for the better; until then, as many surveys and tests indicate, girls in their teens are both more introverted and more neurotic than boys. It may be that the Arapesh girl's five days of rubdowns with stinging nettles is, after all, a cheap price to pay for womanhood.

4 GLAMOUR AND CRISIS

Toward the end of her teens, the girl enters a new age of her life when she leaves home physically or psychologically, or both. She is now in what Talcott Parsons has referred to as her "glamour" phase— young but in full bloom, sought after and seeking, free of responsibility and greedy to drink in experiences, emotions, and new ideas. If she cannot go to college, she goes to work and becomes a young woman of the world; if she can go to college, she becomes a young woman of the special and wonderful world of intellect. Either way, she is not only on her own, but finds herself the equal of men by virtue of a weekly pay check or the honors list; yet she is also at her most attractive now, and freer than ever to try out her personality on young men and to experiment at the game of love. These are the golden days for which she has long waited, and on which she will later look back wistfully.

But she arrives at this interim paradise far from prepared to enjoy it fully. All through adolescence she was far more sheltered than her brother; now rather abruptly she must take charge of herself, guard herself, and make decisions about herself, all of which she finds somewhat scary. The young man who says he loves her, and who eloquently argues that "it isn't right for people in love to deny the natural, beautiful fulfillment of their emotions," alarms her though she yearns to believe him. As time passes, she hears the same story in one form or another and gets over her maiden fright at the idea; yet even if she finally allows herself to sleep with him, and possibly others, she is never really able to believe in her sexual rights. All her previous conditioning conspires to make her feel that she is giving away something precious, and becoming less valuable. At the end of a session of petting or intercourse, the young man feels a sense of accomplishment (another experience tucked away, another point scored), but the girl feels a sense of loss (another time when she let herself be used without attaining the goal of engagement or marriage).

Even while she is wrestling with this new and uncomfortable role, she is also discovering that most people expect her to be much more than an attractive girl: they want her to be intelligent, competent, cool-headed, punctual, self-reliant, and many other things she has long been told she is not or ought not be. How shall she be an executive's efficient secretary without damaging her precious feminine appeal? How shall she make the dean's list without having her male classmates view her in distaste as a cold-blooded grind? It is a role for which neither childhood nor adolescence has readied her.

The unreadiness is manifested in many ways. Despite a generation or more of freedom, young women in creative professions and business are notably less in earnest about their work today than their feminist mothers were. A recent article in *Mademoiselle* aptly summarized the situation as follows: "Today's [female] junior executive is not working for glory. She doesn't want to set the world on fire and, in fact, considers raw ambition in rather bad taste." Meanwhile, in the world of learning, girls show similar ambivalence toward achievement. A study at the University of California, based on interviews with girl scholarship students, concluded that "only a very occasional young woman gave major stress to a career or occupational future." College women far more than college men choose the easy subjects, and half of all degrees recently granted to college women were in the spongy, light-weight field of education. Even their classroom manner is typical: as one professor puts it, the undergraduate boy speaks up, bristling and full of slightly cock-eyed opinions, while the undergraduate girl quotes first what she read in one authority, then what she read in a contrary authority, and concludes weakly, "So—I just don't know!"

Yet it is curious how the taste for competence and intellectuality grows on her. The college girl, like the girl with any sort of job better than routine typing, comes to cherish her daily experience of the wider world and her continual discovery of her own capacities; it seems at times that she has come upon her real self, a self she hardly knew about. But what is she to do with it in the future? A long-range study made at Vassar during the 1950's found college senior women to be more adventurous, liberated, rebellious, broadminded, aware, and insightful than they had been as freshmen—and also more anxious, frustrated, upset, and uncertain about themselves and about life. Professor Nevitt Sanford explained that the latter are the stigmata of an "identity crisis." College men typically experience such a crisis in the sophomore year when choosing their major subject and thereby deciding what they expect to be in life. College girls, in contrast, slowly discover a new identity over the four-year period, and belatedly realize that just ahead of them lie major decisions. They have no clear idea of how to use and maintain

the new self beyond the next few months or years. The old identity
has been put aside in favor of a new one—but the new seems bound
to clash with the old, and to succumb when marriage and motherhood come along.*

5 LOVE AND ADJUSTMENT

To put an end to these perplexities, says Professor Sanford, many
seniors upon graduating "seek immediate relief by going all-out for
some clear-cut but limited identity." Three-quarters of them plunge
into the labor market and get to work right after leaving college,
but the identity so achieved is worrisome and probably impermanent. A far more clear-cut identity is the one achieved through
marriage; one-third of the girls become wives within half a year after
graduation, and about one-half marry within nineteen months. As
they achieve the latter identity, they correspondingly abandon the
former, dropping out of the labor market and relinquishing that
side of themselves with indecent haste in order to embrace the rediscovered familiar self they learned about long ago.

But is it really the old familiar one? There are strange and
troublesome differences. Sex is at last an unqualified good, and now
finally is supposed to be united to love. But this is easier said than
done. The girl has for so long restrained herself, held boys back, and
been the defensive party drawing the line that it is difficult for her
to behave otherwise now, and to react to love-making in any but her
old hard-to-get way. The sexual side of marriage, so simple for
most primitives, is more apt to cause difficulties of adjustment to
Americans than any other major area of marriage, including religious, money, or in-law problems. One out of eight successful mar-

* Without the intervening step of education and the discovery of another self,
daughters of the working class also experience an identity crisis. "One of the
reasons they marry at an early age," writes Dr. Lee Rainwater in his book *And
the Poor Get Children*, "is that when they outgrow the status of daughter they
feel somewhat lost and look forward to the clear-cut status of wife and mother as
a way of securely establishing themselves as *someone* again."

riages never does arrive at a mutually satisfactory sexual adjustment, according to a well-known survey by sociologist Judson T. Landis; among unhappy marriages, the fraction is surely much higher.

Meanwhile, the girl's glamour role—one of her favorite images of herself—has abruptly vanished, often leaving her with a keen sense of loss. She has in a twinkling ceased to be what Max Lerner calls "the overvalued darling of the culture." For she is off the market, no longer a bewitching romantic girl; any man who now expresses admiration for her is in effect suggesting an improper and shameful relationship.

Still, despite the giving up of her single glamour, she is often intensely happy as she and her husband, savoring the intimacies and daily discoveries of married life, enjoy the delicious process of self-revelation and comparison. Why can't he cry at a movie, and why does she so enjoy it? Why does he squeeze the toothpaste tube neatly at the bottom and she messily in the middle? Why does he relish dirty jokes or vulgar expressions which only make her uneasy? They never tire of comparing themselves and indulgently adoring their dissimilarities.

But mutual discovery is not all fun and fascination. It also involves conflicts and difficult constructive work. Americans greatly prize their privacy, and their intimate ways of behaving are not seen or known to each other. The young man and the young woman have only a very limited range of experience of these things, and within marriage must slowly hammer out a set of folkways of their own, acceptable to both of them. For each home has its own rules concerning the permissible tones of voice in which man and wife talk to each other, the allowable gestures and expressions they use toward each other. In one, a man may take his lordly ease with company while his wife does everything connected with preparing and serving dinner; in another it would be out of the question. In one home a woman may tease her husband about his addiction to messy old clothes on weekends; in another it would be lèse-majesté. What is the right way for a husband to approach his wife about love-making, or for her to reply? How do people go about ending one of those interminable late-night quarrels? How can either tell the other about some offensive or embarrassing habit without getting an angry flareback? What about church? How should they deal with their parents? When should they entertain, and how lavishly? Dates and love affairs were only a very incomplete preparation for all this. The strain of the transition affects the woman more intensely than the man, for a large part of his life remains outside the marriage and always will; hers, though, is almost concentric with her marriage, or soon will be.

For on top of all the roles she has acquired almost overnight there comes the most radical new one of all—motherhood. Later on we will look at it more closely; for the moment, we only need to note that this, too, arrives abruptly and causes violent alterations in her way of life and her image of herself. Without ever having had to assume or practice adult responsibility for another person, she now finds herself in total charge of a completely helpless new human being. She feels proud and fulfilled as a woman; her confusions are forgotten, and she seems to know at last who she actually is. Yet the demands of the child and the home sometimes seem to overwhelm and submerge altogether the marvelous self she had discovered in college. "I adore my husband, our neat little home, and our beautiful little girl," writes one very young woman from North Dakota, "but sometimes I keep wondering what has become of the excited, thoughtful, hopeful young woman I used to be." And though she is only twenty-two, she adds, "Sometimes it seems to me as though my real life were over already." It is a mood of despair her great-grandmother probably never knew; but her great-grandmother would not have been the right kind of wife for a man in 1962. Education and awareness of self exact their due; and sometimes the modern woman almost wishes she had never known anything but the time-honored meaning of womanliness. She forgets that in that case she would not have been the woman her husband fell in love with.

6 THE SECOND LIFE

In one way or another, as we will later see in detail, the young wife makes her adjustments to, and choices among, her new roles, settling for a self of one kind or another, or several selves patched together. The difficulties caused by the disconnections between the segments of her life diminish after a few years. She solves her problems or comes to tolerate them, finds outlets for her frustrations or becomes inured to them, achieves her desired satisfactions or settles for only some of them. For all the hustle and bustle of her days, she achieves a certain stability and fashions a seemingly permanent way of life, cementing together youth and maturity, motherhood and outside interests, the accumulation of savings and the enjoyment of spending—this whole structure resting on a foundation of successful married love.

And then, when things have been going along in a known and established fashion for perhaps fifteen or twenty years, the entire lovely creation begins to show signs of impermanence and of still another transition soon to come. She has had her children earlier and closer together than her grandmother did, bearing her last child when she is twenty-six. She is still only in her early thirties when they all go off to school in the morning, and somewhere between thirty-five and forty when they are adolescents, away from home much of the day and becoming highly independent. The nest is not empty yet, but much of the day it has an ominously vacant look. Meanwhile her husband is busier than ever with his work, and his career has in some ways become more important to him than his wife; moreover, he rarely needs her encouragement and advice as he did in his first uncertain years.

All in all, she is close to being out of a job and to losing her carefully built-up sense of self. Unless she has been developing other interests, she uneasily senses her diminishing value, glumly counts gray hairs and studies her figure, worries about the coming menopause, and feels that the rest of life will be a long, slow decline toward the grave. In reaction to this she thrashes around uncertainly in search of new goals, new roles, a new identity; to borrow a phrase from Dr. Ruth Hill Useem, sociologist at Michigan State University, she is that curious phenomenon, a thirty-five to forty-year-old adolescent.

She may become a bustling, harried committee member in a woman's club, try her hand at different sorts of volunteer work, go back to college for refresher courses, start teaching again, or try to find a job she is qualified for. If she built a strong, warm relationship with her husband earlier, she may also be buoyed up to some extent by a return of intimacy and companionship when the children are finally gone. But if she has none of these resources to draw upon, or lives in an area remote from opportunities for new involvement, she may flounder around pitifully, playing unwanted mom to her married children, seeking answers in séances and palmistry, frequenting the doctor's office with ambiguous ills, immersing herself in card playing and gabble, or even distractedly trying alcohol and adultery.

Let us admit that these problems are not insoluble, and do not even become critical for the majority of women. But they are real, nonetheless, and particularly worrisome because they are so new in the history of womankind. Even a quite contented housewife, for instance, who has cheerfully spent the fifth age of her life raising a family and running a home, will be forced to redefine her identity halfway through her years in a way women did not have to do formerly. Once, woman's last child did not leave home until she was fifty or more, at which point she had little life to count on and hence not too much of a problem. But, even at that, she did have an accepted, acknowledged niche for the remainder of life; until recent decades, a grandmother was a welcome and necessary part of her children's home, helping in all the female duties and playing the enjoyable new part of revered matriarch, which compensated for the dwindling part of sexual lover.

That pattern, which existed among many peoples throughout much of the past, has all but disappeared from America today. Young people fight tenaciously to keep their home life as personal and private as their honeymoons. They need counsel, but will not take any from their parents; they require financial and other kinds of help, but want it on their own uncompromising terms; they lightly uproot themselves to follow opportunity, and rationalize it by saying, "It will be a good thing for us and the folks that we're going to be so far from them." Even if they do remain close at hand and make grandmother welcome on her visits, she finds herself not a wise matriarch but a naïve oldster. She cannot imagine why they paid good money for the abstract spatter hanging in the living room, the hi-fi assaults her with idiotic discords which they assure her are music, and all her ideas about raising a child have been completely put to rout by a new generation of experts who studied under, and then refuted, the experts she believed in only twenty-five years ago.

Thus woman entering her sixth age of life stands at the border of the longest phase of all—reaching from, say, forty to sixty-five—and yet the least definable, most poorly structured of all. During this entire time she will be relatively free to come and go, and still will retain the comfort and safety of a husband's love. She will be reasonably vigorous, healthful, and even attractive, rather than prematurely withered by diseases and worn by excessive childbearing. She will be financially comfortable, and increasingly free to use her money for experiences she previously had no time for. This need not, therefore, be the anticlimax of life. In these years, many men are in their very prime—practicing their skills more surely and enjoying their achievements more soundly than ever before. Perhaps it could be so with women too; but since the problem is a new one in history, no one has thought about it much, or yet done any intelligent planning toward that end. For all too many women, the discontinuity of their lives at this juncture strands them, flopping and gasping, on the shore of time, where they take a hideously long while to die. For others—and later we will see that their numbers are growing substantially—it is a period when, as the eminent psychoanalyst Therese Benedek says, growth rather than shrinkage takes place and psychic energy, freed from reproductive functions, is channeled into new activities and new emotional investments. It is, in fact, a second life—a thing man has yearned for ever since he was able to think at all.

7 THE YELLOW LEAF

And so at last arrives the seventh age of woman: old age, final retirement, senility. Once again, her roles fall away from her, but this time no new ones appear to take their place. Old age is not a ripe, royal time of life among us as it has so often been among other peoples. It is a period when the elderly people drift around, warming their stiff joints in Florida (if they can afford it), contracting their possessions and habits into a small efficiency apartment in which they feel all but strangled, and thinking up transparent excuses for phoning their distant children. (The phone companies assure us that it is wonderful to pick up the phone and hear the sound of a dear, faraway voice, but it is hardly a substitute for living near and being important to the owner of the voice.)

The aging woman is better off, though, than her husband. Retirement for him means losing the major identity he has had ever since college, and uneasily trying to accommodate himself to being an idler and a nobody. Despite all the modern emphasis on early retirement plans and the joys of leisure, doctors say that many retired men abruptly develop psychosomatic ailments, heart and digestive troubles, and even suicidal tendencies as a result of their sudden uselessness. It is easier for woman; she has been through all this again and again, and has never been so long or completely identified with any single role as he has. It almost seems as though she may have the better time of it at the end of life. But she is deceived; he dies before she does, and forces on her the new role of widow.

And in that unglamorous, unwanted, inglorious part, for which few of the experiences of her preceding forty years of marriage have prepared her, she has her last difficult lessons to learn and adjustments to make. Those who do not get to play the part long are lucky; for others, who live on and on, in full retirement and far from their scattered children, it is often a desperately tedious time, and the most painful of all waits.

PART TWO

MAN'S LOVER

CHAPTER FOUR

THE RELUCTANT

NYMPH

1 THE MAKE-BELIEVE LOVER

How shall we make sense of this complex and contradictory creature, modern woman, with her many selves, her untidy scheme of life, her curious discontentment in the midst of plenty? We have looked at her thus far as a whole thing; now it is time to disassemble her personality into its component roles, the better to see what each of them means to her and how she performs in it. In the end, we should know somewhat more of how the mechanism works, and even perhaps have a few ideas as to how to make it run more smoothly.

Let us start with woman's role as a lover. (The word sounds awkward, yet to speak of her only as a "beloved" implies a passivity which, as we have seen, is not an essential part of her nature.) Taking first things first, what kind of lover does she make in her fancy-free youth—the very time when she is idealized by her culture as a creature loved and loving?

Idealized she may be, but she is pulled to and fro by irreconcilable contradictions. Unchaperoned and uncontrolled, she is free to play at love—and indeed *must* do so, on pain of seeming a failure if she does not; yet actually she is supposed to limit her own freedom and remain chaste or at least niggardly with her favors. Both biologically and emotionally she is ready for love—Helen of Troy, Chloe, Héloise, and many other famous lovers were teenagers at the time of their celebrated love affairs—but while permitted intense emotional experience, she is required to control or deny its biological concomitants.

Things have often been much simpler for the young woman. At one extreme, she was permitted in many societies to indulge in physical and emotional love affairs as long as she managed them discreetly. In Samoa, for instance, the young girl could choose her lovers herself, arrange to meet them privately at night, and experience both poetry and passion without social disapproval until it came time for her to marry. At the other extreme, the young maiden in some societies had no freedom at all, remaining secluded and ignorant of all sexuality and temptation. In Victorian England or nineteenth-century Spain, she was not even responsible for her own emotional liaisons, since any contact she had with young men was arranged, chaperoned, and undertaken in a sensible spirit as a step toward marriage. She may not have been much as a lover, but her role was at least clear and consistent; in marriage she might later experience difficulties with sex, but in her frozen maidenhood there were neither bewilderments, temptations, nor dangerous freedoms.

The American girl, in contrast, occupies an uncomfortable middle ground, able neither to ignore love nor to indulge in it free from guilt and danger. Her love life is characterized by resulting pretense and compromise, from the teen-age crushes that mean less than she wants people to believe, to the sophisticated sexual practices of her late teens which permit her to experience nearly everything, while remaining ostensibly virginal.

In consequence, she is a lover who would have confused and aggravated most of the men who have lived on earth; they would irritatedly have wanted to know whether she does or doesn't feel the emotions she hints at, whether her glance, her manner, and her banter are mere tricks or convey a real message, and why on earth she should allow a man's hands to explore all her body, and, though she is panting and flushed, regard the last small step as immoral and refuse to let him take it.

But the poor girl is quite as confused about herself as any man could possibly be. She is pulled in two directions at once—one way by residual Victorianism and leftover puritan ideals, the other way by contemporary hedonism and the emphasis on the healthful fulfillment of love. Our social code still consists largely of a watered-down double standard in which female chastity is the ideal; inwardly, however, the girl may slowly discard this in favor of a concealed code more in line with contemporary ideas. She tries to hide the discrepancy between the outer code and her inner one, and feels guilty as a result; she stops short of the full implications of her inner code, and feels both cowardly and frustrated as a result. Possibly the best thing about her performance as a lover, in this period of her life, is that it does not last very long nowadays.

2 DATING AS A MARKETPLACE

The perplexities of the girl's role as lover are due, among other things, to the radically new and unsettled milieu in which she plays her part—that amorphous, unregulated mass of customs collectively known as dating. Contemporary Americans accept it as a natural and inevitable procedure; actually, it is a distinctly new idea in Western culture, and one which contradicts most of the age-old practices in that area.

Until the 1920's young girls of the better classes were practically never at liberty to make their own appointments with young men and to go out alone with them on the town. A girl might meet a young man at a party or ball, dance with him, and essay a few stereotyped coquetries; then she went her way home again with Mother or Nanny. If she were lucky or very daring, she might meet him later for one or two clandestine walks in the garden at night; more normally, he would pay formal, uncomfortable visits to her at home in the presence of her family. Over the centuries there were many variations on this pattern, but none of them set any precedent for a system in which a single, decent girl would go out alone with a young man to public places for recreation, and then to private ones for intimacies.

This radical innovation came about for good reason. When society was relatively stable and communities were smaller and closer-knit, young men and women located their future mates through established and controlled channels. Either the parents themselves prospected around for a suitable mate for their daughter, or the young man saw her at church or learned of her by shopping around among his relatives and acquaintances for a suitable, adequately dowered wife. In either case, when he finally came to call, it was not in pursuit of recreation, but in order to size her up before privately talking to her father about the finances involved.

As women became emancipated, they would have none of this any longer; they were ceasing to be helpless and dependent in other aspects of their lives, and saw no reason to be so in this one. Moreover, the system could not work in a society so mobile and large that a girl's father had no good way to appraise the suitor or his background. Dating was the answer: young people would locate and evaluate each other on a personal basis, arrange their own meetings, and conduct their own marketplace, shopping around without commitment until they found what they liked.

The independence of the girl and the absence of any commitment by the man made dating not only a new technique of mate seeking but an enjoyable activity in itself. To the middle-aged, indeed, it often seemed dangerously shallow and pleasure-bent, and Willard Waller and certain other sociologists of the era—themselves middle-aging—even earnestly argued that it was only a competitive game and a form of status seeking, rather than a real love or courting relationship. They charged that the girl wanted in a boy not a lover, but a date who had good clothes, money to spend, a car, a smooth line, and membership in the right fraternity, and that the boy, correspondingly, wanted not someone to love, but a date who was well-dressed, pretty, a good dancer, and sexy-looking, and who would therefore raise his social rating. The girl, in this analysis, invested much time and effort to be alluring, but yielded as little physical love as possible—enough to keep the boy coming back, but not enough to make him spend less on her the next time.

Something was wrong with this portrait, however. How could such a loveless struggle ever turn into a genuine love relationship and culminate in engagement and marriage? For after all, that is what it did. Waller himself had to make the awkward assumption that at some point, for unclear reasons, the girl's and boy's attitudes underwent a metamorphosis, resulting in a different and opposite kind of relationship. A less tortured explanation would have been that, despite the exploitative aspects of dating, it always involved the testing of one's personality on the opposite sex, the piecing together of the meaning of one's femininity or masculinity, and the search for an ideal lover and overwhelming love.

In recent years, external changes in dating customs indicate that these were its underlying values all along, and that the frigid contest of give-and-get was and is the exterior and lesser part of it. A new generation of sociologists finds that postwar youth, even at the high-school level, overtly recognizes the love-and-courtship values of dating. College men and women both assign low places to money or prestige, when describing what they want in a date, and name instead personality traits such as considerateness, pleasantness, and a sense of humor. Even high-school girls and boys, in one recent survey, gave as their primary reasons for dating such answers as "affection," "gaining poise and ease," "selecting a future mate," and so on; only a minority named "getting to social affairs," and only 6 percent of the boys and one-half of one percent of the girls named necking. The teen-age girl acts pert, coy, flirtatious or sultry in order to be popular and go places, but she never stops looking boys over in the hope of finding the "right" one. When she sees or casually meets a new boy who appeals to her, she daydreams not of being his date at the senior prom and arriving in a flame-red convertible, but doodles his name in her schoolbooks with "Mrs." before it and gets goose pimples at the sight of it.

All of which merely indicates that the original motives behind the invention of dating have come to the fore, while the folly and frenzy of the 1920's have taken secondary place. A great deal has been written about how different the dating practices and the sexual mores of today's youth are from those of their parents, but in truth the differences are those of quantity, not quality; the real shift in the mating pattern happened a generation before that.

It was always part of the pattern (though it came a few years later than now) for dating to lead to an unspoken understanding between a boy and girl; for them to become, therefore, more or less a recognized pair; and for their "seriousness" to justify increased physical intimacies. And today, as a generation ago, the girl faces the same questions: How is she to know when to stop having fun and start feeling seriously about a boy? How can she know when his words and actions are sincere, and allow herself ever more risky explorations in love-making? How should she take initiative on occasion, or express her own opinions, without risking the loss of her feminine appeal to him? How shall she gracefully be both game and game warden at once? They are not easy questions, for there are still no fixed rules or guidelines; the relationship between the sexes is in continual flux, with every girl responsible for the successful outcome of her own personal experiments.

3 THE ART OF BEING POPULAR

What could be more bewildering than the young teen-age girl? In the afternoon she is a graceless adolescent, lounging about in sloppy clothes and grumbling about her homework; in the evening she floats into the living room to meet her date, her mouth painted, her hair carefully upswept, her arms elegantly posturing like those of a fashion model. A man of thirty may notice her figure when she is in a bathing suit, and study it reflectively; then, seeing her face, he is privately ashamed of himself. She herself is as bewildered as she is bewildering. At dinnertime she is sick for love of some boy who never notices her, and advertises her sorrow by saying she has no appetite; in the evening she and her girl friends are all a-giggle about a new fellow in the neighborhood, or gaily rush off to a soda fountain to guzzle frappés and flirt with the soda jerk.

She is obsessively interested in boys, but could not tell you why. Sometimes it seems her aim is only to get to the important Saturday night parties and dances; then again, she may feel a tremulous painful yearning for some one boy that makes her listless and moody, and causes her heart to pound wildly whenever the phone rings. Her feelings are sometimes no deeper than the powder on her nose; all she says, of a boy she likes, is that "he's cute" or "he dances like a dream." But equally often, she may retrospectively say, as one college girl did, "Maybe it sounds silly to say a seventh, eighth, or ninth grader can experience love, but I know that's what it was. What else could it have been when I'd lie for him, or lay awake all night and wonder which way to turn?" She may be made quite distraught by her attraction to a boy she does not even talk to; in a letter to a bosom friend one high-school junior wrote:

Bill was at school this morning. All he will do is stare and smile. He thinks I am snootie because I never see him in time to speak. Bill is just about all I think about any more. All of my grades are going down from not studying. This all may sound silly to you, but I am desperate.

A boy of the same age will seldom talk like that. The adolescent love affair is said by many psychiatrists and sociologists to be an attempt to define one's own identity by casting oneself in the role of a male or female lover, but the boy need not rely on this definition alone. He is aware that soon enough he will be a man, with a clear lifelong identity deriving from his work and position. The girl, as we have seen, is quite uncertain what her real self is in this period of her life; the most obvious and readily available answer is to be some boy's girl friend, some man's woman.

A boy may therefore look to the detached observer like a lumpish, ill-mannered hot-rodder, but to the girl he is a mirror in which she sees the image of a female in love, and worth loving; this quality alone makes him a marvelous creature.* Such self-reflecting love is apt to be easily transferred from one mirror to another, but it is untrue that girls are fickle; they may easily and quickly fall out of love with any one boy, but they are always in love with love.

Whether the girl is dating around, or is momentarily infatuated

---

* Stendhal, in *De l'amour,* said that this kind of infatuation was due to "crystallization" upon the other person of all the imaginary desired traits; hence it succeeded best at a distance. He spoke of it in terms of the man's love of the woman, but it also fits the adolescent girl's infatuations perfectly.

with one boy, her effort to achieve a new identity is complicated by her need to acquire feminine techniques that have ambiguous implications. She must be appealing and desirable, yet not let her appeal signify anything bad. She must learn how to talk and behave with a bit of sauciness, yet neither chase after boys nor imply any improper readiness. Her art is to intrigue, to entice, to wring from the boy deeds or words indicating genuine interest—and then some- how to reply to him without giving away her advantage or losing her hold over him. And in curious contrast to what she has learned of her own abilities in school, she is urged by everyone from her mother to the newspaper columnist to simulate admiration for, and inferiority and deference to, the boy. She learns the need for deceit, sometimes quite early; as one bright fourteen-year-old told me, "A girl has to be smart about it—if she likes a boy, she has to let him beat her at games and arguments. And if he's a creep and she wants to get rid of him, she tries her best to show him up." Did this mean, I asked, that the rest of her life she was going to go around fooling men? "Yeah," she replied with a wrinkled nose, "I guess so. Well, why not, if you have to?"

As the years go by the girl comes to do this with almost automatic skill, yet many a girl can neither forget that she is acting untrue to her actual nature, nor overcome a feeling of anger at the part people expect of her. Some 40 percent of undergraduate girls on two differ- ent campuses admitted to Professor Komarovsky that they "play dumb" on some of their dates, concealing their abilities and knowl- edge by artful ruses. One occasionally spells a long word incorrectly in her letters to her boy friend; another admiringly listens to her date as he explains to her matters she understands far better than he; a third has learned that she must never make suggestions to her in- decisive boy friend as to where to go of an evening, but stick to the "I-don't-care-anything-you-want-to-do" routine.

The tactical advantages thus won may exact a double penalty of resentment of the boy and dislike of self. As one girl said:

> I sometimes "play dumb" on dates, but it leaves a bad taste. The emo- tions are complicated. Part of me enjoys "putting something over" on the

unsuspecting male. But this sense of superiority over him is mixed with a feeling of guilt for my hypocrisy. Toward the date I feel some contempt . . . [or] maternal condescension. At times I resent him! Why isn't he my superior in all ways in which a man should excel so that I could be my natural self?

Despite the immense changes in woman's life in the past two generations, this double standard of the personality still finds its sharpest expression in the sex play of dating. Even though the young girl is now beginning to taste her freedom in the modern world and dream of becoming "somebody important," she is required to play a curiously subordinate and dependent sexual role on her dates. At fourteen, her relationship to the boy can be summarized by a simple two-part question: Will he try to kiss her, and will she let him? (If he doesn't, she feels belittled; if he does, and she too easily lets him, she feels cheapened.) A year or so later the question is different, but reflects the same relationship: Will he try to neck, and will she let him? And later still it reads: Will he try to do something with his hands, and will she let him?

As we saw from the evidence of animal life and of human behavior in other cultures, the female is not innately passive and resistant, but enough diluted patriarchalism remains in our culture to force her to be so in her dating behavior. For it is still the boy who invites her out, calls for her, and pays the costs of the evening, all of which symbolizes his masculinity, and earns him the right to make a try at her. Yet when he does so, it is her responsibility to stop him at some appropriate place, without alienating or offending him. She is the guardian of morality on a date; even when the boy himself goes only so far and no further, the real controlling reason is that he knows the girl will not, and so does not try.

As a result the girl develops a peculiar ambivalence concerning sexual experiences. She reads, thinks, daydreams, and talks incessantly with her girl friends about kissing or necking, yet unlike the boy is rarely eager to try it with a casual date. Even after years of experience this remains so; a study made by sociologist Robert O. Blood of the University of Michigan shows that most college men like, and most college women dislike, extensive necking on dates. The same holds true all the more so of that compromise between opportunity and morals known as petting; several surveys have found that a majority of girls neck or pet only because they fear to be unpopular if they refuse. Neither necking nor petting generally appeals to the girl in itself; she only comes to enjoy it when she and a boy feel "serious" or are "emotionally involved" with each other.

Dr. Winston Ehrmann, in a massive study of University of Florida undergraduate sexual habits entitled *Premarital Dating Behavior,* reports that, on the average, boys derive quite a considerable degree of pleasure from necking, light petting, or heavy petting with casual dates; girls, however, rate the pleasure as being distinctly "below average" compared to other life experiences. But when girls do pet for politic reasons, they carefully conceal their lack of enjoyment, since to be known as frigid would be even worse than to be known as too free and easy. The result is that along with a constant harried defensiveness, the girl's noninvolvement is apt to give her a hidden feeling of condescension toward the boy which would be intolerable to him, if he knew of it. For imagine how the young buck would feel if he read this statement by a coed at another university:

> I don't pet with too many of the boys I date, [and] I'd rather not pet to climax, but a few times it couldn't be helped, and I believe this is natural. I don't think it is fair to the boy to allow this state to develop. I naturally don't know how they really feel, but they look like a pathetic case to say the least and at that point there's not much a girl can do.

4 THE DEFENDER OF THE CITADEL

A significant change comes about when casual dating gives way in the girl's life to pairing off and going steady. This shift always did occur, although today it does so several years earlier than it used to. According to reliable sources, it seems that, from their mid-teens on, about a third of urban and suburban boys and girls are going steady at any given time; when one such affair fades out or breaks up, they cast about anxiously until they begin another. To put it formally, going steady rather than playing the field has become the youth ideal.

Why should young people today put so much store by locating a steady partner so early in life? Analysts have offered many profound answers, including cold-war insecurities, the feeling of personal isolation in the monolithic modern state, the sense of success obtained from being in love at a time when other adult achievements are not yet possible, the challenge to parental authority in showing oneself mature enough to love, and so on and on. All these and other factors affect the girl more strongly than the boy; for years she has been more sheltered, less certain who and what she will be for the rest of her life, and more subject to a shifting and declining estimate of her own value. Going steady both clearly identifies her as a girl about whom a boy feels seriously, and gives her an unarguable proof of her own value to the superior male.

For such reasons, she may start going steady without a flicker of real attraction for the boy. "I just drifted into going steady with Arthur," writes one of my questionnaire respondents, "I wasn't in love with him though I thought he was nice enough. Mainly, I had to pick somebody or other; that's the way it was in our school. Only after months did I find myself wondering if I was kind of in love with him." For some others, the experience may start far more intensely, though still as a matter of ego support. "When I was seventeen and fell in love," writes a woman now in her thirties, "I felt as though I had blossomed overnight into a woman; I was a new and wonderful person whom I had never known. The affair went sour in half a year; I broke it off, and felt miserable for a while. But it wasn't that I wanted *him* back—I wanted the new *me* back."

Some are vaguely aware of their own motives, and feel uneasy about them. A recent college graduate who has been more or less going steady with a man for several years writes, "Nowadays I rarely date anyone else except Jim, and I feel trapped, yet secure. At times I feel very much in love with Jim and at other times want to break up, or wonder what I see in him. This is my problem, probably quite a typical one." Others discover more or less through accident that their love is built on convenience, which is likely to prove a shifting sand; one young man, narrating to sociologist Jessie Bernard of Pennsylvania State University the details of a "sacred" and prolonged teen-age love affair, said that after three years the girl's mother finally insisted she go out with other boys for a while. Both young lovers were heartsick, but were forced to acquiesce; then, mysteriously, in a few weeks their love seemed to dissipate and vanish, and they never dated again. What disturbed the narrator was that, looking back on this affair, he no longer knew whether he and the girl had really been in love, or had merely confused habit and comfort with love.

Usually, however, it does not require direct intervention by a parent, or other outside force, to make an *amour de convenance* disintegrate; it comes unglued quite by itself. Accordingly, the average girl has several such attachments of greater or lesser intensity before marrying and learns a good deal about herself and about love in the process.* Professor Robert F. Winch of Northwestern University, in a study entitled *Mate Selection,* reports that many young people are first drawn to persons who embody a cultural ideal (girls, for instance, frequently yearn for the tall, dark, handsome man about whom there is a faint air of mystery), but later find themselves preferring persons who satisfy deep-lying emotional needs.

This shift often takes the girl unawares. A recent college graduate told Dr. Bernard that after she had been "pinned" for over a year, she felt herself slowly falling out of love against her own will. After fruitless efforts to remain in love with the young man, she finally allowed herself to have some insight: "I need someone who is stable and firm and someone who will tell me what to do. In my relationship with Bud it has reached the point where we have just the op-

* Half of American girls marry before twenty, but the proportion is much lower among middle-class college-educated girls; even though campus marriages are talked about a lot, the average age of college graduate women at first marriage was twenty-three in 1960. The delay is definitely helpful; girls who marry in their teens have three times as high a chance of divorce as those who marry in their twenties.

posite. I am the stable one and he is dependent on me. I do not think
I could ever have a happy marriage with him." And just as love
fades when not built on mutual need gratification, so does new love
appear when needs are met. Writes one college senior:

> All of a sudden I realized I had been dating George much more than
> anyone else. George wasn't what I had always thought of as an ideal mate.
> He wasn't very tall—five feet seven inches—and he wasn't the handsomest
> fellow I had ever dated, but something made me enjoy going out with him
> and wanting to date him more often than anyone else. We could sit for
> hours and talk on various subjects—religion, prejudice, morals, our ambi-
> tions, our homes, and our dreams. . . . This causes our love to grow much
> deeper than just the physical aspect.

The status of going steady brings about a marked change in the
girl's attitude toward sexual activities. If the boy is "serious" about
her and if she likes him very much or feels herself in love with him,
she becomes much more permissive of his sexual explorations. In
Ehrmann's sample of Florida college girls, for instance, only 8 percent allowed casual dates to uncover and caress their breasts, but 18
percent granted this to boys they liked and knew well, and 58 percent granted it to boys they had a love relationship with. Similarly,
only 4 percent ever allowed casual dates to touch their genitals, but
10 percent allowed boys they liked to do so, and 41 per cent allowed
boys they loved to do so. Studies in other parts of the country give
different figures for these activities, but the principle holds good—
the girl feels that love justifies her in granting greater sexual liber-
ties to the boy, without her feeling cheapened or "used."*

What is still more important, the distaste or disinterest the girl
felt about sex play now gradually gives way to excitement and pleasure. It is not so much that she kept her passions leashed until now
as that she has had none to keep leashed; but now she begins to discover that she can enjoy sex play. The same girls who say they get
very little pleasure from petting with casual dates admit to getting

---

* Despite the contemporary sound of these details, the pattern is still remarkably true to the ancient tradition, originating in medieval courtly life, in which
personal attraction on a serious and noble level between lady and knight justified
the lady in generally granting sexual "favors" to her lover.

quite intense pleasure from doing so with boys they love, and may even begin to initiate love-making on occasion, by playfully teasing or enticing the boy.

Yet the girl's feelings about sex play remain ambivalent, for despite her growing enjoyment, her role consists mainly of being defender of the citadel and the doler-out of rewards. The nineteen- or twenty-year-old girl's sexual attitude toward her lover is epitomized by the key phrase that appears time and again in interviews, "I let him ———". Whether she is a girl with a strict private code who draws the line at deep kissing, or whether she has a liberal code that allows for maximum petting, she and he arrive at the permissible limits by a process of slow female retreat in the face of a persistent male offensive. A somewhat conservative twenty-year-old, for instance, states:

I've often allowed the boy with whom I'm in love to feel my breasts even though I did not think I wanted him to because he seemed to enjoy it so much. In fact, when he does it I enjoy it too, but I always have a slight guilt complex about it.

Another twenty-year-old, though far more permissive in her code, expresses a generally similar orientation:

This past summer I let the boy I am in love with now do everything except have intercourse with me. In a way he physically forced me and in a way I did not resist as much as I should because I feel so close to him.

The petting relationship, in sum, whether it goes no further than an occasional touching of the bosom, or as far as spending the night nude together without actual intercourse, reflects the girl's residual misgivings and her incomplete acceptance of her own principle that being in love justifies making love.*

* This parceling out of favors, and the maintenance of a fictitious purity, is far from being an invention of our own age; tenth-century upper-class Arabs, and eleventh- and twelfth-century French lords and ladies, set great store by the practice of *amor purus,* a form of sexual dalliance which included "kissing and clipping" and the nude embrace, yet was said to be "pure" because it omitted "the final solace."

Since she herself is in charge of the artificial limitation of love, and is always intently watching to see that the line is not crossed, she is apt to be nervous, resistant, and guilty, even though her sexual activity falls short of intercourse. Over half the girls in one college study, for example, have felt at times that they had gone too far in their petting; in contrast, less than a quarter of the boys have ever felt so. Even though the girl often says of heavy petting, "I feel it's all right because we're really in love," at other times she says, "Mother would *die* if she only knew." Aggravating her misgivings are her ignorance of what other girls are doing, and how they feel about it; despite the lurid girl-to-girl talk in such modern novels as *The Frog Pond,* most sociological research indicates that girls almost never speak to each other frankly about sexual matters. As one recent college graduate puts it, "Freshman year, the problem girls talk about is what to do when a boy tries to unbutton your blouse; sophomore year, when he reaches up under your skirt; and after that, everybody shuts up."

Yet defensive and uneasy as she may be in her performance, the girl undeniably gains a feeling of power from petting. Her image of her own sexuality centers not about performance, but about her ability to attract the male and make him suppliant and eager. All his vaunted superiority, his right to decide what they should do, his present and future advantages over her in the world, are suspended during petting; he wants what she would like to give him but remains cool-headed enough not to. "I insist on not going all the way," says one girl. "I am saving that for my husband when he *is* my husband. That is something I am really looking forward to." In a sense, she is acting a bit more like a mother than a lover; if he will be a good boy, he will get his candy by and by.

5 THE TRIAL RUNS OF LOVE

Dating, as many an expert has pointed out, is far from an ideal method of finding a potential mate or testing one's love. It is fundamentally fun-oriented and free of cares and duties, and thus involves only part of the personality of each partner. Even after many dates, after scores of shared laughs and long earnest discussions, after half a hundred dances and countless kisses, the boy and girl still have only a very incomplete idea as to how their personalities will mesh with each other in marriage. It is one thing to ride off into the spring night with the top down, or to lie on the summer sands, burnished limbs lightly touching and eyes looking at each other with longing; it is another thing to learn how each will feel about the other when faces are pale and drawn with winter fatigue, when bodies are discovered to have their imperfections and unromantic by-products, when dishes, unpaid bills, dirty laundry, job decisions, and in-law problems are no longer the tedious concerns of older people, but of the lovers themselves. Even such characteristics as life-long mental instability may escape notice during courtship; the forty-year-old wife of an electrical engineer in an Eastern city furnishes this dramatic example:

> My husband is a manic depressive who lives on drugs and has been seeing a doctor for the past two years at my insistence. I only regret that I didn't insist on this years ago when I discovered, through old friends of Bill's, that he was like this as a child, and finally stopped telling myself that his ups and downs were just "war nerves." I thought I knew him just because I saw him socially at church and on dates for seven years before we were married. How naïve of me!

But such cases are the minority rather than the rule. Despite all the worries of the middle-aged, who see with alarm the young lovers walking together, their arms boldly around each other's waists, or hear from their parked cars music and bursts of intimate laughter, the going-steady pattern has some merit. Coquetry, the smooth line, competition, and exploitation of each other are all minimized; affection, loyalty, intimacy, and the exchange of confidences replace them. Boys who go steady are less ready to use force or trickery to gain sexual thrills from the girls they love; they assume some responsibility and do not take all the advantage they can. By and large, the young man's sexual activity actually decreases in frequency and extent when he begins to go steady; the girl's, in contrast, increases.

The opposing views boy and girl have held of sex move slowly toward a common middle ground of compromise and equality, more in accord with the practices of modern marriage.

For such reasons, going steady tends to promote neither bittersweet infatuation nor scalding raptures, but a steadier, more realistic love based on intimacy and mutual trust. A number of major studies of marital adjustment agree that long acquaintanceship or long engagement are associated with a high chance of good marital adjustment, and vice versa. Max Lerner therefore terms going steady a "semi-companionate" relationship—one with some of the characteristics of trial marriage. It has pre-empted some of the meaning of engagement, the distinction between them becoming blurred; both, however, publicly commit the boy, and enable the girl to willingly move a bit further from the artificial pose she adopted in random dating toward becoming a complete lover.

Increasingly, she lays aside coquetry and enticement in favor of intimacy and the exchange of personal revelations. Engaged couples no longer spend all their time in dancing, laughing, bantering, or the maneuvers of sexual offense and defense; they now spend long hours telling their past experiences to each other, or discussing religious beliefs, contraceptive techniques, careers for women versus motherhood, and many other subjects their grandparents would have been aghast to think of as topics of premarital talk.

They learn a hundred things about each other's tastes, abilities, and habits; they see and learn to endure many a small flaw that would have blighted adolescent love overnight as frost would kill a rose. Three-quarters of a group of college women interviewed by sociologists Ernest Burgess and Paul Wallin, for instance, named traits they wished they could change in their fiancés, including such unromantic items as nail biting, underweight, overweight, stubbornness, taciturnity, dandruff, poor posture, protruding ears, and the habit of leaving a teaspoon in the cup. But these girls were speaking of men whom, despite their imperfections, they loved and expected to marry—television and magazine advertising notwithstanding.

Engagement also leads to companionate testing in the area of sexuality. Actual behavior ranges very widely today, extending from that of one newly engaged couple who agreed to cease petting and do no more than kiss so that the eventual delight would be the greater and purer, to that of another who, in the words of the girl, a coed at Florida, began sleeping together "without planning or without any conscious decisions. It just seemed to be the most natural thing in the world to do." The central and typical position of the girl, however, is still hesitant and rather equivocal. Her sexual mood is warmer, more overtly desirous, prouder of being desired and of giving a part of the treasure of herself—and at the same time cautious, worried, talkative, and analytical. With casual dates her basic reason for doing no more than she did used to be lack of desire; now, with her steady or fiancé, it is a combination of morals and fear—fear not only of pregnancy, but of being found out, of being changed for the worse, of becoming cheap, and of having something "show in her face." The closer she comes to accepting the boy's fervent plea to spend a Saturday night with him in a neighboring city, the more intellectual and worried she gets about it and the more she wants to discuss all the pros and cons. She is neither languor nor fire, neither yielding virgin nor pursuing sybarite; she is desirous but as tense as a treed cat, panting but jesuitically analytical. Even if she finally "tries it" with her fiancé, she is apt to have her mind on other things. With exquisitely inappropriate timing she may whisper, "Is the door locked?" or "Are you sure it's safe?," rivaling even Tristram Shandy's mother who asked his father, at the most unsuitable of all moments, "Pray, my dear, have you not forgot to wind up the clock?"

Because of all these impediments, there is only about a one-in-four chance that before the average college-educated woman marries, in her early twenties, she will have given up the arbitrary purity of petting for actual intercourse. (The longer she remains single, however, the greater that likelihood.) Even at that, in about half the cases she has done it only with her fiancé. Once again, it appears that the major shift in the morals of American girls occurred in the generation that came to flower just after World War I, and that the changes from that time to the present are far smaller than today's fretful parents are willing to admit.

Except for those girls who go from high school or college to live alone in big cities, sleeping with a man before marriage continues to be worrisome, hard to arrange, and often downright uncomfortable. Cars are generally thought to be great havens for fornicators; actually, they are too exposed and cramped to be suitable for more serious activities than medium petting. The mechanics of the sex act are such that neither Ovid nor the author of the Hindu *Ananga-Ranga* nor Dr. Theodoor Van de Velde could have prescribed a really satisfactory position for the contemporary automobile, and Kinsey actually found that premarital intercourse takes place far more often in the girl's home than in the boy's car.

Similarly, popular humor would lead one to believe that a continual muffled thunder of copulation comes from every motel and camping ground, every thicket in the public park, the beach beneath every boardwalk, and every porch swing and steamship deckchair. But when the wishful thinking of the young and the envious reminiscences of the old are put aside, the unglamorous truth is that sand, grass, bugs, and plastic cushions are exceedingly unpleasant accoutrements of love; that, moreover, the fear of discovery or exposure is hideously distracting; and that finally the lack of sanitary facilities can make the whole thing highly unaesthetic. All in all, none of the illicit loci of love can compare with the legal bed. The net result is that even if the American girl does give up her virginity, she remains something less than a practicing sensualist; according to Kinsey, nonvirgins under twenty have intercourse only once every five to ten weeks, and those over twenty only once every three weeks or so. In comparison, the stodgily married live in riotous debauchery.

Yet for all these limitations and hindrances, a quarter of the girls do go beyond petting to become lovers in the immemorial meaning of the word. But rather than being a further complication of the lover role, this is an important simplification of it. Even under the awkward circumstances of love-in-the-bushes or the worrisome ones of love-on-the-family-couch, the illogical and contradictory aspects of the girl's behavior are diminished; she ceases having to be simultaneously seducer and virgin, temptress and moralist, rose and thorn. With no fragile purity to safeguard, she can stop intently watching herself and her lover for any misstep or weakness. She can begin learning how to become more or less an equal participant in the love act as she already is striving to be in the rest of their relationship.

Any number of moralists have warned the young that premarital intercourse cheapens or harms their later relationship, but the objective evidence does not sustain them: the most reliable interviews and surveys available show, for instance, that the great majority of women who slept with their fiancés before marriage feel that it strengthened the relationship; that only a very small minority have guilt feelings or regret about it after marriage; and that women who had successful premarital intercourse far more often achieve sexual adjustment in marriage than do those who stayed virginal.

Other critics of premarital intercourse warn that it leads to unplanned pregnancies and thus to forced marriages, the prospects of which are notoriously poor. This may be true of the lower classes, but of girls from the middle and upper classes, fewer than one-fifth of the nonvirgins become accidentally pregnant, according to data of the Institute for Sex Research founded by Dr. Kinsey, and only about a tenth of these get married because of the pregnancy; the great majority seek abortion instead. Shotgun marriages would seem, therefore, to account for only 1 percent or less of all marriages of better-class girls.

It is true enough that gifted women either fail to go to college or drop out early, in order to marry, in far greater proportion than gifted men, but not because of anything so simple and obvious as pregnancy. The major reason, rather, is that the girl's identity as a lover and as her fiancé's woman is much clearer, easier, and more immediately satisfying than any of the other, less socially acceptable, more remote aspects of herself that she has been fumbling with for several years. It is not primarily the latter-day stress on homemaking and early motherhood that impels her to marry young; these are only subsequent efforts to justify having done so. The young women who are nervously marriage-minded today are so principally because they want the emotional security of legal love.*

Sociologist Floyd Martinson studied six hundred girls, one to five years after graduation from high school, and found that those who remained single for a while were the better-adjusted and more self-reliant, while those who rushed into marriage were the less mature and the not-so-well adjusted. The social pressures that push young people toward early engagement and early marriage operate on all alike, but the psychologically weaker are pushed the farthest; to them, being in love and belonging to someone seem like the panacea for all ills and the solution to all difficulties. As one Barnard undergraduate said to a friend, according to a note in *The New Yorker,* "I can't decide whether to get married this Christmas or come back and face all my problems."

Yet fortunately that is not all there is to the modern girl in love and on the threshold of marriage; nor, perhaps, is it even truly representative. Here, for instance, from the casebooks of Dr. Jessie Bernard, is part of a letter from a young woman of twenty-three whose parents opposed her engagement to a young man of a different faith. She had gone home from her job in Pittsburgh during a vacation period to tell them about her plans, and met with considerable resistance; then, following a long conversation with her father, she wrote her fiancé as follows:

My darling:
    How fondly I wished that I might have preceded yesterday's second wire —to put my arms around your neck, to smile into your eyes and tell you not to be distressed or unhappy. I'm sorry, my dear, to have to cause you even one moment's unhappiness; but as we have so often said before, even one day of our married life will make up for a whole past lifetime of lone-

---

* Ninety-eight percent of the married women studied by Locke, for instance, named love as a reason for marrying, while only 38 percent named having children, 22 percent sexual satisfaction, and 12 percent economic security. Blood similarly reports that women name companionship as more important than children, economic security, etc. See below, Chapter Nine, *passim.*

liness and unhappiness. . . . My only answer to Father, and to my own heart, is that people take a great risk even in the case of perfectly matched backgrounds, and that, except for the religious factor (which I assured him you and I have not underestimated) you and I were so wonderfully, happily, remarkably compatible in all other ways and strong enough, we felt, to counterbalance the other factors. He was pretty good about it really and said that I was right—he only hoped I'd feel that way when I was forty years old. David, darling, I love you and we *shall* be wonderfully married! So few people make a worthwhile dent in life . . . [but] our marriage, along with adding to the love and laughter in the world, may be one small step toward the building of future racial and religious equalization and harmony. My dear, let's never lose each other. I hate to think how perilously close we came to it that night in Philadelphia. . . . Our love is such a wonderful thing that small set-backs are all only temporary.

I love you dear,
K.

If K. is closer to being the typical lover than the Barnard girl, there is hope for the species after all.*

* K. and David did marry, despite the continuing coolness of her parents. At last writing, nine years after their wedding, she reported their marriage as being extremely happy and stable.

1 UXORIOUSNESS BECOMES FASHIONABLE

Europeans of the better classes, especially those from the Mediterranean countries, find it remarkable and even laughable that American men so rarely have mistresses, and American women so rarely have lovers. The Frenchman or Italian may suppose this is so because Americans are inhibited, awkward, and puritanical about love, and in part he is right; but in larger part the reason is that the potential mistress in America faces competition of a damnably difficult sort: her opponent is the man's own wife. Incomprehensible as it may seem to the Gallic or Italian mind, the American's wife is something of a mistress to him, as he is something of a lover to her.

This, rather than a rigid morality, is why it is rare for American men or women to seek, or to sustain, any major love relationship outside of marriage. If one's marriage is unsatisfying, the love affair is not philosophically accepted as a supplement, but is considered the raw material of a new marriage. But if one's marriage is satisfying, it pre-empts most of the lover in man and wife, leaving little for the outside; to have both a successful marriage and an important love affair is as difficult as to have two mistresses or lovers at once, without either guessing that another exists.

This is distinctly in defiance of many centuries of Western tradition in which marriage had its proper purposes, and love, a diversion, had no connection with them. The very Athenian gentlemen who discoursed so eloquently of love in Plato's *Symposium* were rhapsodizing about their feelings for courtesans or beardless boys, but uxoriousness—undue love for one's wife—was a term of derision among them, as it was also to Romans in later days. Dante's incandescent and utterly pure devotion to Beatrice, Casanova's earthbound obsession with conquest and copulation, Rousseau's tearful, palpitating infatuation for the Countess d'Houdetot are but a few archetypes of the many fashions in love which lay beyond the borders of marriage.

Indeed, throughout the literature of Western civilization the mistress has classically been a woman outside the tedium and practicality of married life who again makes a man's pulses pound, as he in turn makes her smile at herself in the mirror with glistening eyes and a hectic flush in her cheeks. Traditionally it is not husband and wife, but lover and mistress, whose eyes exchange secrets in public, unknown to others; whose feet or knees, touching unseen under the table, cause a pounding in their ears and a trembling in their hands; who, lying together at last after great difficulties, wake, sleep, and wake again, in their repeated efforts to slake the thirst of love.

It is nothing so simple and animalistic as biological pressure that has made the lover-mistress relationship flourish; most men with mistresses have been quite adequately married, with convenient outlet always available. The lover may have written his mistress tormented letters from abroad and seen her only once or twice a year, or he may have kept a little apartment for her and visited her frequently; he may have stolen into her home at night and fled over the rooftops at the sound of her husband's return, or he may proudly have escorted her to the spas while his dowdy mate remained at home in domestic ignorance; he may have repaid her for her love in jewels, or offered her nothing but his own ardent words and body: but in all these situations she has been the one for whom he preened, smiled, insinuated, strutted, and acted his lordly best. Conversely, he has been the one for whom she considered her hair style, practiced her smiles, and placed a touch of perfume here and there; for whose footstep she waited expectantly every time; for whom she did her best to be enchanting and beguiling, always winning him but never possessing him beyond all chance of future loss. Love, in short, has for the most part had little to do with familial obligation, domestic comfort, or regular sexual relief. As La Rochefoucauld put it, "There are good marriages, but no delicious ones."

Yet he wrote that three centuries ago, not foreseeing a time when men would have no mistresses, and wives would have no lovers— and when each would therefore yearn to have their marriages be delicious, at least once in a while. The larger forces of history have dealt roughly with the traditional division between conjugal love and the love affair. Wherever society has grown vast, competitive, and impersonal; where woman has become emancipated, educated, and approximately man's equal; where divorce law permits each to enforce fidelity in the other; where parental or economic mate selec- tion has given way to dating and love choice; where man and woman alike have come to expect that marriage should be a principal source of personal fulfillment and happiness: there the lover-mistress rela- tionship cannot exist peacefully alongside marriage, but must be in conflict with it.

The American answer has been to absorb the lover-mistress rela- tionship *within* marriage, where it becomes one of the major bonds holding the union together.* Marriage still involves the making of a home and the rearing of children, but its most important goal today is taken to be the achievement of a reasonable degree of personal happiness. That being so, the American man and his wife can think themselves lucky to be lover and mistress, rather than look back nostalgically to the fun and games of naughtier eras; indeed, they serve themselves and their children best when they preserve the relationship as carefully as if it were an old-fashioned love affair.

2 ROMANTIC LOVE VERSUS CONJUGAL LOVE

How successfully can the modern wife play the part of her husband's mistress? To begin with, can she remain for three or more vigorous

* The middle-class amalgam of romantic love and marriage is not an American invention, though it has perhaps gone farther here than elsewhere. In Europe, signs of it were visible in Shakespeare's day, and it made particular progress thereafter in Protestant lands and bourgeois circles. See my previous work, *The Natural History of Love,* Chapters 6 and 7.

decades of life a creature about whom he feels strong romantic emotions, and who feels similarly about him? Habit is comfortable but tranquillizing, and excellent things, grown customary, seem mediocre; anyone can remember his wedding night, but who can call to mind the thousandth night in bed with his wife? Many a volume in the library is filled with turbulent and passionate letters that have passed between lovers; the letters of husbands and wives, however, usually deal with local news, domestic arrangements, and assorted essential business. The ultra-romantic lover is said to be happy for a week if he gets one soft glance from his beloved's eyes; what wife can boast a similar power? Stendhal, that eloquent expositor of the love affair, tells in *De l'amour* how he would tremble, stammer, and blurt out inanities in the presence of the woman he loved, and how at night he would skulk in the street outside her home, the merest glimpse of her at the lighted window setting his heart to pounding insanely; what wife can so affect her husband?

Such necromancy cannot be practiced in the broad daylight of marriage; modern men and women forgo some of the magic for the more reliable benefits of married love.* Indeed, as we saw in the previous chapter, dating and going steady are in themselves a partial training away from imaginary emotions toward a more realistic and functional kind. The question is whether all of romantic love should eventually be junked in favor of a practical partnership, or whether some of its components should be retained so as to make that partnership also a continuing love affair.

For some time, it has been the fashion among marriage counselors and sociologists to say that "romantic love" and "conjugal [or mature] love" are logically antithetical, the former being all folly and fraud, the latter all sanity and truth. Romantic love, states a typical

---

* But there are compensations. Stendhal himself admitted that the intense ecstasies he was describing require solitude and misery, and that such love is wrecked by the least imperfection in the beloved. Of the eleven women he loved during his life, the ones who remained remote seemed wonderful to him to the end, but every one of those who actually became his mistress rapidly came to appear ordinary and unlovable. Stendhalian romantic love may, in fact, be harder for the female to endure than the male.

widely used college textbook on marriage and the family, "is like a drug. Fortunately, its power can be more easily broken than that of drugs. Time and common sense . . . frequently restore even the violently afflicted to sanity—and happiness." "Psychically," states another, "it is attuned to persons who are emotionally adolescent and insecure." A third virtually advocates arguments between new-lyweds in order to "liquidate the effect of the romantic complex."

But there are good grounds for doubting the sense of this seem-ingly sensible advice. In the files of family counseling services and in the interviews gathered by many researchers of marriage, one of the commonest complaints concerns the way in which tenderness, expressiveness, and intensity have given way to stolidity and dull-ness. The man does not so often complain of this; his life offers him substitute satisfactions. The woman, however, typically says, "He's a good enough husband and father, but"—and rambles on about a hundred things, all of which simply mean that "he isn't my lover, as he used to be."

One item in the questionnaire I sent out asked, "How does your idea of love compare with the ideas you had of it when you were engaged?" The satisfied and generally happy women among my respondents replied with statements like, "It's far stronger than I ever knew," or "No comparison—I didn't really have any idea how wonderful it was." But many others revealed a hunger for some-thing that has been lost. "I miss that 'moony' feeling that was so warm and tender," writes one young woman. Says another, "One always believes that her marriage will not be like the ones she has seen all around her; then she learns the truth."

Indeed, a perceptive person can often tell, when meeting a woman the first time, what kind of relationship she has at home with her husband. If it is that of lover and mistress, she is likely to be wom-anly without seeming available, appealing but contentedly owned; if it is only a practical partnership, she may talk with a false bright animation, or wear a mask of cynicism and world weariness, or hint in faint desperation at her availability.

Once in a while a woman will pour out, in all honesty, a confes-

sion of what it is like to try to make a modern marriage work without any romantic components. From Oregon, a Catholic woman who
married rather impulsively, and too young, twelve years ago, writes
in quiet anguish:

> What is it like to be married to a person you don't love, and who cannot
> make himself feel love for you? First, you have to pretend, and this requires
> you to be constantly on guard. For a few years you hope that one day you'll
> wake up and find you've fallen in love with your husband; but slowly you
> realize that although there are brief moments of physical passion, there will
> never come a union of souls. The empty place in your heart grows, and for
> no tangible reason you feel guilty. I sometimes think that being unfaithful
> would not fill me with such remorse as the knowledge that I am not, and
> never will be, in love with my husband. We tried togetherness, but the
> strain was too great; now we gracefully find reasons to be apart, in our
> separate clubs and activities. We never talk about it.

The belief in the antithesis between romantic love and conjugal
love, as this woman has painfully discovered, is frequently unworkable today. Romantic love is not a simple entity, made of fiction,
foolishness, and dreams, but a complex structure, some parts of
which are highly adult and valuable. The palpitations, the sleeplessness, the idealization that sees perfection far off and is disillu-
sioned up close are its juvenile aspects, and as we saw do not even
survive the going-steady process. But these are not all there is to
romantic love. Historically, it brought about a revolution in the
relationship between man and woman: for the first time in many
centuries, it made the woman a human being of value, rather than
merely a sexual object; it stressed the concept that lovers should
serve and please each other, rather than seek to conquer each other;
it made sex more difficult and complicated, but allied it with concepts of loyalty and friendship; it made love no longer merely a game
and a sensuous delight, but a source of reassurance and genuine
affection. The more these notions about love were absorbed within
marriage by the middle classes, the more marriage came to seem an
ideal state and the primary source of individual happiness.

The advocates of conjugal love speak of marriage in terms of
"adjustment," "task specialization," "interhabituation," and "ac-

commodation to a standardized pattern of living, working, and playing together." One can hardly quarrel with them; these are all essential parts of it. But by themselves they are a grossly insufficient portrait of what modern Americans want—and need—from marriage. The young man decides to marry, after a period of going steady, because the girl is, among other things, pretty to look at, wonderful to hold, fun to talk to, and above all makes him feel like a man; she marries him because among other things he pays attention to her, tries to please her, is admirable in any of a number of ways, and above all makes her feel like a woman. It is not dreadful of the young man or the girl to continue desiring and hungering for these things after marriage—it is only dreadful if the hungers are not satisfied by the marriage.

But Americans are curiously embarrassed about any admission of the need for romantic conduct between husbands and wives. A man and wife will rarely show as much affection before their friends as they did when engaged (the Greek scorn of uxoriousness is not dead yet), and any advocacy of romantic attitudes within a marriage runs the risk of sounding like a Listerine ad ("Why do some Honeymoons last year after year? Because some people never stop being thoughtful . . . never forget the importance of a fresh, clean breath"). But it is significant that among the educated and intelligent classes in our society who most strongly value romantic attitudes toward marriage, infidelity is low in the early years of marriage; for both men and women, however, it slowly rises to a peak between forty and fifty, as time, children, habit, and routine wear away at the romantic components, leaving many a man and woman with unsatisfied emotional hungers.

Unfortunately, directions for preserving the romantic components of marriage tend, like detailed descriptions of sexual technique, to sound artificial; the words and deeds that come easily to one man or woman may only make others feel self-conscious and uncomfortable. Writes one woman, rather wistfully:

The most romantic couple I ever knew were my maternal grandparents. I remember that even in his seventies, grandfather would enjoy stealing out of bed bright and early and going into the garden to cut a rose, fresh with dew, which he would hand to grandmother with a bow as she woke up. I can still see her bright little old face shining with admiration when they were going out to a concert as she would needlessly straighten his necktie and tell him how handsome and debonair he looked. Once in a while I try to smuggle a little of that into my own marriage, but all I get is an indulgent chuckle for my efforts; besides, I feel foolish and self-conscious about it.

But another and luckier woman, now widowed, reminisces about her twenty-year romantic marriage with poetic pride:

He knew so much: that there is a way to love a woman so as to make his pride in her the chief source of her strength; that there are ways to make her sure, without arrogance, that whom she loves best loves her best; that there is a way to say to her, "Look at that face—like a May morning," in such a way that she does not mind growing old—and does not even seem to. I hope, though I cannot know for sure, that in my own way I did the same things for him.

The old question, "What on earth does he *see* in her?" has various jocular or ribald answers. The truth, however, is that when a man finds a woman who fills his emotional needs and makes him feel important to her she seems rare and marvelous to him; the same, of course, works the other way round. This voluntary and deliberate belief that he or she is a little finer or more wonderful than is objectively the case is a source of health and life to the ego of the loved one, a tonic to body and spirit. We thrive on esteem, and cannot help loving more the one who esteems us.

This is far more salutary than a hard-headed evaluation of each other; marriage should perhaps be realistic, but not so much so as to kill one's delight in the beloved. Terman, in his classic study of marital happiness, found that even his happy women could mention faults in their husbands such as argumentativeness, a quick temper, selfishness, nervousness, touchiness, and so on; yet by and large they did not consider the faults important. Unhappy women, naming these same faults, found them important roughly ten times as often as did the happy women.

A minority—one out of five women, according to sociologist Ernest

Burgess—do not want any changes in their husbands at all.* They apparently still think their husbands quite wonderful, and though not blind to their imperfections, seem to accept these with equanimity and sometimes almost with enthusiasm. Writes one of my correspondents, a brilliant woman who collaborates with her husband in biological research work, "We've been mad at each other and hurt each other many a time. But I can't think of any way in which I would want to change him, even if I had the power to do so. I think I would love him as much—that is, he would be just as much the man I love—if he didn't go through periods of depression, and I'd be pleased if he quit smoking and biting his fingernails. But it couldn't make me love him any the more."

Marriage assuredly cannot be *continuously* delicious, as the interludes of a love affair might be, but there is time and place in it for many romantic moments. A man needs to feel, occasionally but powerfully, his delight in a woman's presence, his pride in her admiration of him, his pleasure in her efforts to be appealing to him; a woman needs now and again to feel noticed, relished, appreciated, sought after. Even though these interludes are separated by large quantities of diapers and bills, mortgages and medical problems, flooded cesspools and college applications, they are neither unimportant nor impossible.

There are some married couples who, even after ten, twenty, or more years, still act out affection and romantic feeling in a multitude of ways. In public, they may not cling fondly, like new lovers, but they look at and listen to each other with a subtle friendliness; when one speaks, the other is proud of something well said; in a word, they

* The above figures on the perception of faults by happily married and unhappily married women are overall averages. In any one marriage, of course, the level of happiness is not constant; there are days, weeks, or even whole seasons in which things go better or worse than usual, and during which the eye that sees faults is more or less critical than ordinarily. But since the surveys by Terman and Burgess took large samples of women at one point in time, these fluctuations were canceled out. The point remains valid that in an overall sense there is a distinct relationship between a somewhat romantic view of one's mate and happiness in marriage.

admire each other. The wife of an operatic baritone has tried to summarize her own love, after twenty-odd years, in groping but expressive phrases:

> Over the years the meaning of love has been a constant revelation. A oneness between two people; a constant awareness of and sensitivity to each other's moods (be they happy or not), and the desire to share them. Mutual respect, of course. A warm glow that comes over me through a word, a touch, or a look—after all these years, too! It's as though I have a halo given me to wear, by this one wonderful person, my husband.

She neglects to mention what is equally significant: that she herself is always aware of *his* moods and needs, admires him unrestrainedly, subtly reminds him of his best stories or most stimulating views in company, and is as delighted when he then tells them as if she had not heard them fifty times already, and looks at him now and again with an awareness and attentiveness that one usually associates with lovers rather than married people.

Nearly all men from time to time dream of mistresses and of escape from the cares of the home to the exhilarations of the affair; but most men with thoroughly satisfying marriages admit that for them these are only occasional fantasies. "Our wives," one such man writes, "mean to us today what mistresses meant to men in other centuries. That's why I've never sought to have an affair, and may never do so—I simply don't need one." The history of love almost seems to have been pointing toward this synthesis for centuries. Some men tried to visualize the outcome long before it was feasible; Chaucer spelled out the wish six centuries ago:

> Wyf is mannes help and his comfort,
> His paradys terrestre and his disport.

It was only satire in 1388, but satire usually implies an ideal; in 1962 the ideal is possible.

3 PASSION AND INEQUALITY

So much for the romantic aspects of the mistress-wife role; now let us see how well the mistress-wife functions as her husband's sexual lover. For the two do not always go together easily: the medieval troubadours who invented romantic love may even have perfected *amor purus* because of some deep-seated discomfort in practicing earthly love where a heavenly one was felt. It is no mere coincidence that the nineteenth century, which exalted purity and domesticity, also witnessed a great deal of prostitution and sexual neurosis.

The modern practices of dating and going steady, however, go a long way toward amalgamating the two impulses. Step by step, the sexual mores of the unmarried result in a partial synthesis of sex and romantic love, at the same time discarding the unrealistic aspects of adolescent romance in favor of those which are suited to prolonged intimacy. The American girl thus learns, at least in some measure, how to be her lover's sexual mistress as well as his romantic beloved.

But marriage, though it finally brings release from the worries and self-imposed limitations of petting, also sharply changes the pace and focus of love-making. In dating and courtship, the girl was continually flattered and reassured by the wooing process; the slow pace of advance, her own power of refusal and control, her lover's solicitousness and his continual attention to her reactions made her seem to be the epicenter of the process. Marriage makes a difference, as she sometimes abruptly learns the first time she goes to bed with him. This is how one young woman described it to a sociologist:

Finally we were alone. We were in each other's arms with our hearts pounding. . . . We could be ourselves. And this meant being close spiritually as well as physically. We were really together. But all of a sudden something happened: before I knew what had happened Ted had me in bed and I had lost him. It was the strangest experience I had ever had. Nothing like the raped bride cliché. Ted is too sweet for that. Until just a minute before, we were together and then he left me and went off all by himself leaving me there all alone, and in the "alonest" possible way. . . . When he finally returned, relaxed and happy, he was sweeter than ever . . . [but] he knew that he hadn't done what the books said to do. He hadn't made me the star of the performance but just a prop.

(One may admit that the bridegroom's technique was faulty—but simultaneously question the girl's assumption that she should remain the "star of the performance," as she was in courtship.)

After the honeymoon or experimental period, the differences between courtship and married love become even more distinct. The girl had been conditioned as long and thoroughly as any Pavlovian dog to respond to moonlight, soft music, dancing, and the slow prolonged dalliance of necking and petting. In marriage the man who used to spend an hour or two getting her overwrought is likely to spend the evening reading, repairing the vacuum cleaner, or watching television, giving no hint of appetite until they are in bed—at which juncture he may pull her to him, instantly ready for action, and easily offended if she shows surprise or emotional unpreparedness.

It is customary to scold husbands for this and lecture them on the need for adequately courting and preparing their wives, but this is not altogether fair. The mistress awaiting her lover's visit knows that love-making of one sort or another will be in order; she is in a state of anticipation and emotional readiness before her lover begins to practice his art. Literature is full of lovers who rush into each other's arms the instant they meet, and immediately repair to the nearest bed without protracted foreplay. The affair is a special situation in which love-making is necessarily implied, and the first touch follows upon hours of courting in fantasy. Marriage, on the contrary, is a generalized situation without automatic clues for one's emotions on any given night; this works no hardship on the husband, who never needed long preparation in order to be aroused, but the wife, with her long years of conditioning as a *demi-vierge* may be slow to react with passion, slow to unleash her desires without fresh assurance that love is involved.*

She may even look back nostalgically to premarital petting as having been, for all its frustrations and temptations, beautiful and ex-

---

* It is often alleged that the differences in arousability are fundamental and biological. But detailed anatomical studies of the nerve structures of the sex organs and the physiology of arousal show fundamental similarities between male and female, and although in some societies women require hours of foreplay before being ready to copulate, in others they are ready almost at once and consider erotic foreplay "wrong." Kinsey even found the latter view existing among a fair number of lower-class Americans.

citing; when her husband sees two teenagers necking in the back of a taxi, he snorts in scorn, but she sighs in sympathy or envy. A woman who was temporarily estranged from her husband after ten years of marriage, writes:

> We had a few "dates" with each other during this period that no one knew about. On one occasion he sent me a dozen roses, and that evening we went to a very posh restaurant for dinner and dancing, and even did a little necking in the car afterwards. It may sound ridiculous, but I found this very romantic.

It is the same impulse that makes many a woman want to lie in her husband's arms at night and feel loved before falling asleep, whereupon, to her surprise, he responds with a hunger she had not meant to arouse. Lying together is, for her, an enjoyable and loving thing, sufficient in itself; for him it is a cue to action, and definitely incomplete.

On top of the difficulties involved in this transition from courtship love-making to married sex, the wife-mistress tries to find a workable meaning of "equality" in marriage. In part, she already does have equality in such things as the vote, the joint ownership of property, the right to divorce, freedom to move about unchaperoned, and most of the important family decisions. But equality also means a drastic redefinition of traditional male and female sex roles, and sometimes seems to threaten the traditional foundations of masculinity and femininity.

A majority of middle-class women, for instance, consider themselves less passionate than their husbands and feel desire less often (only about a third consider their sex drive equally strong, and only a small percentage think themselves more passionate).* But if most other things about marriage rest upon a basis of equality and partnership, ought the husband not to be required to restrain himself

---

* There is nothing permanent about the disparity, however. The ancient Greeks believed that women derive nine times as much pleasure from sex as men do, and men as dissimilar as the Roman poet Juvenal and the medieval inquisitors Sprenger and Kramer were certain that woman was far more passionate than man. Anthropological surveys of human sexuality show that in various societies the female attitude ranges from mass frigidity to mass insatiability.

when his wife is not as eager as he? Ought she not make love only on those occasions when she wants to just as much as he? And the middle-class husband concedes his wife this right to refuse: as Burgess and Wallin report in a study of nearly seven hundred marriages of college-educated people, "Because the marriage relationship is conceived of as a partnership, many men feel guilty in pressing for intercourse when they believe their wives are getting no satisfaction from it."

Refusals may have any one of many different meanings or qualities. Although marriage manuals give no specific advice on the techniques of refusal, women discover and create their own methods with remarkable ingenuity. Some are crude but effective: as one woman candidly told a clinical case gatherer, "We don't do it much —about once a week, or sometimes twice, if I can't talk him out of it or make him mad enough." A nearly frigid woman from a lower-middle-class farm background remarks, "I think I have sort of cooled him off during the years. If I was tired I would say, 'Now, you turn over there and go to sleep, for I don't want to monkey with such foolishness.' And he wouldn't bother me any more." Still others enlist outside help: the late Marion Hilliard, an eminent woman's doctor in Toronto, said that many women came to her after ten or twelve years of marriage with various vague complaints of a "female" nature, hoping they could return to their husbands with the report, "The doctor says I can't."

Most middle-class wives, however, are neither so crude nor so hostile. On those occasions when they choose to refuse, they are more apt to say, "Not tonight, please, dear; I'm *so* tired," or "Can't we wait for a cooler night?" or "I've got a headache—let's make a 'date' for tomorrow night," or even, "You go on to sleep—I've got to get the ironing finished." Still subtler is the one who, as bedtime approaches and a spark begins to glow in her mate, remembers some gently quenching topic she must discuss with him such as how to handle the three-year-old, or where to go on vacation, or what on earth to do about the living-room sofa. Among the ungathered but fascinating statistics of our time would be the total tonnage of face cream used annually not as an emollient but a detumescent.

According to a generous sampling made by Terman, 10 percent of middle-class wives use these or other means frequently, another 28 percent do so sometimes, and still more do so on rare occasions. Only 21 percent never refuse their mates. A separate study by psychologist Harvey Locke shows close agreement, only 23 percent of his wives reporting that they never refuse their husbands.*

To some conservatives, this whole spectacle is cause for dismay and despair; any and every refusal by the wife is seen as a "pseudo-masculine protest" or a "symbolic castration," while any and every male concession to sexual equality is seen as a failure of masculinity. "We live today," write Ferdinand Lundberg and Dr. Marynia Farn-ham with scorn, "in the era of the apologetic bridegroom, successor to the sturdier rapist of a bygone day."

Before one sighs, like Miniver Cheevy, for the days of old, one should consider whether the price paid, in relinquishing the right of rape, is not cheap, considering what he gains. Locke's data show, for example, that twice as many divorced women as married women had never refused sex to their husband; their acquiescence, far from being a sure-fire technique for achieving happiness, may have been a symptom of a crippling inequality and lack of empathy between husband and wife.

Every major statistical appraisal of marriage made in recent years shows that among the economically lower and less-educated classes, far more husbands neither comprehend nor care about the wife's feelings about sex, while among the better-educated, higher-status classes more husbands understand and are interested in the wife's feelings. The results as reported by various authorities are re-assuring:

—Lower-status women, far from being naturally and hotly sexual, are more frequently frigid or antagonistic toward sex than women in higher-status groups.

* Women, too, make advances or drop hints, and are rejected, but far less often; both Terman and Locke found that about two-thirds of husbands never refuse an overture by their wives, and that hardly any refuse them frequently.

—Divorce, contrary to all popular notions, is far more common among the lower-status, less-educated classes than among the middle and upper classes.

—Lower-class women generally find marriage less satisfying, and married love-making less pleasurable, than do women of the middle and upper classes.

Yet equality is like a sharp-edged tool. It can be skillfully used to chisel out a beautiful object, but the woman who misuses it in revenge, or to establish a parity she has insufficiently won elsewhere in life, is turning it into a weapon which will wound her as well as her husband; the literature of psychiatry is filled with case histories of men who have become partly or completely impotent within marriage, and found their lost potency outside it. A wife's desire to be aroused by the careful techniques of premarital petting can be a stimulus and excitement to the husband—or can be used by her almost as a punishment, exacted in advance, for his pleasure.

The most fortunate woman is she who desires sexual intercourse as often as her husband, or who is easily aroused to that desire by his overtures. But almost equally fortunate is she who comes to value her husband's love-making as a tribute to herself and as an expression of his masculinity, and who exercises her right of refusal rarely and only when love-making would turn out so poorly that he, as well as she, would be disappointed in it. "The satisfactions of a mate's needs may be justifiable even when they are not necessarily mutual," wrote Dr. Lena Levine and the late Dr. Abraham Stone, noted counselors of the Margaret Sanger Marriage Consultation Center. "When the woman's response is slower, as it frequently is, the man's control of so powerful an impulse as the sex force shows evidence of thoughtfulness and consideration. . . . The wife who is willing to accept her husband and give him the satisfaction he seeks, even though she may have little desire at the time, shows the depth of her feeling for him." This is a far cry from automatic submission, with repugnance; it is no endorsement of automatic patriarchal privilege and female masochism, but of a far subtler and more mature relationship. In a burst of confidence, one woman of thirty-nine, who appraises her own marriage as extremely happy despite occasional turbulence, expresses the whole thing perfectly:

> In the first few years, I used to worry and wonder each time whether I'd get involved in the act, that night, the way he always does, or whether I'd remain outside it, and feel annoyed and cheated. But over the years I've learned a great deal. Nowadays I sometimes want it when he does and sometimes not, but I rarely refuse, and I tell him—and it's almost always true—that I love to have him make love to me, that my enjoyment and his enjoyment are sometimes rather different, and that I like it fine that way.

4 THE SEDUCTIVE WIFE

Obviously, the attitude of such a wife-mistress toward the act of love is far from identical to that of her husband. But to be *not-identical* does not necessarily mean to be *opposite*. The female's sexual alternatives are often arbitrarily presented as a choice between the aggressive, competitive striving of the old-style feminist and the placid receptivity of the old-fashioned "womanly" woman. The modern wife is uncertainly evolving an answer which attempts to reconcile her equality as a human being with her need to be sexually appealing. As we have just seen, this conflict affects her arousability and her acceptance of love-making—and that is not all; it also complicates the question of the *activity* she displays concerning sex, and the kind and frequency of *satisfaction* she gains from it.

Activity on her part is a chancy thing; except in an occasional neurotic marriage, a wife realizes that certain kinds of sexual aggressiveness or dominance on her part are profoundly upsetting to her man. The part of the gigolo or male prostitute is almost incomprehensible to the normal male; he is revolted at the thought of the man's being expressly commanded by a woman to perform sexually. "When I say *now*, the answer must not be later," says Princess to her young kept lover in a particularly unpleasant passage from Tennessee Williams' *Sweet Bird of Youth;* "I say now and mean now." Chance complies, but later, when she tells him that a group of men are threatening to castrate him if he does not leave town, he replies, "That can't be done to me twice; you did that to me this morning, here on this bed."

Yet nonaggressiveness in the modern woman is very different from the passivity of the middle-class wife in the last century or the lower-class one today. Her basic attitude is not inert and yielding, but enticing and responsive. This is generally recognized among upper-status people, who, for one thing, approve of the wife who tries to remain sexually attractive and appealingly feminine, and disapprove of the wife who "lets herself go" or forgets to maintain her feminine charm. Natasha, in *War and Peace,* perfectly exemplifies the way in which a woman was once supposed to change after marriage, and the way the American woman is *not* supposed to change. Once the slimmest, gayest, sauciest, wittiest, and prettiest of girls, she shed these traits after marriage almost with relief, becoming thick-waisted, placid, earthy, sexually passive, and quintessentially maternal. A similar change still occurs in the daughters of conservative Spanish or Latin-American people, and in American frontier days it was both unnecessary and improper for a young woman to remain appealing and girlish, rather than hard-mouthed and matronly.

One might even suspect that the more patriarchal a society and the more the wife is limited to the household and to motherhood, the less she can function as her husband's active lover. Patriarchalism seems to set up a conflict between the role of mother and that of lover, not only in the mind of the wife but in that of her husband; his incest fears make him unable to tolerate in this highly maternal person any conduct that is seductive, sexually playful, and passionate.

Here, surely, is the source of power behind the argument that the wife should be quiescent and masochistic rather than stimulating and pleasure-loving, and the ultimate reason men have often divided women into sacred lovers and profane ones, into those they marry and those they frolic with. Such a dichotomy makes the husband uncomfortable about treating his wife as his sexual playmate. He "relieves himself" or seeks perfunctory "solace" upon her unresisting body without much delight or sport—recall, if you will, the dictum of St. Jerome that "He who too ardently loves his own wife is an adulterer"—but for more intense and abandoned satisfactions he seeks outside liaisons (if he has money and leisure enough), leaving his wife to satisfy herself vicariously through children and religion. She sometimes chooses, instead, to love his neighbor, the stableboy, or almost anyone else who is at hand.

In modern times such a pattern obviously will not do. For one thing, the man cannot get away with it; for another, he only half-heartedly wants to, since he really does not *need* to unless his wife abandons her part as lover in favor of good, gray, asexual wifeliness. Modern woman best protects her functions of housekeeper, mother, partner, companion, and friend to her husband not by decreasing her role as his lover, after the honeymoon, but by cultivating it; not by being the waiting receptacle, but the eager mouth and the responsive body.

Like a mistress, her activity begins with continual effort to be attractive to her mate, and to guard against seeming unappetizing. To some thinkers, this indicates that the love between her and her husband is not "mature," for mature love should be godlike or at least parentlike, forgiving all faults and flaws. The noted psychologist A. H. Maslow of Brandeis University writes that in real or conjugal love "there is much less tendency to put the best foot forward [or hide] physical defects," and Theodore Reik has said, similarly, that in genuine or mature love one no longer needs to practice pretense or concealment.

Godlike love, however, is suited chiefly to gods; the rest of us, being human, have human needs in our loving. If a man hungers for and enjoys the presence of a lovely woman, and a woman the presence of an attractive man, it can only be selfishness and thoughtlessness—hardly mature qualities—to refuse or deny each other what is so important. A man cannot help knowing—and therefore must decently accept—his wife's physical functions and limitations; it is the same with a lover and his mistress—yet a mistress tries to appear attractive and pleasing as much of the time as is feasible.

This is only the first of the active components in the wife-mistress role. She does not always wait, for instance, for her husband to show signs of gathering sexual hunger, but excites or signals him in any of a hundred ways. One woman slips on a filmy gown at bedtime rather than her usual pajamas, another acts kittenish in the course of the evening, a third nuzzles her husband in some special private fashion that "lets him know." One asks her husband to walk her around the block before bedtime, another sits at her vanity brushing her hair out instead of putting it up for the night, and yet another regards her husband's body, as he undresses, with a soft, sly admiration that pleasantly surprises and arouses him each time anew, just as though she had not been doing it for ten or twenty years.

And in the act itself the modern mistress-wife is not a compliant, utilized object, but an active partner. This is actually the human norm; only a very few cultures have ever prescribed impassivity and inertness—our own being one of them. A best-selling marriage manual of the mid- to late-nineteenth century, for instance, warned wives against "excessive ardor," and enjoined them to "complaisance, tranquillity, silence, and secrecy." One nineteenth-century gentleman, introducing his bride to the rites of love on their wedding night, is said to have stopped short and admonished her, "*Ladies,* my dear, do not move!" As recently as 1959, a psychoanalyst named Marie N. Robinson was still advocating that woman be "the passive instrument . . . stretched out supinely beneath him, taken up will-lessly by his passion as leaves are swept up before a wind." But although the upper-status sophisticated male may be dismayed to have a woman "run the show," he finds it equally disagreeable today for her to lie still and receive him passively, without words, gestures, or movements.

Precise prescriptions of what she should do may not be very helpful, since our culture is so rapidly changing and so inclined to privacy that individual men and women react differently to different details. Nevertheless, there is a whole armamentarium of touches, words, movements, sounds, and facial expressions which most better-educated men find exciting and yet not threatening, responsive and yet feminine. This has been true in many another culture: older collectors of anthropological sex data like Havelock Ellis and William Graham Sumner, and modern ones like Clellan S. Ford and Frank A. Beach, have listed scores of details of how women in different lands tease, provoke, touch, bite, scratch, or otherwise arouse their men. Such behavior usually differs from the male's in kind or at least in manner, there being in each culture a set of appropriate feminine sexual actions; many of them might not seem particularly appealing to us, but that is no matter—the important point is that they are *actions,* and that they seem feminine and exciting to the men involved.

As wise a statement of this general principle as can be found anywhere was written sixteen centuries ago by the Hindu scholar Vatsyayana in his *Kama-Sutra,* a great classic on the art of love. "In sexual congress," he wrote, "one is apparently active and the other apparently passive. There is, however, no fundamental difference between them, for they are both equally indispensable to one complete act of intercourse. Really, neither partner is passive or indirect; they are both equally active." He thereupon lists a great variety of complementary kinds of biting, kissing, caressing, and slapping, all of which are mutually though a little differently performed. The precise details may seem a trifle bizarre to us today and not to everyone's taste, but the underlying ideal is the same as our own— mutual, though differentiated, activity in the sex act.

This is the goal toward which the great majority of better-educated upper-status Americans are moving today. For these people, to a measurably greater extent than most of the less-educated and lower-status Americans, spend time kissing, touching, and admiring each other's bodies, in their separate ways, before joining them. These men tend to prolong intercourse to please themselves the more, but especially to await the right moment in their wives, and these wives are likely to sensuously do various "forbidden" things on occasion and to playfully try variant positions from time to time. These men and women whisper expressive words to each other during the act and feel affectionate and talkative afterward, rather than copulate with monosyllabic expressions and fall asleep in silence. These are the people who have overwhelmingly accepted birth control, not in order to be childless, but in order to enjoy the lover-mistress relationship, begetting children by choice and not, like the animals, involuntarily.*

5 THE MEANING OF "SATISFACTION"

So much for the kinds and amount of activity of the wife-mistress; now, what of the satisfactions she expects from the act of love? Here again she is involved in a seeming conflict between equality and difference. Only a few decades ago, when feminists were fighting to liberate women from shackles of Victorianism, it seemed to them that man had selfishly appropriated to himself sexual pleasure just as he had political power. Like suffragettes fighting for the vote, the sexual reformers ringingly demanded that woman be given the orgasm; in the context of their general struggle for equality, it was natural for them to feel that woman's climax should be very much like man's, and just as unfailing. Mrs. Marie Stopes, in her radical manifesto of 1918, *Married Love,* proclaimed that the wife must be given full gratification every time; Havelock Ellis repeatedly stressed the moral duty of the husband to guarantee his wife's satisfaction; and in one of the best-known marriage manuals of the 1920's, still popular today, Dr. Theodoor Van de Velde solemnly warned men that "every considerable erotic stimulation of their wives that does not terminate in orgasm, on the woman's part, represents an injury."

A literary tradition came into being in which the female orgasm was not only exalted, but made to sound much like that of the male in violence and significance. Mrs. Stopes herself wrote in another book that "the critical pinnacle of the orgasm broke like the towering crest of a sun-sparkling wave," and D. H. Lawrence, writing bet-

---

* About 80 to 90 percent of better-educated Protestants and Jews, and nearly as many better-educated Catholics, make efforts at contraception or regulated fertility. Less-educated and lower-status Americans of all faiths know less about fertility limitation, are less favorably disposed toward it, and are haphazard in their practice of it when they employ it at all.

ter but just as wetly, said that the woman felt "deepening whirlpools of sensation, swirling deeper and deeper through all her tissues and consciousness till she was one perfect concentric fluid of feeling, and she lay there crying in unconscious inarticulate cries." Moving ashore, Tennessee Williams recently had the young wife in *Streetcar Named Desire* see colored lights flashing, and a currently popular marriage manual asserts that the woman's "whole being is a full orchestra playing the fortissimo of a glorious symphony."

But these and a hundred similar lyrical efforts are wishful thinking rather than objective reportage. Clinical studies report again and again that female orgasm is vastly more variable in intensity and meaning than the male; this is only natural, since it does not involve ejaculation and so does not always or necessarily include highly localized violent convulsions such as must occur in the male prostate and urethra in order to expel the semen.

The unscientific equating of the female's orgasm with the male's has been partly if not largely responsible for many of the alarming statements about the frequency of frigidity in modern women. A generation ago the psychologist G. V. Hamilton direly reported that 46 percent of the American wives he had studied had "a very inferior or wholly lacking orgasm capacity," and scores of other writers followed his lead in the ensuing years. Even very recently, the psychiatrist and popularizer Frank Caprio began one of his books by saying that "the prevalence of [frigidity] is high enough to account for a large number of divorces (400,000 a year)," a statement as ambiguous as it is alarming.*

Such data, though intriguing, are highly misleading, since by using the female orgasm as the prime measurement they perpetuate the feminist error. No one can deny that orgasm in the female is *related* to general sexual satisfaction, but it is far from being *identical* with it, or invariably *necessary*. It is true that women who persistently fail to reach orgasm in their married love-making often come to clinicians and marriage counselors to complain and to ask

---

* No one else attributes all of the 400,000 annual American divorces to frigidity, as Dr. Caprio seems to do.

for help, but in part their discontent is caused by an acquired cultural expectation that has not come true. If a woman has been assured that she will, that she ought, that she *must* see colored lights, feel like a breaking wave, or helplessly utter inarticulate cries, she is apt to consider herself or her husband at fault when these promised wonders do not appear.

Any wider look at human sexuality proves the parochialism of this attitude. Margaret Mead reports that some cultures have no idea that women can or should experience orgasm, although the women in such a culture may have active sexual appetites and enjoy coitus thoroughly. Anthropological studies in general show that there is an immense range of female sexual response and orgastic capacity, and that the women in each society generally believe that their own set of mores represents the right, natural, and proper way to be. Clinical data show that a wide range of differences exists even among American women. Some can reach orgasm within half a minute and experience it repeatedly during one act of intercourse; others never know it in a lifetime, despite the best efforts of attentive husbands; and the majority are somewhere in between.

A fixed expectation concerning the "right" orgasm frequency can do as much harm as a husband's ineptness or a rigidly puritanical upbringing. The typical upper-status woman with no more than the usual inhibitions, and a normal physical endowment, is justified in expecting that at times she will know wild abandonment and the violent purgation of desire; that more often she will know a milder, somewhat blurred climax that dies away gently; and that some of the time she may find resolution and satisfaction in a mere dying-away of her own heat after the man is done. ("A woman in love," writes Simone de Beauvoir in one of her rare gentle moments, "can find in the man's orgasm a conclusion that brings appeasement and satisfaction.") The woman who, however, is fixated on the attainment of explosive orgasm in herself may, despite a fury of activity, seem a poor lover to the man, for she does not make love to him at all—she is remote, alien, and absorbed in herself, relegating him to the status of an impersonal mechanism.

Valuable as are the data on female orgasm frequency, the important question is: How many women like and find satisfaction in the role of married mistress? The data of Kinsey and half a dozen other investigators are in general accord: even after years of marriage, only some 40 percent of better-educated middle-class wives achieve orgasm almost all the time. Nevertheless, 62 percent of 1,000 such women surveyed some years ago by Katharine B. Davis said that sexual relations were definitely pleasurable to them, and only 26 percent said they felt neutral about sex or found it distasteful. A review of nearly nine thousand women patients of the Margaret Sanger Research Bureau showed that only a third of them usually reached orgasm, yet three-quarters exhibited healthy, positive attitudes toward their sexual life.

The proportion of women who find sex pleasurable even when not invariably productive of male-type orgasm seems, in fact, to be increasing: Harvey Locke's data, published twenty years more recently than those of Katharine B. Davis cited above, indicate that nowadays as many as 90 percent of better-status wives call their sex relations "enjoyable" or even "very enjoyable"; only 8.2 percent say they "tolerate" it, and 1.2 percent find sex disgusting.*

The further the dust and clamor of the feminist battle recede into the distance, the more a balanced concept of female satisfaction seems to be emerging. The data above are one indication of that. Another is a change in the tenor of much professional and popular advice to wives. Some of the newer marriage manuals no longer aggressively demand that the husband furnish the woman with orgasm, measure for measure; a recent book was even entitled *The Sexual Responsibility of Woman*. Advice to women is appearing of a type the feminists would have rejected out of hand: Dr. Hilliard, for instance, has urged wives to pretend that they have reached orgasm on those occasions when they have not. "It's the worthiest duplicity on the face of the earth," she wrote. "It gives a man his

---

* But almost 27 percent of divorcees, in the same study, called sex disgusting. Still, it is not clear whether they became divorced because of that fact, or found sex disgusting because they did not love their husbands.

manhood, a quality of glorious robustness that cannot fail to reward the giver. Thousands of women who have begun this sort of benign sham have discovered that their pretended delight rapidly became real."*

Such is the tone of some of the latest professional advice, but the married mistress herself occasionally expresses it even more convincingly. Here, for instance, is part of a recorded clinical interview that conveys the attitude about as well as is possible:

Married love is infinitely bigger and more wonderful than I ever dreamed back in my dating years. Including the sexual part. I used to be all stirred up and unsatisfied by petting before we were married. Even after, it took months before I began to have any of those "perfect times," and to realize what the poets had been writing about. But on those times that weren't perfect—you know, the times when I didn't make it—I used to be upset, or sleepless, or get a splitting headache, just as I'd been told I would. Well, somehow—I don't quite know how—our love has grown and I've changed, and nowadays when I do have it, which is about half the time, it's tremendous, but when I don't, I've so enjoyed being made love to and being terribly close to him that I feel very good anyhow. The oddest thing is that now at such times I usually fall asleep after some talk and affection, just the way he does.

* Her advice has ancient precedent. Ovid, in his famous *Ars amatoria*, counsels women who fail to achieve orgasm to "counterfeit the sweet bliss with lying sounds, movements, even your eyes. Let your words and panting breath make clear your pleasure."

CHAPTER SIX

THE WOULD-BE

ADULTERESS

1 DECADENCE: IMAGINARY AND REAL

Despite the foregoing demonstration that the American woman plays the role of lover to her own husband, one hears a great deal to the effect that she is more and more inclined to do so to other men as well. If some pedantic bookworm of A.D. 2500 ever undertakes to reconstruct the social life of the 1960's from our popular art forms, he will surely come to the conclusion that in our era female adultery had become commonplace and well-accepted. Fidelity, he will state, was still ostensibly the standard; actually, however, a woman unshakably faithful to her husband was considered lackluster, timid, or prissy. Such a one, in speaking of her sexual morals, felt the need to defend or to apologize for her code, as though it implied that she were somewhat wanting in personal desirability. Our scholar's diligent search through fiction, drama, TV, and movies would convince him beyond all doubt that adultery was all but universal; he might point up his finding by quoting from a novel of the period, *Strangers When We Meet,* by Evan Hunter, in which one character, a practiced philanderer, says:

It's a big procession, an American Marching Society. From bed to bed to bed they march. March, march, march! And everybody looks the other way and pretends not to see the parade. Half the people in the world are out there keeping time to the music, and the other half are itching to march, too, but they haven't got the guts. And do you know who's leading the procession? A woman. Any place you've got a housewife, you've also got a potential mistress for [some] stranger.

If one were to accept the evidence of popular art forms, the major reason for the prevalence of adultery is that it no longer poses moral problems to women, but only tactical ones—the choice of how and when, and the avoidance of detection. The heroine of Stephen Birmingham's novel *Barbara Greer,* whose friends talk about affairs as being "modern" and perfectly permissible, is about to have one herself when her lover (her brother-in-law, Barney) drowns en route to her cabin in a canoe; later, confessing her thwarted intentions to her husband, she explains that she felt sorry for Barney, was lonely, felt depressed by family feuding, and was jealous because her husband had not been registered in the London hotel his schedule called for. But, having offered all these excuses, she promptly admits that, in reality, "there wasn't any excuse, or any reason. I wanted it just because I wanted it—the way a child wants something." She assures her husband she has never yet been physically unfaithful to him, but adds, "That isn't because I've had any *moral* feeling about it. No—you've just been lucky." And this comes not from a slut or vixen, but from a lovely, sensitive, well-educated young woman of a good New England family.

A vast mass of popular writing offers much the same picture of middle-class woman: novels like *The Chapman Report, From the Terrace, By Love Possessed, The Young Marrieds;* plays, murder mysteries, and movies by the score; and TV dramas beyond counting. As a theme, indeed, ordinary adultery has come to seem rather tame; a generation that has grown accustomed to everything from the clinical minutiae of *Lady Chatterley's Lover* to the outright perversion of *Lolita* is not likely to be startled by simple infidelity; to regain its savor, it now almost has to be linked with violence, abnormality, or bizarre and gruesome circumstances.

All this would surely lead a scholar of the twenty-sixth century— or even of our own—to suppose that modern woman is not unlike the "gallant dames" of the Renaissance court of Francis I, or perhaps the naughty ladies in the court of England's Merry Monarch. Yet astonishingly enough, despite the wealth of fictional evidence, every careful scientific survey of American sex habits indicates that among the middle classes throughout this country female adultery is still the exception rather than the rule. The surveys vary widely, for many reasons, but the figures for better-educated women are as low as 6 percent (Locke) to 31 percent (Kinsey), with other findings lying somewhere in between.

Even taking the Kinsey figure, in order to play the devil's advocate, upon closer examination one finds that it does *not* indicate that 31 percent of American wives are currently cheating on their husbands. The figure refers to *accumulative incidence;* it is the summation of all infidelities over the years, however infrequent or long past. We would get a fairer idea of the situation by looking at the incidence of adultery in any given five-year span of life; and when the data are subdivided this way, we find that even in the 36-to-40-year age group—the peak years for female adultery—only one out of five married women ever sleeps with a man other than her husband. Even that figure, however, gives a wildly exaggerated idea of their behavior, for a large fraction of all unfaithful wives commit the act only once or at most a few times in their whole lives; 42 percent confine their extramarital experiments to a year or less of their marriage; and 41 percent are unfaithful with only one man.* The averages are pulled up by a few hard-working adulteresses, but the statistics, properly analyzed, make it plain that the majority of American women never stray, and that most of the minority do so relatively few times.

Adultery has not become a way of life for the American woman, the testimony of fiction notwithstanding. She does not view sexual straying as one of her rights, nor adulterous love as a pleasure she deserves to enjoy in addition those of her married life. In our society adultery does not coexist with marriage, but combats it; the affair rarely achieves balance and equilibrium, but nearly always is a cause of change and upheaval which ends in its own termination or in remarriage. Despite our seeming libertarianism, we Americans

---

* La Rochefoucauld's remark on this point—"You can find women who have never been guilty of an indiscretion, but seldom women who have been guilty of only one"—is witty, but not particularly applicable to American women.

are the true inheritors of the Tristan and Iseult legend, rather than the southern Europeans; for us, adulterous love is fraught with difficulties, pleasure-pain, tragedy, and sorrow. Perhaps this is the clue to the reason for the astonishing discrepancy between the fictional portrait of American female sexual behavior and the reality. Let us see what we can discover by pursuing it.

2 ADULTERY IN THE HEART

In much of the past literature of adultery, the great danger is that one may be found out: hence the thousands of stories and books dealing with, or hinging upon, ruses, intrigues, deceits, suspicions, secret messages, hasty departures by the window, concealments in the closet or under the bed or down the well, accidental give-aways, violent quarrels, duels of honor, disgrace, and death. For the contemporary American woman, however, the danger has shifted its locale; it now exists within herself. She fears adultery not because she may be caught at it, but because it may change her feeling about her husband, her home, and her carefully worked-out pattern of life; it may overturn everything she has arranged for herself, bringing sorrow, disorder, and loss in the wake of her secret new joy. Yet undeniably marriage grows placid with the years, losing what was most piquant and exciting about dating and falling in love; the pulse rarely races, the game of feint and retreat is laid aside, the feeling of being wanted and carefully pursued is all but forgotten. And so, despite her outward fidelity, the wife cannot help thinking about other men and other love.

Her antipathy to actual infidelity is so strong, however, that she hates to admit even anonymously the existence of these fantasies and leftover desires. Burgess and Wallin, Terman, and others have asked married women how often they long for extramarital love; generally speaking, about three-quarters of the women have replied that they *never* have such feelings or thoughts. This is in striking contrast to the answers of married men, some three-quarters of whom candidly admit that they do have adulterous yearnings and speculations anywhere from once in a while to nearly all the time.

This sharp difference has often been taken to prove that men are promiscuous by nature and faithful only under duress, while women are monogamous by nature and unfaithful only under special stress. The survey by Professors Ford and Beach of sex habits in 190 different societies shows that in only a minority of them have married women chased around, though married men have done so, to some degree, in most of them.

Yet this does not at all prove that women are instinctively monogamous; it may just as easily indicate that most societies, for the preservation of order and the minimization of sexual competition, have conditioned women to be more nearly monogamous than men. Fidelity in either sex is a matter of cultural shaping rather than instinctive biological drive; as evidence, Professors Ford and Beach point out that "in those societies which have no double standard in sexual matters and in which a variety of liaisons are permitted, the women avail themselves as eagerly of their opportunity as the men."

There is thus good ground for the suspicion that women have the same fundamental capacity for illicit desires that men do, and that their upbringing is what restrains their actions and even censors their thoughts. But unconsciously, or in guarded and masked form, they feel adulterous wishes a great deal more often than they admit in response to forthright, objective-type questions. Many psychologists and psychoanalysts, skilled at using subtler and more penetrating tools of inquiry than the multiple-choice questionnaire, feel that nearly every human being has latent or repressed promiscuous desires which the process of growing up and becoming socialized drives into hiding. "The destiny of every man and every woman," wrote the psychoanalyst Robert Lindner, "is to be torn between the imperative of fidelity and the pressure of human bio-psychic nature." Freud himself, in one of his most significant works, *Civilization and Its Discontents,* described unconscious sexual restrictions and our resulting discontent as part of the tribute demanded of us all for civilized progress.

Precisely because the aboriginal wishes are deeply buried, many women refuse to admit feeling them and deny that it is part of the female nature to feel them. But what gives these women away is their almost unappeasable appetite for syrupy stories involving adultery or near-adultery. In fiction, the sinful desire is safe because it is someone else's desire; and even if this vicarious dalliance is only a pale shadow of delight, it is blameless. Consider, too, the hordes of women who come to ogle and clutch at matinee idols and movie stars, or recall the astonishingly personal grief felt by millions of women at the death of Rudolph Valentino in 1926, and of Clark Gable in 1961.

My own questionnaire asked, among many other things, whether women have any one continuing secret from their husbands that is comparable to the male's recurrent daydream of other women. The response was most intriguing. One-fifth of the respondents flatly denied having or knowing of any such secret, but two-fifths omitted the question altogether; no other question produced anything like so high a proportion of nonresponse. Nearly another fifth coyly wrote laconic answers like "Naturally!" or "What else?" but offered no explanation, the import apparently being plain enough. Finally, about one-fifth frankly admitted having secret fantasies concerning other men, but from the details they gave, these would seem to be rather unlike the salacious four-color, anatomically precise male daydreams of seduction and intercourse with specific women. Instead, they tend to be vague and amorphous speculations, or escapist and romantic visions; in either case, their avoidance of clinical detail makes them more nearly acceptable to the internal censor.

"Certainly I dream of being desired and loved by other men," writes a forty-year-old social worker from Buffalo, who describes her marriage as nearly ideal, "but it very rarely involves any specific person. I think I so dream only because of a dread of growing old and a need to be reassured that I am still desirable, because in fact I'm very happy sexually and can't really envision an actual affair." The sexual aspects of infidelity fantasies are sometimes repressed almost to the point of vanishing. "Here's my dream," writes a woman from Miami. "I'd like to be somebody's kept woman, ensconced in the Plaza Hotel in New York, and have strawberries and cream for breakfast, and an unlimited expense account—I'd just charge EVERYTHING—and delightful luncheon dates with him, and afternoon naps—sometimes the naps would be 'matinees' with him (of course, we'd really go to the *theatre* only at night). And then dinner, and out on the town. I'd just *love* to be a kept woman for a while."

Less innocuous than these fantasies, but still within safe bounds, are certain forms of overt activity which offer a token gratification of the hunger. Mock gallantry is one such: a man may offer highly charged compliments to another man's wife or make good-naturedly seductive or suggestive remarks to her in her husband's or his wife's hearing, this condition being the assurance that there is no harm in it. The woman may reply in kind, or mockingly squeeze his hand, or press closer to him while dancing—still within earshot and view of one or both spouses.

A little further on, however, are compliments and playful remarks exchanged out of sight and hearing of their respective mates; and while this makes her somewhat apprehensive, it has correspondingly greater erotic value. Such flirtation, even if innocently intended, gives her that marvelous half-forgotten feeling of using her charm upon a man, and of having it work. It permits her to pose the hypothesis, "*If* I wanted to—" without going on to the consequent; it reassures her that she is still in her flowering, still worth something as a woman; it provides some of the excitement of the chase without any of its dangers or guilt feelings. At least, it does all this as long as it remains on the level of playful make-believe.

But let the man shift his mood ever so slightly and ask—meaning it—when he may phone her, or let her drop her bantering manner for a moment and appraise him with frankly admiring eyes, and the whole situation will change in hue like a scene on the stage when the electrician shifts the colored gelatin. Or suppose while shopping in town she chances to meet a man she knows, who invites her to have a drink in a nearby cocktail lounge: what could be more innocently flattering, and yet more poised on the brink of danger? Will he merely admire her, be charming, act terribly interested in her—

or will he hold her hand at some point, reach for her knee under the table, or offer her a key to the little place he keeps in town for nights when he works late? All during her drink with him she wonders what he will do, and fears that her harmless moment of quasi-flirtation will be spoiled by his trying to start something. And the hairline difference exists to the very end, when he says either, "Thanks for having a drink with me"—or "Can't we meet again?", and when she, for her part, wavers between "It was so sweet of you" and "Maybe I'll run into you again next Tuesday."

In upper-middle-brow circles there is a concerted attempt to encourage this art of erotic brinkmanship. As Louis Kronenberger points out, when two working-class couples get into a car, the men sit in front and the women in back; two middle-class couples pair off as marriages; and among the sophisticated, husbands sit with each other's wives. The latter kind of woman, when acting as a hostess, will reprove a guest, "Now, you know you just *can't* sit next to your own wife." If a pair falls into an intimate conversation, it is a gaucherie for either one's mate to come over or to show irritation; and it is bad manners for a man to do more than laugh and tease when his wife reappears after a long walk in the garden with another man.

Even the walk in the garden, of course, remains harmless as long as it is all done in a spirit of pretense. But the line between pretense and reality is so fine that a man and woman, especially after a few drinks, may easily waver across it. At this point, however, women usually react with astonishment and alarm, as though they had been unaware of where they were going. A woman who thoroughly enjoys the pseudo-innocent game of flirtation may act surprised, indignant, and upset if the man kisses her or puts his arms around her. Or she may respond at first with a rush of passion, only to pull violently away a moment later, genuinely frightened, not by what he did, but by her own response.

In *The Split-Level Trap,* a study of the stresses of suburban life in Bergen County, New Jersey, psychiatrist Richard E. Gordon recounts how the rather strictly brought-up wife of a young executive steadfastly refused the advances of an attractive divorced man she met at community activities while her husband was working late in the city. Finally, however, at a New Year's Eve party, her husband was acting sullen and disinterested and she began to drink and dance with the hopeful wolf. She was dumbfounded to find herself feeling pliant, excited, and eager for something to happen. Midnight struck, and as he was about to kiss her for the first time she felt such a sudden wave of sexual desire that in panic she broke away from him, fled to her husband overwhelmed with guilt, and tearfully begged him to take her home at once.

Not all women react with alarm; some enjoy and prolong these preliminaries. In fact, several authorities report that some wives permit themselves to extend flirtation all the way to petting, and manage to hold it at that point; like a teenager, such a woman will sit in a parked car and allow the man to fumble around her body but never permit him to have intercourse with her, though what she is preserving is not quite clear. It is not known how widespread this practice is; it seems to be a marginal activity, although possibly on the increase. But the meaning of it, if not the incidence, is clear enough: it enables the woman to gain the excitement and ego satisfaction of an affair while remaining technically faithful. "I've kidded around a bit now and then—hasn't everyone?" one woman explains. "Once in a while I fool around at a party, or a beach barbecue, with some attractive man, and if we neck a little or he has a fast hand, it's just for kicks, and nobody's been hurt. What counts is that I can really say that I've never been unfaithful to my husband, and I can look him in the eye and swear to that. I doubt if he can do the same."

The real question, of course, is why most women do no more than indulge in fantasy, mild flirtation, or dubious borderline experiments. Almost all the classic external controls of female behavior have been weakened or discarded in recent decades. Woman's emancipation gives her the right to go almost anywhere alone; the automobile makes it possible for her to get far from home and back again with great ease; contraception insures her against disastrous after-effects; easy divorce and manifold job opportunities mean that even if she is found out and abandoned by her husband she can make her way in the world; and finally, although society may whisper about her, it neither punishes her nor brands her with the scarlet letter.

It is true, of course, that a suburban housewife with one or more small children is fairly well confined to the home, and it is furthermore true that the movements and meetings of people in the suburbs are far more visible to the community than they are in the city. On both counts, therefore, adultery may not seem so easy to arrange. But this is all relative; in comparison to the women of most other eras, ours have quite a lot of maneuverability. In any case, the voluminous literature of infidelity over the centuries is proof enough that neither children, slaves, doorkeepers, mothers-in-law, duennas, bailiffs, majordomos, chaperones, stewards, seneschals, nor private detectives have been able to prevent a wife really bent on adultery from contriving to meet and disport herself with her lover.

All in all, a cautious and well-organized woman can expect to "get away with it" nowadays. Why, then, if the desire is basic, are adulteresses so few in number and so sporadic in their activities? The answer most often given is that it is due to the lingering influence of American puritanism; yet although there is some truth in this it is not a sufficient explanation. For five or more decades, psychological and anthropological ideas have been filtering into the body of popular thought, making women—especially the better-educated ones—aware that sexual enjoyment is not harmful per se, that prudery and inhibition are a matter of social fashion rather than a universal requirement of female nature, that frustrated desire may be as hurtful as overindulgence, and that Victorianism, beneath its façade of sweet domesticity, concealed a great deal of misery and psychosexual illness. The sophisticated woman rarely offers God's Law as a reason for moral behavior; she prefers to say that there is nothing intrinsically evil about adultery, but that those who truly love each other will be faithful for aesthetic and rational reasons.

Yet most real or even would-be adulteresses *do* suffer from guilt—

but today's guilt is of a curiously new species. The God-given moral commandment no longer imparts to woman a scalding sense of sin; yet the thing she wants seems wrong in some important way, and she feels guilty for not having a clear emotional revulsion against it. Her guilt feeling, one might almost say, seems to come from her not feeling guilty.

There is no expiation of such guiltless guilt by prayer or repentance, yet inwardly it seems that there *must* be some settling of the score. In fiction it may take the symbolic form of bad luck—not God's design, but accident. In Mary McCarthy's novel *A Charmed Life*, the heroine, remarried, allows her ex-husband to possess her after a party at which they had drunk too much (she struggles at first, but reflects ironically that "one screw, more or less, could not make much difference, when she had already laid it on the line for him about five hundred times"). She feels no guilt about the act afterward, but she becomes pregnant, and while driving to Boston to get an abortion she is killed in a head-on collision. Similarly, the near adultery in *Barbara Greer* results not only in the would-be lover's death, but the exposure and disgrace of the heroine, and severe damage to family prestige and the family-owned paper company. These are symbolic representations of the American woman's feeling that a love affair—unless it happens to be totally justifiable for special reasons—will somehow lead to harm.

But why *need* harm come of her infidelity? In certain European countries unfaithful wives manage their affairs with tact and finesse, maintain them over a period of years with no one the wiser, and deftly avoid bringing shame or harm upon anyone. Nor do they conceive of this as a dangerous practice. Although it is not easy to be quantitatively precise about national differences in sex attitudes, the data of various American surveys indicate that some five-sixths of American women do not expect or intend to seek extramarital relations, while 36 percent of a sample of French and Belgian women —though not asked exactly the same question—said that a wife's fidelity is unimportant to the marriage, and another 37 percent termed it desirable but not necessary.

For these European women, the erotic traditions of antiquity still survive in modified form: marriage is one matter, love and sex a couple of others, and friendship still another. Neither husband nor wife expects all things of each other, but only a sharply demarcated relationship; it is therefore psychologically feasible for them to maintain other forms of intimate male-female relationship outside of marriage. A love affair does not seriously invade such a husband-wife relationship, nor wall off certain areas of the soul which previously were open to the mate.

Modern married love in America, however, is becoming an extremely complex and demanding interaction in which each partner is nearly all things to the other and has virtually unlimited access to the inner reaches of the other's mind and heart. This is why enlightened young husbands and wives are startled to learn, for instance, that a neighbor of theirs never tells his wife how much money they have saved, or are amazed to read in the paper that a murdered lawyer had been involved in large-scale contraband operations for years and that his tearful young wife had had absolutely no idea what he was up to all the time. And what is true of money or business is true all the more so of the erotic life; illicit love-making, especially from the woman's viewpoint, is not just a voluptuous physical experience, but a subtle, compound relationship with a man which easily laps over into many of the areas of emotion and thought central to her marriage, competes with it, and thus is virtually impossible to keep truly secret from her husband.

The American woman's affair is therefore curiously unstable; she is not likely to succeed in being both one man's mistress and another man's wife for years. She may start out looking for a sexual thrill, an escape, a fling—but if the affair remains nothing more, she quickly finds it tawdry and breaks it off, ashamed of the cheapness of it. If, on the other hand, it prospers and lives up to her requirements of love, it rapidly absorbs most of her romantic ideas, her excitement, her energy, hopes, and dreams. It becomes too good to be just an affair; she begins to want her lover to be her husband. The typical affair of the American woman is thus either worth too little to be continued, or too much to be kept only an affair.

This is why the occasional experiments in liberalized or permissive marriage, in which each partner is considered free to indulge in outside affairs, have so generally come to grief, engendering bitterness or misery in at least one of the partners; it is also why the key-swapping parties of certain suburban communities begin as sophisticated lechery, but shortly generate alcoholism, neurosis, divorce, and even murder. Several marriage counselors have told me of a number of cases in which one-night wife exchanges that began as mere half-drunken hedonism ended in double divorce and double remarriage of the adulterous partners to each other.*

It is just because the American woman senses this progression of events that she is so reluctant to admit her desires to herself or to put them into practice. Her pragmatic morality, which in effect balances potential harm against potential gain, is not as simple and reassuring as old-fashioned conscience, but it is fairly powerful all the same; in any case, it is the morality she now principally relies on.

3 ADULTERY IN THE FLESH

Most American women, in order to function effectively as wives and mothers and to remain integrated as individuals, thus maintain strong inhibitions against adultery and even, to some extent, against the overt recognition of the wish for it. But what of the minority who fail to do so? How do they get that way? What personal or social factors permit an American woman to become another man's mistress, and how well does she play the part?

Some authorities—principally psychoanalysts and psychiatrists— view infidelity as an illness, terming it "the acting-out of neurotic conflict." This interpretation quite properly applies to such types of female adultery as the vain search of the psychologically frigid woman for a satisfying sex experience, the insatiable demands of the nymphomaniac, or the random adulteries of the immature narcissis-

---

* Still, some authorities, including Carney Landis, Lindner, and Kinsey, state that there *are* certain mature, independent women in American society who can maintain rewarding affairs without disrupting their marriages. They give no statistics, but admit that this idyllic combination is very rare.

tic woman who is plagued by an immoderate need to feel admired and wanted.

But this purely clinical interpretation of adultery is surely too narrow, and results from the clinician's daily contact with emotionally disturbed types. History is filled with proof that adultery can be normal, rather than abnormal, conduct; in the Middle Ages and the Age of Reason, to cite but two examples, infidelity was the fashion, and to be faithful a woman had to be either emotionally deviant or very homely. The testimony of comparative anthropology likewise makes it certain that in some societies female adultery (as well as male) is not the product of emotional disorder, but is part of a stable, accepted pattern of sexual practices, and exists alongside marriage and family life without undue conflict.

Our own society is not one such; yet it does have within it special subcultures and particular combinations of circumstances which make adultery appealing and provide ready-made justifications. Though adultery is not the American norm, it is nevertheless true that a certain number of American women cross the borderline and go beyond fantasy or flirtation out of motives that must be called essentially normal rather than neurotic or emotionally disordered. It is with these women, rather than the demonstrably ill, that we will concern ourselves here.

Fortuitous circumstances, to begin with, may conspire to rob a healthy, affectionate woman of the love she needs: her husband may be removed from her side and her bed for months or years by accident, mental illness, or war, and after a while loneliness, passion, and sorrow may make her susceptible, even though not deliberately seductive. In answer to my questionnaire item about the secrets women keep from their husbands, an anonymous Southern correspondent in her early thirties wrote this unusually frank confession:

I have one secret which Bob will never learn if I can help it, because it would only wound him and do neither of us any good. Besides, it's way in the past. He was away during the Korean thing for nearly twenty months, and that's a long, long while for a girl as young and warm-blooded as I was then. It was *so* damned lonely in our little apartment, and even if I went out visiting I still came back to the silent rooms, and thrashed around in my lonely bed trying not to think what it would be like to have him there. Finally, when I'd been feeling really wretched for months, I accepted a dinner invitation from a shy, quiet, rather attractive man in the office who had recently been separated from his wife. I guess I wasn't very tactful about hinting that there would be nothing in it for him, but he just laughed and I relaxed about it. Then, as the evening went on, we danced and drank and laughed and said many serious things and opened up to each other. I felt myself sort of falling in love, which was ridiculous because I was in love with my husband. But there it was—and I could tell that he felt that way too. But he was a perfect gentleman for five such dates; then one night, suddenly we were holding hands, and kissing, and right then we stopped asking ourselves questions. We just looked at each other and left the restaurant, and went quietly and trembling back to my place and became lovers. It was wonderful and the most tremendous unburdening— but why did I cry, afterwards? It happened about half a dozen times in all; then I got panicky, thinking that I was going to destroy my love for Bob, and on an impulse I quit my job overnight, wrote my lover a little note, and moved in with my mother for a couple of months until I got over it. I told her I had war-bride jitters and couldn't stand being alone.

The fact that it takes an unusual and potent combination of circumstances may account for the surprising percentage of adulteresses who have strayed only once or a few times. Such a woman, as the thing is happening, watches with a numb, helpless fascination, hardly believing what she is letting herself do. Then it is done; physically, it probably hasn't been very different from what she already knew, but emotionally it has been delirious. But then come the afterthoughts when the blood cools—the fear, the inner shame, the secret of such tangible weight that breathing is difficult. To ease her pain, she either unburdens herself of the secret to a minister or priest or even to her husband, or else encases it in rationalization and walls it off slowly from the rest of her being. Such adultery therefore often does little or no harm to the marriage because it is isolated and neutralized, or is made known to an understanding husband and so expelled from the body of their union.

In contrast to accidental adultery there is the kind that comes about, almost inevitably, as a concomitant of life in a community or group whose mores permit and all but require extramarital adventures as a proof of membership. In such a milieu, moreover, adultery is usually rather easy to arrange and get away with, and prefabricated rationalizations are freely offered the novice by the initiates. Writes a young woman recently married to a film writer:

I must be awfully old-fashioned because I haven't yet got used to the way the married women out here, when they get together, talk about affairs as casually as though they were discussing the weather. I told my feelings to one girl I've come to like very much, and she laughed at me and said, "Don't be ridiculous—everyone does it. What makes you think you're any better off for denying yourself a part of life? In twenty years it won't matter a bit to anyone that *you* kept yourself so pure—but *we'll* have had the fun." I went home all upset that night, and I can't honestly say now whether I'm being faithful out of love, or morals, or just plain lack of guts.

And in a moment of extraordinary frankness induced by three martinis a young married actress burbled to a female friend of mine rather pridefully, "Well, at last I've *tried* it. I *had* to—it was really just too *square*, the way I was fighting off the passes. I took a good look one day at the way people live, at least the really *honest* people, and decided, 'What the hell, who am I to be holier-than-thou?' So I let something happen just for kicks a few times this past summer. Now I feel more mature, and part of it all."

When adultery thus becomes a mark of status, and fidelity is the stigma of personal failure, women who stray will have far less inner conflict than adulteresses in other parts of American society. But whether it works out well for them is quite another matter; even in these special subgroups, much the same security needs exist, and much the same difficulties arise from the attempt to fragment and subdivide the emotional life. If Hollywood, Greenwich Village, café society, the hard-drinking horsey upper class, and the theatrical world are special spheres of sexual permissiveness and personal freedom, they are also more afflicted than the rest of America with alcoholism, ulcers, insomnia, and divorce; it is reasonable to suppose that the phenomena are somehow related.

Quite a different reason for normal adultery is the sexual incapacity or incompetence of some husbands. Unlike neurotically frigid women, some wives with normal sexual potential fail to be satisfied by marital lovemaking, though they may be aroused and wrought up by it. This is often put forward with great assurance as the leading cause of infidelity, particularly by those social critics who do a brisk business in condemning American men *en masse* as unmasculine. Novelists, too, are fond of this motivation for adultery, since it is simple, clearcut, and classic. The recent novel *The Devil in Bucks County* by Edmund Schiddel, for instance, portrays a devoted wife in her late thirties who is married to a television producer; he, working too hard and under constant strain, has been unable to carry through their love-making on seven different occasions in recent months, and we are asked to believe that his wife is therefore in such a condition of lubricity as to yield with only nominal protest to the advances of the bakery truck driver, and time and again copulate with him on a purely animal level. (E.g., "It was the quickest she had ever had in her life and exultantly satisfying. If he had said one word to her, she would have burst into tears.")

It is doubtful, however, that things often work out this way; the intelligent, well-reared woman with an impotent or sexually inadequate husband is far more likely to compound her sexual hunger for another man with a sophisticated and aesthetic set of feelings, in order to justify it to herself. In a casebook of typical marital problems edited by members of the American Association of Marriage Counselors, the narrative of an impotent husband and a normally sexed wife has quite a different flavor from that of the novel. The marriage under scrutiny had lasted nineteen years although Louis, the husband, was a moody, adolescent person with severe sexual inadequacy. College-educated, and a successful salesman, he was nevertheless plagued by self-doubt which found its worst expression in the form of partial impotence and premature ejaculation. Indeed, even in the early months of the marriage he rarely sought intercourse with his wife Sandra; when at last she asked him about it, he explained that sex should be indulged in as rarely as possible, and she, being naïve and puritanically raised, took his word for it. But it was not easy for her to stifle a naturally affectionate and passionate nature, and she sought out books on the celibate life and studied them, developing a good deal of rigid self-control.

Then she met a physician—a witty, intelligent, and mature man—of whom she became very fond, and with whom, inevitably, she began an affair. He urged Sandra to divorce Louis and marry him, but she felt too strong a sense of obligation to Louis to do so; instead, they corresponded regularly, met at long intervals in between his many trips, and from time to time went to bed together joyously and with great contentment. After ten years, however, they agreed to part so that she might try to work out a better relationship with her husband. But Louis, despite his and her efforts, remained a petulant, fearful child, and although he now tried hard to be a virile lover, his lack of success was grimly described by Sandra to a marriage counselor:

> The physical part of our life together is a nagging, smothering arrangement. . . . I go to bed and lie so rigid every muscle aches so that we can pretend the courtesy of being asleep. I know in advance I'll be awakened during the night, and that in the last analysis it won't work and I'll spend some hours encouraging Louis and persuading him that this is a temporary insecurity and not to worry. With always the futile knowledge that it wouldn't make any difference if it did work.

Not surprisingly, she drifted into a second affair; this one, however, threatened to break up the marriage. Yet it was not primarily sexual love she was seeking; her second affair, like her first, involved relatively few episodes of actual passion, but a great deal of emotional and intellectual stimulation. Moreover, when Louis, through marriage counseling, began to gain some self-assurance and to expand as a personality, Sandra decided to stick with him and see less of her lover, even though Louis had hardly become any better in bed.

Indeed, unappeased sex hunger rarely seems to be the real or major reason for adultery in women. Authorities who have studied female infidelity have found a number of reasons for it, of which sexual dissatisfaction with the husband is only one, and not usually the leading one, and most probably does not contribute at all, in the majority of cases. Psychologist Carney Landis of the New York Psychiatric Institute, in a comparative study of normal and emotionally ill adulteresses, found that in general the normal ones had perfectly adequate sexual relationships with their husbands. Even more tellingly, Kinsey found that 58 percent of adulterous women admit to a better (or at least as good a) chance of reaching orgasm with their husbands as with their lovers; and at almost every age the great majority of unfaithful women continue to obtain most of their sexual outlet not from illicit, but from marital, coitus.

Though sexual discontent may play a part in normal adultery, most of the time the real reasons lie deeper. One of them, and it is an unpleasant one, is woman's hostility or ambivalence toward her husband (about which I will speak at greater length in Chapter Ten) . There is almost no way of getting even with a difficult, selfish, or thoughtless husband so satisfactory as giving away behind his back his right to the exclusive sexual use of his wife. Even if he is not particularly disagreeable, a woman may feel vengeful for his slow transferring of his attention and interest to his career instead of herself, or for her own nagging sense of her relative unimportance in the world. She may be unfaithful not out of love or even desire, but out of exasperation. As Simone de Beauvoir puts it, "A wife may even be likely to feel that in yielding to another man—if only once, in haste, on a sofa—she has gained a certain superiority over her legitimate spouse." Alfred Adler, the first of Freud's followers to break with him and establish a separate school of psychology, went so far as to claim that all infidelity was a mode of revenge. The exaggeration has a hard core of truth to it; let a woman state it as only a woman can, in this passage from "Cruel and Barbarous Treatment," a story by Mary McCarthy about a young woman's adultery:

For her husband she had, she believed, only sympathy and compunction. She got no fun, she told the Young Man, out of putting horns on her darling's head. . . . It was as if by the mere act of betraying her husband, she had adequately bested him; it was supererogatory for her to gloat, and, if she gloated at all, it was over her fine restraint in not-gloating, over the integrity of her moral sense, which allowed her to preserve even while engaged in sinfulness the acute realization of sin and shame.

And yet important as is the revenge motive, there is still a more important one—the wife's need to experience once again the unbearably sensuous thrill of feeling terribly important to someone, having him urgently want her, being the image of his thoughts by day and the elusive phantom of his dreams by night.

It is, of course, the same motive that in her early teens made her think about boys and dates more than anything else, in her later teens made her dwell obsessively on infatuations and love affairs, and by her early twenties drove her on to the ultimate goal, marriage. Yet having achieved this quietus, she finds as time passes that her husband gradually achieves more and more of *his* major satisfactions through the other part of his life, and that she is slowly becoming his comfortable companion rather than his *raison d'être*. Within many a woman there appears, little by little, a gnawing, unsatisfied hunger for the inner excitement, the feeling of personal value, the bursting triumph she once felt when love was new and she was all-important to him.

The result may be anything from a mild, low-grade discontent that emerges only as an occasional fit of pre-menstrual tears to a sharp burning hunger that becomes a conscious readiness to have an affair with the first reasonable prospect. As a typical middle-of-the-range case, the late Dr. Abraham Stone, an eminent marriage counselor, cited the story of a young woman whose marriage was a success, who loved her children, and who was interested in her home, her husband's work, and her community—but who no longer felt valuable or precious to her husband. Explaining why she drifted into an affair, she told Stone, "Evenings, he [her husband] wants only his dinner and his newspaper. If I make any affectionate gesture, he just pats me on the head as if I were a child or a pet. If he would only make his touch mean something! I know he loves me, but I need to be loved with some passion." A man she met while on vacation with her children offered just that; and before the resultant affair was over, her marriage had been nearly torn apart.

Of course it was not just a meaningful touch that she hungered for; it was an entranced companion who wanted both to talk to her and to listen to what she had to say. From Iowa, a mother of four children who has somehow found time for an affair writes that her husband takes her for granted and treats her like a cherished servant—"but this other man excites me—he *talks* to me. I'm not stupid; I realize what he's doing—but it's so nice to have a man's full attention, it's so nice to feel you're attractive to another man, and if you feel attracted to him, it's even nicer." "There have been four other men in my life in my twenty years of marriage," writes a woman from Richmond, Virginia. "Each time, I have let it happen because it made me seem to be alive in the way I was when I was eighteen. Each time I see the leaves and smell the air more vividly, I hear music keenly again, I float about with my lovely secret—a man is in love with me, and I am falling in love with him. I hope it never wrecks my home life, but it's too good to do without."

The yielding of such a woman is thus less the result of her lover's seductive powers than of the sense of importance he brings her. It was, above all, this sense of importance that Mary McCarthy's young adulteress relished when lunching with friends and casually dropping her secret lover's name into the conversation. After a while, alas, this grew flat—"The audience of two no longer sufficed her; she required a larger stage"—so she began to confide the secret to dear friends, one at a time. And when this, too, palled, she found an intense new delight in preparing for, and finally playing out, the scene of revelation to her husband—the beautiful moment when his love, ordinarily rationed out thinly day by day, showed itself briefly in its entirety, accompanied by tears, understanding, renunciation, heartbreak, and separation. Next came civilized encounters among him, herself, and the lover at the homes of friends—oh, they were whispered about by everyone!—and when that, too, became stale and tired, she at last left for Reno. At that point, she abruptly recognized beyond any doubt that her lover was vacuous and unworthy—an imposture, a mirage she herself had created out of her own need. But by then, of course, it was too late.

As time passes, this kind of need is apt to grow more acute. For aesthetic reasons, writers of fiction make their adulteresses quite young, but in actual fact, among middle-class women in their early twenties the incidence of unfaithfulness is very low. But it rises gradually and consistently with the years and reaches a peak in the 36-to-40 bracket, showing only a slight downturn in the next two five-year segments.

There are many reasons for this. The average woman attains her peak of sexual responsiveness slowly; as she leaves girlhood further behind she feels less need to act maidenly; simultaneously, she becomes ever more emancipated from parental disapproval and the force of conscience; and so on. But more important than all this, since her early teens she has valued herself primarily as an attractive love-object, and derived much or most of her feeling of personal value from that fact. Many husbands and wives, however, allow the married–lover relationship to gradually become dull and routine; many women fail to grow in breadth and experience along with their husbands; and many husbands become increasingly involved in business and their ambitions, and correspondingly less involved with their wives. The net result is that the woman—unless she has found other values to replace those of being a love-object—suffers from Time's depreciation of her worth, and sinks into the moody despairs of *Eheu fugaces*. The reassurance of her desirability may be the only kind of ego prop she thinks of looking for. Recently at a large, elegant party I was struck by the fact that all of the various attractive thirtyish housewives I talked to were flirtatious and provocative, while two others, of the same age and attractiveness, were womanly without being arch, and delightful without being teasing: both the latter, it turned out, were married, mothers of several children—and practicing physicians.

But lacking such a source of ego gratification, or a surprisingly good marriage, a woman is much more susceptible in the 35-to-45-year bracket than she ever was earlier. Close students of woman refer to the pre-climacteric as the "dangerous age," when she is likely to do something foolish in order to make up for the loss of her husband's attention, her children's dependence upon her, and her own youthful looks. It is dangerous, however, not because she may sleep with another man a number of times, but because while doing so she may delude herself into thinking she has found a better way of life, rediscovered the "Real Me," and found an antidote to pessimism, despair, bewilderment, and uncertainty about the future.

Love, as so often before in her life, once again seems a salvation and the solution to all riddles. Thus the affair that starts as mere hedonism or as an emotional fling runs the considerable risk of being crushed by burdens it was never designed to bear—the rupture of her marriage, the loss of many of her friends, the suffering of her children, the breaking up of her home, the making of a new life. The adulteress in America generally makes a rather poor mistress, even when she is sexually responsive and suitably flattering to a man's ego, because she wants too much of her lover—she wants him to be her mainstay in life, her be-all and end-all, and, inevitably, her legal mate. It is enough to frighten any sensible philanderer away.

4 THE FUTURE OF ADULTERY

To judge by the Kinsey data, the younger generation of women is more prone to accept and experiment with adultery than the older one; extrapolating, a number of people have predicted that adultery will continue to increase in popularity until it is nearly universal. Even as much as three decades ago, Bertrand Russell, Havelock Ellis, and a number of others argued that this was inevitable, and therefore proposed permissive forms of marriage which would openly acknowledge the right of each partner to have outside love affairs. Alternatively, others argued for greater freedom of divorce, for companionate marriage, and for free love. Even quite recently Mlle. de Beauvoir has asserted that all forms of marriage inevitably defeat love and so produce adultery; her recommendation is that we abolish marriage (presumably in favor of free unions), and thereby eliminate adultery entirely.

None of these drastic suggestions has struck a responsive chord among the American middle class. American men and women have come to prize marriage and conjugal love more than ever, and have proven deaf to all suggestions for simplifying, easing, or uncomplicating it. Their divorce rate, though it continues to be high compared to other countries, indicates not so much a frivolous sensuality as a compelling need to find a partner with whom to build an enduring and satisfying sexual-emotional relationship.

The internal logic of the situation thus seems to contradict the prediction that adultery will soon be a national pastime. Everything about modern marriage—its importance, its complexity, its totality, its legal fragility—makes it more likely that most men and women will continue to forgo illicit pleasures they long for. No doubt adultery will be ever easier to talk about, read about, and daydream about than it has been in the past, or is even today, but that is not to say that more people will act it out. Merely because we can freely discuss mental illness, sexual perversity, or homicidal impulses today, we do not necessarily act insane, perverse, or murderous; as in psychotherapy, indeed, the ability to deal consciously with the words may be the key to control of the emotions they signify.

The emerging ethic concerning adultery is a pragmatic one, relying not upon commands from on high nor the dictates of a stern conscience, but on a prudent appraisal of the situation and the potential consequences of an action. There exist for modern woman more temptations and fewer internal safeguards than for her grandmother, more risk and greater anxiety, more complete identification with her mate and greater concern for his feelings. The net result is that, like premarital behavior, extramarital activities have changed little in quality or meaning in recent years, though the statistical average may have risen somewhat. Adultery by American women is, or soon will be, on a plateau; some will do it and some won't, but by and large it will continue to be rare, unstable, and more of a threat to happiness than common sense can usually justify. Writes one of my correspondents with admirable directness, "Marital fidelity is certainly the *simplest* answer. Affairs have a way of getting out of hand and destroying the way of life they were only meant to spice. And yet I don't deny that married love must fade and become drab—unless the partners grow and change with each other. This takes work, but at least I believe it is possible—and well worth the effort." It may not be a sublime ethic, but it is at least a workable one.

1 JUST A HOUSEWIFE

If being her husband's lover is complicated and difficult for modern woman, at least it is something she wholeheartedly wants to do, and from which she eventually derives a good deal of satisfaction. A far greater part of her time, however, goes into being his mate, a combination of roles—housekeeper, mother, and companion—about which she has mixed feelings, and which yields dreary boredom as well as intense satisfaction, frustration as well as fulfillment, guilt as well as pride. For the housekeeping part of this trinity frequently turns out to be time-consuming, dull, menial, and even hateful; her real self seems wasted on it and withered by it; and, worst of all, she is ashamed of her dislike of it, and thinks that it means she must be unfeminine, selfish, and even unnatural.

In the past, the great majority of women thought of housewifery as one of their proper female activities, but modern women regard it as a price they have to pay for being married. In many a bygone era woman took pride in the practice of her housewifely skills and would have felt lost if freed of her duties, but today she can think of a hundred things she would rather do than scrape dishes, fold laundry, or battle dust and fingerprints. Girls growing up in America today are not conditioned to take pride in making an oaken floor gleam, darning an Argyle sock, or producing a perfect bouillabaisse; their set of life goals either omits such things or assigns them low value. In a survey, 90 percent of a group of high-school girls said they wanted to marry—but 85 percent of them said they did not want to be housewives; the modern girl likes to envision herself as a slim, girlishly appealing young mother, mistress of a charming, immaculate home, and perhaps part-time teacher or author—but not as her own housemaid. She does not choose housekeeping as a role in life; she chooses marriage and motherhood, and has housekeeping thrust upon her.

Nor does experience lead her to radically change her opinion of it; when a Cornell sociologist asked a broad sample of women in Ithaca what gave them the most satisfaction of life, only about one-third chose the answer "Doing things around the house." Similarly, most of the women who replied to my own questionnaire find housekeeping either partly or wholly disagreeable, and say so in curt, edgy terms, such as: "bores me to tears," "hate housework, but there's no escaping it," "despise picking up, dishes, sewing," and "general cleaning, straightening up—ugh!" On the other hand, nearly all of them agree that the "creative" sides of housekeeping, such as cooking for a special dinner, decorating, and gardening are more rewarding, but some women accept even these gratifications with curious self-consciousness; a former journalist, who hopes to return to that field, writes, "I must confess"—note her choice of word—"that appreciative comments about my cooking do give me pleasure."

Many critics of modern woman censure her for her dislike of housewifery, but she is only reflecting the value her whole culture places on it. Thousands of advertisements and commercials show the happy housewife at her duties—while promoting the idea that housework is not something to revel in, but to get done with; the touted virtue of Lestoil, Ajax, Mr. Clean, and Lux is that they will get her through the hateful tasks soon, still wearing a smile and looking adorable and girlish. As a recent ad for scouring pads put it, "One thing about cleaning roasting pans, you feel so good when you're finished. With S.O.S. you finish faster!" Florence Kluckhohn sums it up by remarking that in all our communications media "the household is pictured constantly as a mild variety of penal institution." And in truth, whatever miracles the manufacturers promise, housework for a servantless woman—particularly if she has small children underfoot—*is* apt to feel like imprisonment; the very term "the trapped housewife" has recently become commonplace in magazine articles on women's problems.

Not all women feel trapped, to be sure; by virtue of personality or social environment, some find domesticity an agreeable and tranquil retreat, not unlike the cultivated garden to which Candide retired after his many adventures. "I am a slow, one-sided woman who has to live at her own pace," writes a young mother from Lakewood, Ohio. "Perhaps I'm wrong, but if I am, don't tell me; I live in a rose-colored world of happiness at home. The outside world comes in at 6 P.M. with my husband, and with friends on week-ends, and that's enough; I'm never bored. I've never been more contented than I am now that I can stay home." Like her, a considerable number of women find suburban living gracious and pleasant, enjoy the traffic and bustle of children and visitors, and feel a snug, tidy pleasure in running their homes.

Yet the evidence of polls, surveys, and the reader mail of women's magazines indicates that a larger number of middle-class women, though they deeply enjoy some aspects of domesticity, all too often find it dull, fatiguing, and deadening to the soul. But they rarely state it so plainly to themselves; as one thoughtful woman puts it, the feeling that comes over them in the midst of bedmaking, dishwashing, and errands is the vague, troubled self-query, "Is this all?"

What is wrong with modern woman that she cannot enjoy those functions that women have cheerfully performed from time immemorial? Is she selfish, spoiled, and childish? Is she a pseudo-masculine neurotic, devoid of real femininity and womanliness? Or should one blame not woman herself, but an educational system that opens her eyes to things she will have no time for, gives her hungers she will be unable to appease, and fails to equip her emotionally for her essential business in life?

Before one leaps to easy conclusions, let him note several contradictions about modern woman which make pat answers doubtful. First, modern women detest many aspects of housekeeping, and yet generally try to be the best housekeepers they can, neither shirking their duties nor indulging in consciously bohemian disorder. Next, though a liberal education may predispose women to feel frustrated in the role of housewife, they almost always remain wholeheartedly in favor of just such schooling, and say they would not have wanted it to be otherwise. Again, the middle-class women who are so often charged with pseudo-masculine ambition are the very ones who overwhelmingly elect to become homemakers in suburbs remote from domestic help and far from part-time career opportunities; they are, in short, not so much trapped as self-immured. Finally, these same women, though they are far more aware of their own problems and discontents than working-class women, are in general much better pleased with their lives, and rate them higher in happiness. Philosophers are forever trying to understand the mechanism of human happiness; could it be that a useful clue is awaiting them in so prosaic an area as housework?

2 *THE BACKWARD SEARCH FOR FEMININITY*

Upper-class women alone, in earlier centuries, could afford to regard housekeeping not as their proper business but as menial work of no great virtue, and to fob it off on slaves or hired help. It took the industrial revolution, however, to make nearly all women look down upon housework and consider it ignoble. The coming of the industrial age meant that much of woman's valuable traditional work could be done more cheaply and easily by canning plants, bakeries, clothing factories, and various agencies of the state. At the height of the feminist movement several decades ago, therefore, homemaking was often radically portrayed as a form of slavery, a view that was advanced precisely because it had become partly possible for others than the very wealthy to escape from it.

Some of the avant-garde fled from it altogether by taking to careers, and maintaining free-love relationships or none; other careerists married but remained childless, or had a child or two who became the servants' responsibility, along with the other household furnishings (the fact that childbearing itself could not be delegated was called "woman's biological tragedy"). Many better-off women were not career-minded, but nevertheless held housewifery in such low esteem that they let the maids run their houses, and battled their ennui with mah-jong, bridge, and the movies.

But successful revolutions have a way of slowly turning conservative and adopting some of the attitudes they set out to destroy. For the past decade and a half there has been a distinct return toward certain traditional—or, more precisely, neo-traditional—views concerning marriage, homemaking, and careers for women. Neo-traditional ideas, some of which we glanced at in Chapter Two, have been put forward in literally thousands of movies, plays, TV shows, novels, articles, and short stories which ridicule or castigate modern woman, warn her against her false, pseudo-masculine ideals, and exhort her to give up the unwomanly desire for achievement and to rejoice, instead, in "real femininity"—a warm, savory blend of homemaking, motherhood, and obedience. In the neo-traditional view, these are essential and interrelated parts of the feminine character; it is impermissible for woman to like one and not the other. Not idly did the Nazis link the orthodox employments of woman in the alliterative phrase *Küche, Kirche, Kinder*.

"Before the Industrial Revolution," writes neo-traditionalist Dr. Marie N. Robinson, "[woman's] experiences were fully satisfying to her body and mind. . . . If woman is to find true happiness once again, she must return to her real and joyful self. She must relearn that surrender to her biological destiny is . . . a wonderful privileged condition." Harry and Bonaro Overstreet, writing for the readers of *Good Housekeeping*, offer a similar recipe for happiness: "The woman's role is the nurturing role. . . . What she lets people persuade her or browbeat her into taking on outside the home should be rigorously put to this test: Is it part of housekeeping, neighboring, nurturing? Or it is just something that someone thought up and is now telling her that she ought to want?" Moss Hart, in *Lady in the Dark*, stated the neo-traditional argument in the neat, idealized terms of fiction: his lady was a top magazine editor, chic, successful, bossy—and loveless; when she slowly realized the secret of true womanliness, she gave her job to the handsome bachelor who had been her assistant, married him, and moved off to the suburbs to be her real and joyful self.

In addition to psychological and historical arguments spiced with quotations from St. Paul, the neo-traditionalists borrow what they can from sociology. Certain sociologists claim that in every known society marriage is based not only upon a sexual relationship, but upon a classic division of labor in which the woman performs the biological and nurturant tasks, and the man performs the far-ranging, food-gathering, and problem-solving tasks. George Murdock and other sociologists have described this as a "cultural universal," a label which greatly comforts anyone who finds the present-day overlapping of roles unnatural.

Some neo-traditionalists feel that it is primarily middle-class women who have forgotten their ancient wisdom and lost their instinctive way to happiness; lower-class women, they claim, have neither lost sight of the verities nor become unhappy. History professor Eric F. Goldman of Princeton asserts that "almost everything that has happened in America in recent decades has conspired to turn feminism into a blueprint for stripping the middle and upper-middle-class woman of the usufructs and pleasures of being a woman. . . . [In contrast,] the truck-driver's wife has no problem about her 'role in society.' She's there, she cooks the dinner and runs the house, sleeps with the old man, raises the children, and when she gets a little weary of it all, plops down in front of the TV. She has no need of a creative career. Her creations are all around her, scratching up the furniture, clouting her eardrums, making her feel the most important person in the world."

A logical outgrowth of this view is the belief that woman is harmed by exposure to ideas and experiences unrelated to homemaking; college education for females should, therefore, be revised in the direction of home economics and child rearing. "I have come to realize that I was educated to be a successful man and now must learn by myself to be a successful woman," writes an embittered college graduate quoted by Lynn White, former president of Mills

College, who believes that girls should be educated primarily in subjects related to "family, food, beauty and warmth, shelter and security." Others make the ultimate deduction that girls ought not go to college at all, and essays and articles to this effect have appeared both in this country and in England. White himself has quoted an intelligent woman as saying to him, "I do not believe that either women or Negroes should be educated. It can only make them more unhappy than in any case they must be."

Today's young neo-traditionalist doesn't want a girl just like the girl that married dear old Dad, for she was probably a hell-for-leather feminist. What he does want is a good old-fashioned girl of the kind they still have in Europe, where women are said to be still truly feminine. Depending on who tells the tale, European women are chic, sexy, intriguing, adorable, and let their escorts talk while they tinkle with appreciative laughter; or are sturdy enough to rise at 6 A.M., scour the markets for bargains, carry staggering loads home, and bear babies without a whimper; or can simultaneously turn the cuffs on a man's shirts, whip out *truite amandine* for dinner, and keep four children silent and neat, all without any sense of strain. It is not quite clear whether all these traits are to be found in one and the same woman, but it *is* absolutely clear that neo-traditional man thinks the European woman knows her place—and allows him *his* place, without any contest.

The pressure of all this propaganda is partly responsible for the nervous haste with which middle-class American women rush into early domesticity, with a consequent loss of position in the world of business and of intellect. A little over 6 percent of U.S. doctors are women today, which is no larger a proportion than in 1910; a distinctly smaller proportion of today's public-school teachers are women today than was true thirty years ago; and although women earned one out of every six doctorates awarded in 1920, they earn only one in ten today. The middle-class educated woman who is most likely to feel frustrated by housekeeping is also the most likely to have read all the neo-traditional arguments and chosen a suburban way of life which all but forces her to confine herself to domesticity.

Yet it is doubtful whether the propaganda itself can really be given all the credit for the emphasis on domesticity among today's young women. More likely, there are basic reasons why women are now susceptible to arguments they would have laughed at a generation ago. Many have been suggested: for one, militant feminism led to biological and emotional frustration on a broad scale, against which there is now a reaction; for another, wartime separations and cold-war tensions have made women reappraise and set great store by normal family life; again, the two sexes are beginning to overlap so much in their roles and personalities that women are taking to domesticity in order to clarify the situation; finally, since men now see fit to lean upon their employers and their government, women accordingly are willing to lean upon their men. Daring, individualism, and ambition are not currently in vogue, and woman's partial withdrawal from emancipation is only part of a larger pattern.

3 STUMBLING BLOCKS ON THE ROAD BACK

If the neo-traditional arguments were sound, the present interest in domesticity which they have helped bring about should already have led to a decrease in feminine neurosis and discontent, as well as in adultery, divorce, and juvenile delinquency. Since this has not happened, something must be wrong with the neo-traditional position.

But we might have suspected, even in advance, that the neo-traditional philosophy would not prove functional today; men have often tried to turn the river of history backward, but time makes it flow on, despite their pitiful exertions. Furthermore, for all the reasons we saw in Chapters One and Two, we may legitimately suspect that woman's historical preoccupation with domesticity has in large part been the result of economic necessity rather than of instinct. Dr. Robinson is right in saying that pre-industrial woman derived a sense of value, importance, and status from her household labors, but what she did *had* to be done by her, which makes all the difference. Woman's life in colonial America, for instance, was no cozy idyll made up of spinning wheel, crackling joint on the spit, rosy-cheeked darlings playing before the fire, and snug, wholesome evenings at petit-point while the lord of the house read aloud a bit of scripture; instead, it was likely to be a backbreaking round of duties such as aristocrats have always assigned to slaves or indentured servants. Here, for instance, is the complacent testimony of Christopher Marshall, a thrifty, prosperous Philadelphia Quaker, whose diary for 1778 includes this note about his wife's activities:

> From early in the morning till late at night she is constantly employed in the affairs of the family. . . . This calls for her constant attendance at getting prepared in the kitchen, baking our own bread and pies, meat &c. [and] also on the table. Her cleanliness about the house, her attendance in the orchard, cutting and drying of apples of which several bushels have been procured, add to which her making of cider without tools for the constant drink of the family, her seeing to all our washing done, and her fine clothes and my shirts, the which are smoothed [i.e., ironed] by her; add to this her making of twenty large cheeses, besides her sewing, knitting, &c. I think she has not been above four times since her residence here to visit her neighbors.

Goodwife Marshall could hardly have suffered from role conflicts; when on earth would she have had time to think about such things? But whether or not she was content, the real question is whether woman today could find contentment in a similar life, though living in a radically different milieu. It seems unlikely: wherever social change makes woman's traditional labors unnecessary, women cease setting store by them and strive to abandon them. The Indonesian woman has responded enthusiastically to President Sukarno's promise that Socialism will bring her electricity and appliances, and so give her some free time; the impoverished Mexican woman who formerly arose at 2 A.M. to grind corn and make a hundred tortillas by hand for the day's meals now sleeps later and buys mill-ground meal, or even ready-made tortillas, in the stores; and in Paris the frugal housewife who used to shop and haggle every day for the evening's meal is beginning to turn to the new supermarkets, stock up her freezer (if she can afford one), and so experience unprecedented leisure.

A history professor, from his comfortable remove in Princeton, may view the life of the truck driver's wife sentimentally, but she herself may see it otherwise. Here, for instance, is a representative working-class mother in Levittown, New Jersey, telling an inquisitive sociologist about her days and ways:

> Crowded, just crowded—that's what every day is like. They're all busy. They're just dull, too. . . . All I ever seem to do is mess around. I get up at eight—I make breakfast, so I do the dishes, have lunch, do some more dishes, and then some more work in the afternoon. Then it's supper dishes and I get to sit down for a few minutes before the children have to be sent to bed. . . . It's just routine. Humdrum. Just cooking and cleaning, washing the dishes and mending clothes. Then the biggest part of the time I am chasing kids.

Case workers and others who have studied the lower classes have repeatedly attested that lack of empathy between man and wife, the view of sex as a "relief" for the man, wife beating, desertion, divorce, and psychosis are all more frequent among lower-class and less-educated groups than among middle-class and better-educated ones. The warm, happy life of the traditional lower-class woman has been much exaggerated; it may even be nine-tenths a literary myth.

As for the sociological thesis that a universal division of labor exists between man and woman, Professor Murdock's own research hardly justifies the use neo-traditionalists make of it. In a survey of published data on 224 primitive societies, he reported that in 100 percent of them war was a male job, hunting and trapping were male jobs in 97 percent and female jobs in 3 percent, trade 74 and 26 respectively, agriculture 48 and 52 percent, pottery making 18 and 82 percent, and cooking 8.5 and 91.5 percent. Division of labor, yes; but universal direction to that division, no. Moreover, even this finding pertains to primitive societies and economies of scarcity, whereas our own society has multiplied the power available per human being twelvefold in one century, and is on the way to becoming a society of abundance. "Patterns which made sense for a division of labor between men and women in a society dependent upon human energy," comments sociologist Ruth Hill Useem, "do not make sense for a power energy society."

Indeed, they make nonsense of an unfunny sort. Thirty-five million American women—one and a third million of them college-educated—currently devote full time to housewifery, ignoring all the modern opportunities of making domesticity a part-time concern; meanwhile, the nation is short at least 12,000 psychiatrists, 70,000 nurses, 135,000 schoolteachers, 35,000 social workers, and 50,000 medical technicians, to say nothing of its huge shortages in engineering, physics, and other occupations women rarely consider although they have the requisite abilities for them. With a life-and-death competition going on between our capitalist form of modern society and the Socialist one, the squandering of this immense reservoir of talent is so short-sighted that future historians may be unable to imagine why we permitted it, and speculate as to whether it was incompetence, gross stupidity, or willful suicide.

Still, the argument that college education for the woman should concern homemaking and nurturant tasks is advanced on the grounds of its suitability for her, if not for her society. Yet it conflicts with major pertinent facts of her life: (1) she will have only about fifteen intensely nurturant years, five or ten of transition, and then about thirty in which she has only herself and her husband to care for: (2) as various studies have shown, the interests she develops in college are apt to be her lifelong ones, but if her college experiences are narrowed to homemaking she will have few inner resources or skills of value to her when the nurturant years are over; (3) the further apart her interests and educational background are from those of her husband the greater the likelihood that their marriage will be unsatisfying or unstable; the girl who learns only to be a wonderful housekeeper and mother may, after a while, be an utter bore to her husband, and so lose him in part—or altogether. The neo-traditional prescriptions for woman's education are thus excellent advice for a world that no longer exists; but in the one we do inhabit, David Riesman says, such prescriptions are not only patronizing but seriously maladaptive.

Ultimately, however, the best evaluation of the neo-traditional doctrine is the record of what happens to women when they attempt to apply it today. Let us now look at their experiences, their joys, and their frustrations in more detail.*

4 THE BUSY YEARS

Even if we suspect that the neo-traditional prescription for woman's education is maladaptive, this is not to say that all preparation for homemaking is bad and should be avoided. The thesis of this book is that in the modern world woman functions most adequately and has the best chance of happiness when she defines femininity in terms of a multiplicity of roles, finding ways to handle them more or less simultaneously with a minimum of inner conflict, sudden shifts, or unpreparedness. And if this implies that the girl, at school, ought not be discouraged from liberal, scientific, or business studies, it also implies that she should be taught enough about housekeeping at home during her formative years to be comfortable and competent at it later on. Unfortunately, compared to music and novels, hairdos and clothes, poetry and psychology, dates and dances, housekeeping is dull and unreal; like old age and death, it is inevitable—but not worth worrying about yet. One professor, who asked a number of undergraduate girls in liberal arts how much they knew about cooking and homemaking, reports getting the almost standard reply, "I'll learn all that when I have to."

This attitude is reinforced and sanctioned by the general American belief in progress, which regards whatever is new as better, whatever is old as worse. Why should the girl bother to learn techniques from her mother when there are bound to be more modern ones that will make her a superior homemaker in a twinkling? Advertisements tell her that whether it is a question of wrapping up leftovers or of furnishing a house, whatever was done a generation

* The balance of this chapter will focus upon housewifery; the next one will consider mothering. It is worthwhile to view them separately, insofar as we can, the better to know precisely what things are the sources of modern woman's discontents, and what things the sources of her fulfillments.

ago is outmoded, clumsy, and even laughable. New improved techniques are available which require no training—all she need do, when the time comes, is pull the tab, plug in, rinse and drip-dry, spray it on (no wiping), add water and stir, use and throw away. She will be a more up-to-date, efficient homemaker than her mother, without having to give it a thought until the time comes or do more than follow the easy instructions on the package.

All her plans and expectations about housekeeping have this same unrealistic quality. Though she does not want to be a housewife, she has no alternative plans—neither for an active career nor for keeping hired help in her house.* She assumes that she will do the cooking when she marries, yet in her teens, according to a survey by the Eugene Gilbert Company, she practices it in her mother's kitchen only three or four times a month. Somehow everything will get done: togetherness, frozen foods, electricity, plastic bags, spray cans, and a little intelligence will make housekeeping effortless and the housekeeper charming.

Then she marries and confronts reality. From Indianapolis a former schoolteacher, now in her late twenties, writes that she had never bothered to think about how to clean, cook, or manage a home until she became engaged; at this point, she says,

> I entertained visions of myself dancing lightly about the house with my little dustmop, having coffee with the neighbors, baking Christmas cookies, and effortlessly putting a hot tempting meal on the table. Instead, when the time came, I found myself swamped with all the household and baby duties, and frantically at work from morning till night. I grew desperate in my efforts to keep the place decent and get everything done; I tried schedules and systems one after another with no benefit, and got to the point where I was greeting my husband like a weary, ill-tempered wretch when he came home.

Many a young middle-class wife simply is technically unequipped for the chores she must do; they are time-consuming and exasperat-

---

* A survey of high-school girls hoping to go to college showed that only 13 percent were primarily career-oriented; a survey of the better-off girls at the University of Minnesota showed that two-thirds of them had no plans to have servants when they married.

ing because she does not do them well, and emotionally fatiguing because, lacking experience and habit patterns, she must continually make decisions. How should she arrange a linen closet properly—do the most recently laundered things go on top of the stack or underneath? How does one manage to use up leftovers in the refrigerator without having them go bad and guiltily throwing them away? Is it better to clean a little every day or do a big job once a week? How does one get a coffee stain out of the living-room rug, and will the same technique work for a dog's or baby's indiscretion? How will she ever learn to buy enough of each thing, so as not always to have to run to the store for one last little item?

Many a woman, faced with all this, reacts by frantically gathering up a thousand bits of technique from magazines, books, friends, and neighbors; then, trying to make up for her beginning ineptness (and perhaps for her stifled dislike of housekeeping), she overshoots the mark and becomes a perfectionist—compulsively neat, fanatically orderly, strictly regulated. Such a woman will wipe away fingerprints all day long, set each piece of furniture in place to the quarter of an inch, nag her husband about cigarette ashes, and shout at her children for leaving toys around. Now and again she hears herself and is startled, or even horrified; if she is lucky or wise, she eventually learns to assign housekeeping its proper place, not as the purpose and end of married life but as part of its machinery. But combatting her own compulsive orderliness may prove as long and painful a job as dieting or conquering fear of the water.

But others never acquire enough technique to face this problem; their problem, rather, is that their lives and homes remain in a state of perpetual disorder, disarray, and crisis. Such women describe homemaking as "exhausting," "hectic," "disorganized," and "bewildering." Their lack of preparation is made all the more painful by the modern emphasis on early motherhood. The contemporary haste to wed, set up house, and immediately produce a brood of delightful babies results in an overpoweringly sudden encounter with all sorts of problems; there is not even time for some women to collect minimum household skills before the arrival of the baby adds an average of forty-four hours of work per week and all but over-whelms them.

Sociologists often call this period of woman's life "the busy years," yet advertisers and many others repeatedly say that labor-saving devices have freed modern woman from time-consuming chores and liberated her for a host of leisure interests. To many young sub-urban housewives this is a sour joke. Granted that the dishwasher does the dishes, the washing machine does the clothes, and so on, she still is busy all day long. "Don't tell me the modern housewife has it so easy," the wife of an old friend in Fort Lauderdale writes tartly. "I get up at 6 A.M. every schoolday to start fixing food for all those mouths—six including mine, seven if you include the dog—and from then on it's washing up, straightening the house, buying more food, doing beds, filling the mouths again, washing dishes again, putting in the laundry, taking it out, rushing off to different stores and doctors, and so on without end. We have lots of expensive gadgets, but I still don't seem to have half an hour free until I drop in bed at 10 that night. Liberation? Show me some!" Mrs. Mark Van Doren, reminiscing recently about her own active life as mother, writer, and editor, remarked that in her day the young homemaker actually had more chance to get around and see people than the young homemaker does now. "I had a housekeeper for twenty years," she said. "I think the girls today do a wonderful job, but they never see anyone but the milkman."

Yet it is impossible wholly to sympathize with modern middle-class woman's plight, since in part she brings it on herself. For she rushes into domesticity and compounds it with motherhood before being ready, technically, emotionally, or financially; on top of this, she almost always chooses to live in her own home, suburban if pos-sible, and far removed from relatives who could help, as well as from the domestic labor supply. In the long history of the family, there has rarely been a time when each young wife was as totally isolated and as solely responsible for her house and her children as is the modern woman. In almost all of the past, she had parents, in-laws, unmarried sisters, slaves, servants, concubines, or other adults around to help; today she has only herself and electricity. But she is the one who chooses to have it that way.

Some social scientists, moreover, feel that many a modern woman, having decided to back away from feminism, refuses to allow the labor-saving devices to give her free time; as fast as they do, she fills the time up with newly concocted duties and increased demands on herself. Alva Myrdal and Viola Klein, studying women's patterns of housework, comment dryly that there are grounds for "the suspicion that housewives often unconsciously expand it in order to [provide] evidence that they are fully occupied and indispensable." The colonial housewife accumulated dirty laundry and did it when she could, once a month or even less often; the housewife of a generation ago did it once a week; but today's homemaker, with her automatic washer-dryer, does it every other day and keeps her family cleaner than hygiene or aesthetics require. Where the nineteenth-century woman served good plain fare six nights a week and put forth a special effort for Sunday dinner, the modern housewife feels that every night her table should look like something out of the four-color section of a woman's magazine. She is, in short, one more example of Parkinson's Law that "work expands so as to fill the time available for its completion."

A classic survey made at Bryn Mawr found that farm wives, who give their husbands some help, spend sixty-one hours per week on housekeeping, while big-city wives, with no such double demand on them, spend eighty-one hours at it. The latter may be more perfect housekeepers, but they elevate their standards of housekeeping either because they have little else to justify their existence or because, being tied down by small children, they cannot get out of the house anyway. Certainly, after the children have gotten beyond infancy the modern woman does not have to remain enslaved by housekeeping; even a relatively conservative magazine such as *Ladies' Home Journal* published an article about a Texas housewife who adores music, reading, and cards, and therefore efficiently runs her lovely home for her husband and two growing sons on one hour or so of housework per day, plus some dishwashing, some help with the cooking from her husband, and a big once-a-week clean-up.

Not everyone can pull off this kind of sleight-of-hand, but most women, if they dared, could at least keep from being submerged and suffocated by housework. "If women were convinced that a day off or an hour of solitude was a reasonable ambition," writes Anne Lindbergh in *Gift from the Sea*, "they would find some way of attaining it. As it is, they feel so unjustified in their demand that they rarely make the attempt." The modern wife encloses herself in a vicious circle; having chosen an identity a part of which she finds disagreeable, she feels ashamed of herself and redoubles her dedication to the part she dislikes. She is a little like that sixth-century Irish saint, Scuthin by name, who, the better to assert his chastity, regularly slept abed with two beautiful virgins. Only very holy people ought to try themselves so sorely; American women, being no saintlier than most, might well reconsider their efforts at self-mortification.

5 PRIDEFUL ACTIVITIES AND NOT-SO-PRIDEFUL ONES

It is extraordinary how many women elect to play the part of the housekeeper so intensely as to eliminate those other aspects of themselves that both they and the men they married used to like. This lopsided choice of roles, particularly noticeable since World War II, is part of the domesticity syndrome. I have called this latter-day mood neo-traditionalism, but others use harsher terms; sociologist Kingsley Davis, for instance, calls it "neo-primitivism." Primitivism, neo- or other, is grossly inappropriate to our society. Early marriage, high fertility, and exclusive concern with nurturant functions might make sense for the woman living in a grass-thatched hut or even in a frontier cabin. In our contemporary world they solve some immediate problems, but at the cost of making many later ones; someone has aptly called early marriage a kind of installment buying, the motto being, "Marry now, pay later."

When, for instance, a young woman is isolated in her home with several small children, obsessed with housework, and cut off from all her previous activities and interests, her homemaking functions may interfere seriously with her functions as a lover and a mother. To be mistress to one's husband and to be mother to one's children are, for most women, fundamental sources of satisfaction and joy in life, but it is impossible to do either thing well when exhausted and embittered by an excessive burden of housekeeping, whether or not self-imposed. Nor can a woman who is drugged by fatigue, cut off from outside contacts and interests, jealous, petulant, and ashamed of her feelings be to her husband the many other things he needs her to be—companion, playmate, intellectual partner, confidant, and adviser. Nor, finally, can she be to herself what is most important of all: an embodiment of the image she once had of herself.

Still, must housekeeping hamper all these other functions of the self and be utterly lacking in fulfillment? Why doesn't modern woman enjoy her housekeeping as she is supposed to by birthright and instinct? Why doesn't she arrive at the end of each day tired but fulfilled, her exertions having yielded a sweet weariness each evening, like that of a skipper who has skillfully brought his boat through a storm and now lies at anchor, safe, relaxed, and garrulously pleased with himself and his day?

It *should* feel that way, women are told; but for many of them, disturbingly, it does not. "What is *wrong* with me?" writes the wife of a commercial photographer in Cleveland. "What is missing in me? Why don't I enjoy these things as I should?" She says that she does get a genuine thrill from successfully trying some new recipe for a special occasion; and now and then, when she goes on a veritable binge of cleaning, rearranging drawers, and throwing out things, she derives a fine, savage feeling of accomplishment. "But that's only once in a while," she says. "Most of the time I just drag myself through my routines and feel my duties to be a great awful bore. But I'm *ashamed* of feeling that way, and I don't tell anyone about it for fear they will think me unnatural." Not everyone would. "The blunt fact," writes Clifton Fadiman, in a rebuttal of the neo-traditionalist praise of domesticity, "is that today the 'life that feels natural to the sex' is . . . a succession of ever-repeated, mentally and emotionally stultifying and degrading chores, most of them filthy, none of them adequately appreciated. . . . If [women] cannot love their fate, let them at least react to it with the only suitable emotion: absolute, unmitigated, icy hatred."

And this is the heart of the problem: the intelligent, educated modern woman, even when she conquers housekeeping technically, recognizes it to be for the most part a menial, tiresome, low-grade job, far beneath her real qualifications and personal value. Advertising men sometimes deftly touch this female sore spot in their copy. An ad in the Spring, 1960, issue of the *Barnard Alumnae Magazine,* for instance, portrayed an intellectual young lady, saucepan in hand, and demanded of her: "Is this the fulfillment they told you about at Barnard? . . . How is your mind faring these days? Does your daily regimen include enough food for thought? If all work and no mental play seems to be dulling your sensibilities, order home delivery of *The New York Times.*"

More serious for the intelligent woman, therefore, than the labor, dirt, or unaesthetic aspects of housekeeping, is the feeling that it is causing her to "go to seed," to "rust," to "wither on the vine," and to "waste away" (to cite only a few of the phrases she actually uses). "I am turning into a vegetable," was one expression Professor Komarovsky reports hearing fairly often, in a series of interviews she conducted. "I am horrified to realize that I begin to like daytime serials," says one housewife with a degree from Columbia University. A talented woman of thirty who lives in Las Vegas has confided to me that she put aside her collegiate dreams of becoming a writer in favor of homemaking, only to find herself feeling cheated. "Life should be an adventure," she says, "hazardous and exciting. Yet I discovered what was wrong with modern woman—we live in our little boxes, snug and shut in, we busy ourselves with idiotic chores, we pop a frozen steak in the broiler, add water to a cakemix, and wait for Hubby to come home, we are dull, plain downright dull, and it is little wonder we turn to divorce courts and mental institutions to make life bearable." The routine of cloistered domesticity, so comforting to some women, seemed to her like an exile (she later escaped it via a part-time job). "I felt as though the world was passing me by," she writes. "Each night as I tucked my sons in bed, I thanked God that they would grow up to be *men,* that they would be able to teach, write, heal, advise, travel, and do anything else they chose."

She and the others all manifest, in their various ways, a common ailment—the loss of identity. The self that she has lost is that of the college girl or career girl, sought-after, fancy free, and involved in the larger world of ideas and events; she has, of course, gained a new and less equivocal identity, but the former one seemed, once, the better, the more real self.

Compared to the old self and the laid-aside identity, the new one —or at least as much of it as concerns housekeeping—is unimportant and somewhat embarrassing. The industrial and urban development of the nation greatly simplified homemaking, but devalued it; when one can buy a loaf of bread or a pair of socks for small change, there is little glory in making them at home. Some housewives recognize this and state it plainly. From Princeton, a woman writes that her mother, who had to work far harder than she ever does, was filled with vitality and a zest for life that the daughter finds lacking in herself, and which she explains as follows:

> Hard and difficult as my mother's life was, the work she did required a great deal of creativity and ingenuity. In contrast, though machines have relieved me of the more arduous tasks, the jobs that are left offer little in the way of creative satisfactions, and produce tension rather than relieve it.

There is no single housekeeping function for which the wife today is irreplaceable; any urban bachelor or widower can buy all the products or hire all the services he needs. And even the jobs left to her are low in cash value; all her labors can be performed just as well by a full-time hired woman, the value of her housekeeping thus being at most about $4,000 a year in New York, and more typically $1,156 (the national average pay of full-time houseworkers in 1960).

This, then, is a large part of the reason housekeeping is aggravating, embarrassing, dull, and unrewarding to many women. Tedium, messiness, and arduousness are not the whole or major trouble after all, for they characterize many a job men find satisfying and worthy;

the fact is that woman's job as housekeeper is no longer a source of prestige and status. It is not, in Dr. Kluckhohn's phrase, "a prideful activity."

Exhortations to women to rediscover the real and joyful self in housekeeping—Dr. Farnham and Mr. Lundberg actually urge women to go back to baking their own bread and canning their own fruit, as a step in regaining their womanhood—ignore the fundamental fact that one cannot healthfully live insulated from the values and the inherent logic of one's own society. Or rather, only the occasional hermit can—but such defiant withdrawal is a solution inapplicable *en masse*. In the nature of things today, housekeeping can bring only limited status and psychological reward to most intelligent women; the technological basis of our society cannot be wished away, and its consequences cannot be dealt with by playing games of make-believe.

6 *THE ENJOYMENT OF HOUSEKEEPING*

The psychological and social pressures in favor of housewifery conflict sharply with its lowly, unsatisfying nature in the modern world; together these constitute the horns of a difficult dilemma for modern woman. One extreme solution is complete avoidance, in the form either of full-time careerism (which we will look at in a later chapter), or of indolent dependence on servants—an attitude psychologically and financially possible only for the very rich.

The far more common extreme solution is complete acceptance. For some women this comes easily and naturally, but for others it may, like religious conversion, come only after a period of struggle and doubt which ends in a highly emotional decision to see housewifery as necessary, right, and good. "This is my job," writes a woman from Hicksville, Long Island. "I married, got a house, had children, and this is my place in society, with all its duties and obligations. Let the others have their golf clubs, their easels, their drama scripts. I have made up my mind and spoken my piece; I will resign myself—cheerfully, I hope—to the daily humdrum."

Such a conversion often imbues the woman with an evangelical fervor. "I would like to shout out to all other young mothers, *Commit thyself!*" writes a woman from a suburb in southern California. "Let's stop considering that our happiness depends on self-identity. Let's see it as depending on our professional success as homemakers—a career we have been committed to ever since a discontented Eve first reached out for forbidden fruit."

Like other forms of conversion, this resolute acceptance is apt to produce some intolerance in the convert. Discussions in print of the "loss of identity," the proper type of college education, or the career-homemaker dilemma always bring forth a rash of letters from housewives who are scornful of or angered by women who feel trapped, or who seek to escape entrapment. The *Wellesley Alumnae Magazine,* after running a series of articles not long ago about the frustrations of the college-educated homemaker, came under such counter-fire from contented women that the abashed editor raised a white flag in print, saying, "We now believe that the so-called frustration must indeed be a myth."

This was politic, but hardly accurate. A *Fortune* survey conducted by Elmo Roper revealed that 50 percent more women think man's life more interesting than think their own is. Thirty percent of the housewives in two different communities, in a sociological study cited by Dr. Marie Jahoda, said they would like to work if a job were available that would enable them to hire household help, and a Gallup poll reported that less than half of all wives derive much pleasure or satisfaction from housework.

But between the two extreme answers of complete avoidance and complete acceptance is a middle-of-the-road compromise favored by a majority: it consists of admitting a dislike for the lowly or brainless chores in housekeeping, and doggedly looking for compensation in its "creative" functions. "I'm not crazy about scrubbing the kitchen floor," writes a fifty-year-old former book store saleswoman, "but there *is* a deep satisfaction in taking fragrant golden loaves of my own home-made bread out of the oven and presenting them to my family at the table." Writes a thirty-five-year-old Wellesley alumna, "The same initiative and creativity that researched a paper on Spinoza can also cook a gourmet dinner, arrange a novel center-piece, plan a memorable party, or devise a unique Halloween costume for a child."

These things may, to some extent, be self-expressive and satisfying, yet in truth they remain an imperfect answer. The meals and the flower arrangements are ephemeral and disappear, leaving no residuum of accomplishment or advancement; home décor is more permanent, but has a very limited audience and, once done, cannot be done again every week. Most important, these creative activities are apt to be indulgently regarded by the society around the woman not as serious endeavors but as nice little skills, on a par with the genteel parlor singing and reciting expected of upper-class young ladies in the nineteenth century.

Unquestionably, many women find certain pleasures and some fulfillment in their housewifery; for the majority, however, it remains in large part an unavoidable, under-rewarding, and frequently demeaning part of their lives. Though many of the latter may try to convince themselves that they should deeply enjoy housekeeping, the more functional attitude would be for them to view it honestly and assign it a realistic value, accept it as an integral and occasionally enjoyable part of the mechanics of daily life—and make every intelligent effort to incorporate into their lives other activities of a genuinely prideful and potentially more fulfilling nature.

CHAPTER EIGHT

THE NOT-QUITE-IDEAL

MOTHER

1 THE ENIGMA OF MODERN MOTHERHOOD

Nothing about modern woman is more thoroughly paradoxical than her attitude toward motherhood. Although a kind of sociological law holds that fertility decreases as the standard of living rises, the fertility of American women of all classes has shot up sharply in the sustained prosperity of the postwar era. The former battles over birth control exist only as fitful rear-guard actions, and contraceptives are easily available in all the states except Connecticut and Massachusetts, but at last counting women in their fertile years were bearing 48 percent more children per year than women did in 1940. Since this dovetails with the renewed emphasis on domesticity, one might suppose that some basic feminine drive had reassertd itself in middle-class women, and that motherhood was again their whole-hearted goal in life. This wholesome assumption is rather soured, however, by lengthy studies made at a number of hospitals and maternity clinics which reveal that the great majority of all women pregnant for the first time feel depressed, anxious, or disappointed on discovering their condition, but keep their feelings to themselves.

Attendance at maternity classes given by the Red Cross and by hospitals, the tremendous interest in articles and books on child care, and the growth of P.-T.A.'s all evidence the strong desire of modern woman to be a competent, informed mother; yet the air resounds with charges that she emasculates and sissifies her sons, secretly rejects her children while openly tying them to her with the silver cord, psychologizes about them instead of mothering them, and either coldly abandons them to the maid or hotly suffocates them with an excess of maternal devotion.

There are undoubtedly deep roots nourishing the revival of motherhood, but the plant is not exactly the old one come to life again. Bosomy, sturdy, broad-hipped motherhood is not what modern woman really wants; she is intrigued by the image, yet fearful of its effect on her future sex life, her figure, and, if she has one, her career. She may be talked into breast feeding her child, only to have her body betray her real feelings. A study made by psychologist Niles Newton in a Philadelphia hospital disclosed that mothers who wanted to breast feed their babies gave an average of fifty-nine grams of milk by the fourth day of feedings; those who disliked doing so could give only an average of thirty-five grams, and most of them had to resort to supplemental bottle feedings. In olden days a woman would blame the faulty flow on natural causes, weep bitterly for the loss of her baby, and eventually recover; today she keeps her child alive on formula, and for the rest of his childhood stuffs food into him in an effort to make up for it.

The revival of motherhood thus has a certain resemblance to the revival of religion, with its increased church membership and decreased piety. Max Lerner, for one, attributes the great eagerness for children not to any praiseworthy excess of maternal instinct, but to a desire to feed those emotions starved in us by American success hunting and sexual repression. Others allege that women bear children in a spirit of performing a disagreeable social duty; Dr. Newton —a woman, by the way—acidly asks, "Who has not heard young matrons talking about having their children early in their marriage and close together in order to 'get it over with'?" Still, in survey after survey American women themselves rate children and the joys of motherhood high on the list of marital values, far above economic security, sexual satisfaction, understanding, and so on. Of nearly a thousand women queried in one study, only one mother said she would have no children if she could live her life over, while all but 3 percent of the childless women said they would want children if they could live theirs over.

When women are asked what their children have meant to them, their answers are couched in terms such as "companionship," "they make you happy," "they're fun and entertaining," "it's a chance to relive my own life," "they give life a purpose," "it is the creation of a new human being that is so fulfilling," and "it is a joy to watch them maturing." The advocates of larger families sometimes grow lyrical and even saccharine about it; a Wellesley graduate and mother of five, after attributing the increase in fertility in part to various social and economic causes, concludes:

> I've left the biggest reason till last—the children themselves. There's no doubt about it: children are a source of endless delight and consternation. But delight far outshines consternation! Once we've known the joy of motherhood, even the annoyances and worries that go with child raising can't discourage us from wanting more babies. . . . In a mother's heart there is always room for one more.

Yet if a statement like that is uttered or read aloud to any group of intelligent and sophisticated modern women, many of them will feel faintly embarrassed, much as they would in the presence of someone fulsomely boasting of his personal salvation. The revival of motherhood is not pure and simple, but impure and complex; it is symbolic that our country was the first to make a great to-do about Mother's Day, and the first to make "mom" a dirty word.

2 *MATERNAL INSTINCT: A FEW NON-FACTS*

The preceding antinomies express the conflict between the realities of woman's life today and the ancient conception of motherhood which is currently being sold in shined-up, neo-traditional form. We have already seen that the neo-traditional psychology of woman is, by and large, parochial and inaccurate; now, more specifically, let us see to what extent this is true of the renovated image of motherhood. It is a touchy subject; one discusses Mother, God, or Our Country only at the risk of being thought damnable and dangerous, if his data contradict any part of the culture myth. Nevertheless, at the risk of being damned, let us see how the conservative assertions compare with the available factual evidence.

To begin with, the neo-traditional view holds that maternal feeling is a natural, instinctive, ultra-powerful drive in every normal female creature, and that any deviation from this signifies an ailment or a defect. Do not all sorts of female animals spend themselves instinctively, generously, and skillfully in the role of mother? The salmon exhausts herself in the upstream fight to reach the right waters in which to lay her eggs and then die; the eider duck lines her nest with down torn from her own bosom; the cat, though she has never seen it done before, finds a warm, dark place for her coming kittens, carefully licks them clean after they are born, lies down to give them suck, and prowls around uttering warning and worried sounds when human beings come to see. Surely motherhood must be the primal goal of the normal female of every species, including mankind; and to the extent that any woman is not instinctively competent at it and totally fulfilled by it, she must be neurotic, unwomanly, and a failure.

But analogies between animal and human behavior are risky. Unlike other animals, the human being is born almost completely unequipped with rigidly patterned instincts; we have powerful amorphous drives toward food, comfort, sex, and so on, but no inborn, predetermined mechanisms which automatically come into play to satisfy those drives. But this is something to be proud of; it is why we are so highly educable, can manipulate our environment, and have built great civilizations. The mother instincts of the animals are marvelous to observe, but although they work well enough as long as the surrounding conditions are normal, let there be an abnormal circumstance and the beautiful mother love may suddenly appear in a different and less noble light. In artificial breeding ponds the bass will eat her own young unless there is an abundance of other food both available and visible, and the guppy in a tank will eat her newborn offspring unless immediately separated from them; a worker wasp, if kept from collecting food for the young, may play the good parent by biting off the hind end of a grub and offering it to the front end; and the mother bird of many a species will feed an open artificial mouth of painted wood just as readily as her own baby's mouth.

A woman, in contrast, is not naturally impelled to behave in specific ways; she does what she has learned and seen and read about. Russian mothers "instinctively know" that the only right way to care for an infant for his first six or eight months is to swaddle him like a mummy, rendering him immovable the major part of the day; American mothers just as instinctively know that babies should freely kick and wiggle to their hearts' content. In some cultures, women have felt it natural to let a child remain at the breast at each feeding as long as he wants to; in others, they have felt it natural to give him a few minutes and then snatch the breast away. Colonial Puritan mothers felt that children were basically sinful and needed continual discipline and chastisement for their faults; just a few years ago, however, many mothers were sure that children could do no wrong, and needed untrammeled self-expression, whatever the cost to adult ears, nerves, and furniture.

These variations are possible because woman acquires her so-called "maternal instincts" from her culture, not from her genes. Bit by bit, from the time of her own infancy on, she absorbs the meaning of motherliness according to her own world. Unlike the animals, she has to *learn* how to be kind and loving, and how to want and to care for a child. She does have certain biological links with her past; her nipples, for instance, do protrude when her breasts are full, and her skin does find the feel of the baby wonderfully agreeable. But the full meaning of human motherhood is not automatically determined and called forth by these things; it is too complex, subtle, and rich for that, for it is in large part a learned, intelligent pattern of behavior.

The recent fads in motherhood which call for a return to simpler, more "natural," and allegedly more womanly behavior imply that motherhood should become again what it used to be, and that there is only one natural way for mothers to behave—the same way most mothers have behaved from Homeric times until half a century ago. The advocates of natural childbirth, for instance, have enthusiastically claimed that the pains of labor and childbirth are largely the result of overcivilized living and of a fearful or rejecting attitude toward normal womanly functions; women in primitive societies, they assert, rarely have such troubles. One enthusiast writes, for instance, that when a Bushman or Australian tribe is marching to a new food-gathering area, sometimes "a woman falls out, gives birth to her child, catches up with her companions, and behaves as if nothing much extraordinary had happened." But surveys of anthropological literature show this to be more the exception than the rule, childbirth being dreaded and difficult in many a present and vanished culture; such diligent researchers as Amram Scheinfeld, George Murdock, and the German scholars H. H. Ploss, Max Bartels, and Paul Bartels have all reported that the belief is a myth.* What better disproof of it could there be, for that matter, than the words of Genesis, "In sorrow thou shalt bring forth children"?—which, with apologies to any fundamentalists present, excellently indicate how childbearing seemed to one semiprimitive people.

There is little doubt that many of the techniques involved in contemporary natural childbirth are useful, and that an unworried and joyous attitude toward the process of childbirth does make it physically easier for the average woman (and a source of great exhilaration to some). But when natural childbirth becomes a moral obligation, it may harm more women than it helps. There is no evidence at all in the medical literature that a woman loves better a child she bore without anesthesia, or enjoys her motherhood significantly more for having done so; but there *is* a great deal of evidence to show that some women come to hate the process that so disappointingly did involve severe pain, feel deeply ashamed of themselves for not having achieved easy delivery, and even harbor strong resentment toward husband, love-making, and child for having brought this about.

It is somewhat the same with the recent revival of breast feeding. From both the medical and the psychological viewpoints, breast

* In part, though, it may indicate a very real difference between the primitive attitude toward pain and our own; an early traveler among the Dakota Indians, for instance, reported that a squaw might be in difficult labor a whole day without uttering a cry, since to reveal her pain would mean that her child—if he were a boy—would grow up a coward.

feeding has many practical arguments in its favor—but so does bottle feeding, particularly for women who dislike the idea of nursing. We need not weigh these aspects of the controversy, however; the only questions that matter here are whether breast feeding is necessarily a superior expression of mother love, and what effects it has upon the practice of motherhood.

Advocates of breast feeding speak of it as the foundation upon which true maternal feeling rests. One author asserts, for instance, that "genuine mother love and maternal care are based upon the pleasure of gratifying a fundamental structural and physiological function in the mother, suckling." It is certainly true that in subhuman mammals the pressure of milk after the young are born creates an urgent need for relief, thus linking the mother to her young symbiotically: what she does for them is good for her, what they do for her is good for them. But the human mother in the modern civilized situation does not necessarily experience this need, since by simple medical techniques the "structural and physiological function" can easily be suppressed.

Is this a violation of the body's wisdom, and an abdication of the meaning of love? If so, then alarm clocks, razors, clothing, dinner hour, monogamy, the police, and law are all violations and abdications of our built-in biology, for they defy or control our "natural" impulses. We evolved from lower mammals, and still possess many jungle mechanisms, but our humanity derives essentially from the higher functions we have added to them. The dimensions and meaning of the human mother's love for the child grow for many years after he has ceased to gratify her breast; and, thanks to her humanity, this is true even if, for medical reasons, she never was able to breast feed him. Indeed, it is true even if she neither conceived, bore, nor suckled him, for adoptive mothers—who, by neo-traditional reasoning, ought to be almost incapable of mother love— very often succeed in becoming excellent ones.*

---

* Statistically speaking, it is not yet known whether they do so as often as natural mothers, but Dr. H. David Kirk of the School of Social Work of McGill University, who has been directing a major study of adoptive parenthood in

What all of this means is that motherhood in the human being takes its character and emotional power only in part from innate biological sources; it is a malleable, subtle experience that varies tremendously from era to era, nation to nation, and class to class. For the middle-class contemporary woman living in a highly technological society, motherhood therefore need not, and ought not, be patterned after the lineaments of motherhood in earlier rural, patriarchal society.

When a contemporary woman decides to have several children close together while she is very young, or becomes convinced that she must produce her baby without anesthesia, or decides to breast feed her new son all the way to weaning, she is not merely saying yea to motherliness, but strongly affecting most of the aspects of her being. When she quits college to rush into motherhood, abandons all outside interests, and immures herself in the home, she is not only deciding in favor of the maternal role, but making many long-range decisions as to her future role as a lover and companion, as an intellectual human being, and as a post-motherhood citizen. Because the experience and fulfillment of motherhood need not involve this neo-primitive constriction of her life, she may later feel that she made a bad bargain; this is the source of her ambivalence, her internal contradictions, and her paradoxical qualities as a mother.

The neo-traditionalist brushes this all aside by saying that nothing in woman's life counts except her service as a mother. "The main function of women," writes Dr. Edward Strecker, "is to give birth to children, and to 'make' a home in which they may be reared." "Marriage, *I* think," asserts Philip Wylie, "exists primarily for the procreation of children. . . . *Kids* are humanity's *main reason for existing*." Even God was less patriarchal; according to His own

Canada and the United States, writes me: "As far as I know, there is no reason why a non-fecund woman could not become a good mother, if she set her mind to it. . . . The adoptive situation is thoroughly different along several crucial points of reference. If adoptive mothers can come to understand these points, if they can relearn the maternal role along the lines of these realities, I see no reason for them not to do as well as other mothers do. . . ."

statements, He made Eve primarily to keep Adam from being lonely ("It is not good that the man should be alone; I will make him an help meet for him").

From the neo-primitive premises one must conclude that nearly everything most worthwhile about man—his ability to wonder about the universe, and to learn; his sensitivity to the beautiful; his capacity for decency and love—is less important that fertility per se.

Even on a practical level it makes no sense. Our American society, our whole world, needs an intelligently regulated fertility rather than an outpouring of babies. Men and women urgently need goals and alliances larger than their own private, insulated, self-centered family lives. Children need parents who are child-oriented, rather than child-obsessed. Women need not a neo-primitive conception of themselves that will serve them for perhaps two decades, but a more complete conception that will serve them for their five decades of mature life—a view of themselves that will multiply their sources of fulfillment, and not place the whole responsibility for their happiness upon their children.

3 MOTHERHOOD AND HAPPINESS

There *is* an advantage to being a female animal: one is ready for pregnancy when it occurs, and ready to be a mother at the end of term. One of the most remarkable things about modern woman is her unreadiness for either.

In the mythology of our culture, every woman is flushed, coy, and radiant the first time she discovers she is pregnant; in actual fact, she is very likely to be frightened and depressed, masking these feelings in order not to be considered contemptible. This is not to be explained by mere incompetence at birth control; most of these women, according to data gathered at the Harvard Family Health Clinic and elsewhere, wanted the pregnancy, or at least passively allowed it to come about. Nor do their feelings indicate any deep-seated antagonism in these young women to motherhood per se; most of them do want children—"only not now." But the arrival of pregnancy interrupts a pleasant dream of motherhood and awakens them to the realization that they have too little money, or not enough space, or unresolved marital problems, or have not yet acquired the skills of housekeeping, and so on.

To some extent, these feelings are heightened by chemistry: the increased secretion of progestine in the pregnant woman affects her metabolism, and may account for some of her lassitude, introversion, mood swings, and those heightened sensory perceptions that are popularized as mad midnight cravings for dill pickles, shrimp salad, and strawberry mousse. But the chemistry of pregnancy has always existed without necessarily making women nervous or depressed, and it exists moreover in those 15 to 20 percent of women who are unsurprised and genuinely delighted by their first pregnancy. The intriguing thing about the negative reactions of many a modern woman is not their physical basis, but their psychological one.

All during her girlhood, she looked forward to the coming of real love and the totally intimate one-to-one relationship of man and woman; marriage was the culmination of all those years of dating, dreaming, and going steady. It is real; the baby she longs for is only a golden fantasy who does no harm to her love. Then suddenly he becomes real in her womb, and however much she had expected to welcome him, she knows that he will change things. Love will never be the same again—at least not for twenty years or so. Too soon! she cries inwardly. "I *want* the baby, but I'm afraid," is her whispered confession to the doctor. "We can't afford it yet . . . and we've had so little time together, we're so happy as we are. . . ."

These first reactions, happily, give way in a few months to other and more agreeable ones. To begin with, her body adjusts to its new metabolism and she becomes fairly comfortable, which makes everything look better. Meanwhile, she starts gathering clothes and planning for the baby, feels the first tiny movements, and becomes sharply aware that a genuine living being is growing and flourishing within her; with this, her initial rejection and anxiety give way to acceptance and gladness. Yet already the intimacy of the husband-wife twosome, enriched as it may be by their shared expectations, is being invaded by the third party and turned into a triangle. She is often dreamy and contemplative, an inward-turned look on her face where once there was only flattering interest in him. Other women visit her and chatter of babies and baby things; she is caught up in a new kinship, she is a "member of the club"—and he is good-naturedly but firmly excluded. Her breasts begin to swell and her belly to enlarge, and it begins to seem that her body, once his possession, has its own destiny. She and he both secretly wonder if she will ever again be as she was, when he used to admire her extravagantly while making love to her by some soft light, or if he will get love over with brusquely in the dark, without joy or pride. She may turn her eyes away when she passes before a mirror naked, but look stealthily and apprehensively at his face to see what is mirrored there.

Her sexual desire, less than his in the first place, now decreases faster than his as the months go by. He and she make love less frequently, and finally stop altogether. They offer each other absurd excuses for doing so; in a survey made at Michigan State College a few years ago, many young couples claimed they ceased to have intercourse because they feared to hurt the baby or because it gave the wife pain, although medically neither reason makes much sense. A more likely explanation is that the more a woman comes to look like the archetype of motherhood, the more their sexual activity makes her and her husband uneasy at the deepest levels of the unconscious, where incest fears dwell.

The approximate equality or balance of power that existed between man and wife is also affected. While they were childless she had a hypothetical independence of spirit; they did things for each other out of love, yet each could have taken care of himself. Pregnancy and motherhood change this; she leaves her job, spends more and more of her time at home, and grows increasingly dependent on her husband emotionally as well as financially. As a result, according to sociological surveys of family decision making, she carries distinctly less weight in major economic decisions, even though she may retain or increase her influence in other areas; the net effect, however, is a certain retreat from her former equality. This contradicts the constantly sounded tocsin about woman's alarming ascendancy over American man, an alarum never more wildly rung than in *Generation of Vipers,* in which Mr. Wylie, the Terrible-Tempered Mr. Bang of American letters, stated that America is a matriarchy with that harpy, mom, sitting on a decaying throne and presiding over a life that has become a nightmare.

This is known as social criticism, and is fun to read; it happens, however, to be poppycock. Almost every sober scientific inquiry into the matter has found that, on the average, American middle-class marriage is now nearly equalitarian—but that there remains a small distinct balance of power in the husband's favor. America may look like a horrifying matriarchy to social critics who take Victorian or Old Testament marriage as their baseline, but no serious student of society would call it one in the legitimate anthropological sense.

Curiously enough, this alarming ascendancy is ascribed particularly to upper-status, well-educated suburban wives who toil not, neither do they spin; yet sociologists Robert O. Blood and Donald M. Wolfe, in their large-scale study of marriages in and near Detroit, found that such women have *less* control over family decisions than women of the very lowest status, or of less education, or than women who work or live in the city. All in all, the very woman who is said to be a modern matriarch is one of the least matriarchal women in the land; any knowledgeable sociologist or social worker will tell you that the truest specimen of matriarch in America today is the employed, laboring-class, urban Negro wife.

Despite the pregnant woman's loss of independence and equality, despite the changes in her body, her psyche, and her relationship to her husband, despite her apprehensions or mixed feelings about natural childbirth and breast feeding, when the new baby arrives she is genuinely suffused with love and transported by the sight and touch of him. He is perfect, unspoiled, an idealized piece of herself; all the self-admiration she once indulged in somewhat shamefacedly she transforms into permissible admiration of this now-detached part of herself. She holds him close and is amazed, as millions of women have been before her, at the perfect minuscule fingers, the absurd face that is both strange and familiar, the limbs that flail about and the mouth that seeks—all of it a thing that blossomed within her. And above all he is so flattering to her—so helpless without her, so grateful for her breast or her arms, so ready after a month or two to smile when she enters or to cry when she leaves. A young woman whom I first met when she was a teenager, and who married an engineer in Seattle after having had a fling at acting and television production, sentimentally conveys this fairyland mood:

> He is three months old already, and I'm so thrilled with this little character that I hardly mind the work involved. Every day is exciting and fun with him; watching him grow and develop is terribly rewarding. I love to dress Jamie with special care, even for a trip to the market, and see the heads turn in admiration of our fine little boy. Jamie smiles at me, I talk to him, and we accomplish our chores. Of course I complain when I can't find a minute to myself, or when the housework piles up and the baby is yowling; and I wish we had a washing machine and a cleaning girl and more money for frivolities. But these are superficial nuisances. When my husband walks in at night and hugs Jamie and me, and we settle down for a quiet dinner and evening together, then life is really wonderful, warm, and full. I only pray it will be ever thus.

But for the majority of mothers life is not ever thus; serene and gracious moments stand out against a background of tedious routines, minor crises, and long-term anxieties. Some of these difficulties stem from the fact that the new mother has neither animal instincts nor human training to draw on for the techniques of handling her young. As Dr. Marion Hilliard once wrote, "If she can't hear her baby breathe she knows he's dead, and if he breathes noisily she's sure he has pneumonia. One of my first night calls, at three in the morning, was to treat a baby who turned out to be suffering from hiccups."

Every step of the way she is uncertain and must strain to acquire

from books, magazines, friends, and the pediatrician the knowledge
and skills which come instinctively to animals, and which girls in
the past acquired long before marriage. In the first half-dozen years
or so of motherhood all this is at its most intense; each new joy
seems accompanied by a new problem. The baby who thrilled his
mother so by taking a few teetering steps seems something of a monster once he is walking well; after the twentieth near-disaster of the
morning (vases, lamps, sharp-cornered coffee tables, the stove), she
pops him into the safety of the playpen and rushes off for a long-
delayed visit to the bathroom—yet even there his howls of outrage
do not allow her the simple pleasure of unhurried relief. The child
who was a delight in the crib and the stroller progresses to outdoor
play, the kindergarten, and the neighborhood child pack, all of
which is exciting and marvelous to his mother—but he also comes
back with dirt, colds, mumps, nasty words, sassy talk, and split lips.

After a few years of this (or sometimes even just a few months)
the young woman may feel as though she hasn't had time for an
adult nonbaby thought for ages and is suffering mental atrophy.
A possibly apocryphal story tells of the young mother who, after
several weeks of unrelieved mothering of her two be-measled children, went to an elegant dinner party, was seated next to a distin-
guished and attractive novelist, and during the first course heard
herself saying to him brightly, "I'll bet I can finish my soup before
you can!"

The "trapped-housewife" syndrome we looked at in the last chapter is particularly acute when the children are small, especially if
they have been bunched closely together. Some women live for about
a decade in a state of continual fatigue, lurching from one minor
crisis to another; these incidents seem trifling to men, but cumu-
latively have on women the effect of the well-known water-drop tor-
ture. Such women may enjoy their children in a hundred ways, seeing their growth, glowing over their ever-increasing command of
words and ideas, teaching them to skate or swim, sensing the young
minds feeling their way to the verge of important understandings;
but these joys are all too often soured by a sense of harassment and

incompetence. As one woman writes, "I was continually exhausted, crying, had no time for myself, even to think. I sometimes feared I might have a nervous breakdown—and would have welcomed it as a way out. People say, 'Don't wish your life away,' but some parts are better gone." A mother who chose to have four children close together comments, "It was all wrong—I can say that now, twelve years too late. Not one of the children has had a decent chance at the right kind of childhood, not one has had enough attention, space, or privilege. We've struggled with them more often than enjoyed them. If I only had it to do over, I'd do it a lot differently."

Other women, though they are not so overwhelmed by logistical problems, find that their complete commitment to motherhood entails a sense of irretrievable loss of part of the self—a part they feel *could* have been salvaged somehow, if they had only thought about it and planned for it. One mother of three in her mid-thirties, who had been deeply interested in political issues in college, told Dr. Komarovsky that she was seriously worried about her loss of mental power, and shocked to realize that she had to ask her husband how to vote because she didn't know what was going on. "I have acquired such an inferiority complex," said a Phi Beta Kappa alumna, "that I am afraid to ask a question at a public lecture. And to think that in college I used to preside over meetings of my college class!" And one of my own correspondents, who vacillates between fervent domesticity and brief forays into commercial designing, tried to explain the problem in this fashion: "I adore my children, and I try to be a good mother but most of the time I'm a grouch to them. Maybe it's because nobody told me the truth when I was a girl; I was always talked out of, or belittled out of, the things I wanted to do, the things that were the core of *me*. Everyone assured me that motherhood was woman's whole life. So I married a few months after college, and had four kids in our first seven years. If I had only known enough to cling fast to myself! Of course I would have married and had children anyhow—but I would have planned it so as to hold onto the things I prized. Now I can't—it's too late. Every time I try, I'm defeated by everyday problems of too many kids.

And maybe by my own feeling that I never developed my talents enough to make them worth fighting for."

Actually the average middle-class marriage does not produce children this rapidly or in as large numbers; yet the trapped-housewife syndrome (it could also be called the trapped-mother syndrome) affects women with one child or two almost as often as those with three, four, or more. The feeling of entrapment is due only in part to the volume of work that is required; in the intellectual woman, it is due in larger part to boredom, alienation from the world, and the disuse of her higher faculties. For some, no amount of devotion or desire to be a good mother will serve to overcome these symptoms. But such a woman may only redouble her maternalism in the effort to make it suffice; like the compulsive housekeeper, she becomes a compulsive mother, denying her own needs—and feeling all the worse for it.

Some of these women recognize after a while what they are doing, and are astonished to find that they *can* make time for themselves, once they admit they need it. A former art student writes that one afternoon, when both her children were resting, she came across her paints in the course of cleaning out a closet; on an impulse, she dropped everything in order to sit down and spend an hour dashing off a water-color. Dinner was late that night and the children got rather perfunctory baths, but she was in high spirits, had color in her cheeks, and all but seduced her husband by 10 P.M. Ever since, she has scheduled time for herself as faithfully as though it were an urgent doctor's appointment, and the household and the children get along just about as well as they ever did.

Others exultantly tell of taking to the piano, clay modeling, a literary discussion club, tutoring high-school children in some subject they know well, teaching Sunday school, or becoming active in a choir or drama group. These and other activities are certainly easier when the children are older, but even the harassed mother of two or three preschool children can usually find a little time for herself, if she feels justified in doing so. Some women view their megrims as an ailment, and consider some self-indulgence a bonafide treatment: a woman who lives near Salem, Oregon, for instance, says that she leaves her husband in charge of the children once in a while and goes to Portland by herself for a concentrated "cure" of concerts, shopping, art exhibits, and good restaurants. "The best part, though," she says, "is to spend an hour or more at a time gazing down at the city from my hotel room and thinking, 'There's half a million people down there and not one is depending on me for a single thing.' "

Along with the feeling of imprisonment, modern motherhood often takes its toll of the modern husband-wife relationship; the diverting of their attention away from each other which began in pregnancy continues until the last child has left home a generation later. Children bring major delight, love, and fulfillment to both man and woman; but despite all pious platitudes to the effect that they bring husband and wife closer to each other, the truth is that they cause a distinct decrease in the amount and intensity of communion between the former lovers.*

For one thing, the number of new duties to be done force husband and wife to give up, in part, playing the game of togetherness, and to specialize in family tasks done efficiently—which often means done separately. The fond young husband goes with his wife to help her buy a dress, but not after there are children; he stays home to baby-sit instead. The fond young wife spends all her evenings with her husband as if she were on a date, but not after there are children; she has ironing, mending, and straightening up to do, after which she wants to read—she is always *trying* to read and never quite making it—so as to have something to say to him when finally he puts aside the work he now brings home from the office.

For another thing, lovers talk to each other all the time, but par-

* Nor do they "hold a marriage together"; indeed, social workers feel they often increase the strains on a weak union. Locke compared divorced and married people, matching them for the duration of marriage; there was no difference in the average of childlessness, or the average number of children born; the presence or absence of children therefore had no relation to the continuation or break-up of the marriages.

ents simply don't get the chance. A study recently completed at
Cornell University has collected detailed data proving that husbands
and wives talk to each other a lot less after the children arrive—
but it needed no social-science survey to convince any mother of
this; since her first child was a couple of years old, she has hardly
ever been able to finish a sentence, or hear what her husband was
trying to tell her, before the static of the young broke in and garbled
the message.

   Love-making is the activity in which man and wife approach nearest each other, but under the impact of the busy years this too may
suffer both in frequency and quality. A young woman from Arizona, fuming about her husband's interest in an unmarried woman,
reflects bitterly on her own wifely shortcomings as a lover:

> Before going off with him to some lush hotel room, *she* enjoys a romantic
> dinner for two at a restaurant, with background music—after spending all
> day lying around getting into the mood. But I, after a day of working like
> an ox, have to fight my way through a hectic dinner complete with scream-
> ing kids and burned potatoes; then I clean up the mess, battle the kids
> into bed, sprinkle the clothes, put out the trash, and fall exhausted into
> bed—and romance. Hah! How can I compete with her? I haven't got a
> chance.

A certain number of women, particularly those who have borne
more children than they wanted because of religious or other objections to birth control, even begin to lose their sexual desire and
increasingly find excuses for putting off love-making. Some actually
find it repulsive, though once they thought it beautiful. Medical and
psychological literature abounds with case reports of such women;
a recent one, in the *North Carolina Medical Journal,* tells of a
woman only in her mid-thirties who had two planned children and
then two unplanned ones, and who now finds herself involuntarily
cringing when her husband kisses her. Though she used to enjoy the
sex act she now feels sickened by it, has become totally frigid, and as
a result feels sinful for having "turned against" her husband.

   This is, to be sure, an extreme and not very common effect of
motherhood. But Dr. Blood, summarizing the data on all the marriages in his survey, finds that the average woman reports definitely

less satisfaction with the total husband-wife relationship after the advent of children; this average level of satisfaction does not rise again until the children leave, at which time there is, for some people, a kind of second honeymoon.

Many social scientists have tried to measure the overall relationship between marital happiness and the presence or absence of children, but have found only inconsistent correlations or none. The explanation is probably that marital happiness is a sum of many different satisfactions, some of which can only be increased at the expense of others. Nor is science yet able to be precise as to the net happiness children bring us; happiness has never yielded to careful measurement, even though Jeremy Bentham long ago proposed a calculus of happiness and Professor Hornell Hart of Duke University a couple of decades ago invented a graph he called the "euphorimeter." No one can, at present, really prove that most parents have a greater total of happiness in their lives than most childless people.

Still, there is hardly anyone in our society who would seriously deny it. Certainly, the regrets of middle-aged childless women and the satisfaction of middle-aged mothers with the way they have spent their lives, as reported by many a researcher, would seem to give the answer. But let no one smugly assert that motherhood today is therefore an easy and natural route to happiness, or an unalloyed pleasure. Modern woman has not yet developed any clear definitions or traditions concerning her complex modern way of life; she therefore often throws herself into motherhood impulsively, without planning, and with a disregard for the other aspects and periods of her life. In consequence, she is astonished at the discomforts that are intermingled with her joys, and dislikes herself for being so often resentful of—well, of whom? She hardly knows; but the one most responsible is the one she is least likely to blame: herself.

4 ACCEPTING AND REJECTING MOTHERS

These are, of course only broad generalizations; women actually react to motherhood in widely differing fashions. At one extreme,

some take to it totally and easily; at the other, some never take to
it at all; and the majority, in between these poles, adjust to motherhood with a good deal of pulling and hauling, deriving joy and
major satisfaction from it, plus a frequent uneasy feeling that their
mother love is not as boundless and their hearts not as ideally maternal as they had expected them to be. Curiously, however, in this
middle ground lies the best hope for a balanced, successful life for
modern woman—and for successful mothering of her children. Let
us investigate this seeming anomaly.

First, there is the totally accepting woman; motherhood is the
only role she envisions for herself as an adult, and it does not bring
about any conflicts or second thoughts in her, nor any sense of de-
privation. Yet such a woman may be defensive about the fact that
her attitude is not the norm. "I'm beginning to wonder if I need
psychiatric care," one writes to me sarcastically, "I can't seem to
realize that I should be unhappy." "You could dissect and analyze
me," writes another, "but you could never convince me that I am
trapped. I am contented as a cow; I wouldn't want to be anything
but a young mother." Higher education does not necessarily rule
out such acceptance; a number of college graduates claim to be
completely satisfied by motherhood, and maintain that their education is not wasted, but enables them to be better mothers throughout the whole day. One hangs art prints in the bathroom, passes on
a scrap of Greek history at breakfast, keeps a bulletin board for current events items, and the like. Another says that her walks in the
woods with her children, her trips with them to concerts and mu-
seums, and her discussions of morals with her teenager are all far
richer because she has so much to give them; so viewed, she says,
"the career of homemaker and mother is the most satisfying, interesting, and challenging one a woman can have."

Yet this type of middle-class mother is apt to bristle when asked
about her role, particularly if she has been well educated. Let an old
classmate meet her at a reunion, for instance, and ask her what she
is doing these days, and she will take the question to be a criticism
of her way of life. A young mother who graduated from Wellesley
in '54 tells of being asked just such a question in just such an en-

counter; she testily comments, "Marriage and motherhood as alternatives to the master's degree and the forty-hour week take no back seat in my book. Right now, family and home give me all the challenge, adventure, interest, and satisfaction I want. Don't ask me what I'm Doing; right now I may not be Doing anything, but I'm awful busy."

Others vigorously attack women who are less satisfied and domestic than they. From a pleasant New Jersey suburb the thirty-seven-year-old wife of a mechanical engineer writes me to describe her idyllic family life: she avows that she has no fault to find in her husband, likes everything about homemaking except cleaning, considers her life with her children to be "fulfilling God's plan" (she is a devout Catholic), and faces no real problem of any sort in her life—no split-level trap, no tyranny of the children, no feeling that she is wasting her talents by being a homemaker and mother. But she is genuinely exasperated by the many women who are not as happy as she:

> I'm so tired of listening to unhappy, frustrated, complaining housewives that I could scream. I realize that there are women who have real problems to contend with, and I sympathize with them, but I have nothing but scorn for those who have good husbands, nice homes, few financial worries, and still are unhappy. Phooey to all of them!

Articles about career women who are childless do not particularly annoy such a woman, but articles about mothers who have careers or important outside activities frequently make her wrathful; a typical comment in a debate in an alumnae magazine, for instance, is that "a woman who wants a Ph.D. or a career ought to wait until her children are grown. How dare any woman run out on a child and leave him with the maid? What makes her think she comes first? That kind of woman ought not marry or have children at all."

As happy as the total accepters say they are, there are at least two serious drawbacks to their all-out commitment to motherhood in addition to the others I have mentioned. First, as we saw earlier, modern woman has lost many of her crucial productive functions and duties; practically all her time, energy, emotion, and intellect are free to be devoted to her children, with the result that she over-mothers them. So intensive a relationship between one woman and her children is rare in the annals of mankind; according to Margaret Mead, there is no cross-cultural evidence that it is really good for the child, but plenty of evidence that he does better when cared for by a number of warm, friendly people.

A great deal has been written about "momism" in the past two decades, much of it exaggerated alarmism, some of it mere scurrilous billingsgate—with at least a nub of truth behind it. For there *is*, in the opinion of many fair-minded authorities, a good deal of over-attachment, overprotection, and overmothering in a number of American homes, which hinders the process of emotional maturing in children, especially in boys. This pattern is most likely to be found in just those homes where the wife has no need to earn money, considers outside activities or vocations wrong and unmaternal, and directs the full power of her hungry personality toward extracting the major part of her satisfaction in life from her relationship to her children.

Undoubtedly this is also true of other kinds of mothers, but in much lesser degree. In the great mass of communications from American women which I have examined and the many interviews I have conducted, it has most often been the traditionalist total-accepters who spoke smugly and proudly of woman's indirect but ultimate power—as the Victorian poet put it, "The hand that rocks the cradle is the hand that rules the world"—and inadvertently revealed what has been called "smother love." This is how they sound:

The mother is the one on whom the day by day responsibility rests for guiding and interpreting her child's experiences so that her children's views are set by her beliefs. It is the golden opportunity of her life . . . her chance to influence the future. She is the one person in the world who has the time to do the job of parenthood.

I submit that we homemakers are serving our communities and justifying our exalted education as much as—and maybe more than—the woman who has thrown the household reins to a hired mother and leaped into an office and at a paycheck. What would the world come to without us?

It is the haggard, chapped-hands "little woman" who is really putting her education to the end for which it was intended. There in the kitchen scrubbing the macaroni dish, there, from morn till night, kissing, spanking, and listening to her children, is the foundation of our tomorrow.

The second serious drawback to all-out motherhood is, as I noted earlier, that the joys of motherhood end all too soon in the modern span of life. By the woman's early thirties, her youngest child has started school and begun having a life of his own. From then on, though motherhood becomes ever more rewarding in certain ways, at the same time the children become ever less dependent, malleable, and childlike—and she, accordingly, is not as essential. After a few more years they become adolescents—thinking human beings who are exciting to deal with, and wonderful to watch flowering, but who remain away from home much of the day, and struggle for their independence all the rest of it. Mother is only forty or so, and yet the end is close upon her. For the time being, to be sure, she is a regular dervish, whirling the children from school to dentist's office, friends' houses, dancing class, scout meetings. There are hems to be lowered, knees to be bandaged, teachers to be seen, homework to be supervised, parties to be arranged, moral issues to be discussed. And yet she needs no gift of prophecy to know that she is on the verge of losing her job and her purpose in life; this knowledge, Dr. Hilliard has commented, is "the deep dark water under the thin ice of her composure." And by unhappy coincidence, this happens just when her change of life is close at hand—a symbolic and physical confirmation that she is finished, and, to borrow Caitlin Thomas's phrase, has only a leftover life to kill.

Now, when the house is quiet and the children's beds never need to be made, now in the time of the empty nest, she begins like a wounded bird to flutter about pitifully and aimlessly, all the more wildly if she invested all of herself in motherhood, derived none of the meaning of her life from other functions, and made no preparation for the second half of her life. Many a woman clings to her husband now like an insecure teenager, only to find that she is no longer a good match for him: he has grown, advanced, is vital and active, has much of his success still ahead of him, while she has remained intellectually where she was, and is now dependent and semiretired, her real life already behind her. Some women try to cling to thir vanishing maternal role by desperate means—many "change-of-life babies" are unconsciously managed "accidents." Some women, to their own dismay, become unappeasably libidinous as a reaction to the groundless fear that menopause will mean the end of sexuality. Though only a minority ever try adultery, this is the time of life when more do so than ever before, not out of biologically caused hunger, but out of an emotional need for reassurance that they are not valueless.

It is in this period that women, particularly those who have nothing left to do, exhibit so much of the foolish behavior familiarly spoken of as "typically feminine"—the visits to astrologers, palm readers, and spiritualists; the letters to columnists and advice givers; the haunting of movies, bridge tables, the country club; the addiction to television; the lemming-like migrations to see visiting movie stars; the mysterious need for extra sleep (coupled with sleeplessness) ; the compulsion to expensively redecorate rooms that are already perfectly attractive. Even shopping, which was once a necessity and a productive act, now degenerates into a way to kill time. Any saleslady in a quality store can spot from afar her *bête noire,* the "regular shopper"—the middle-aged woman who comes in, time and again, to look, feel, ask, try on, but not to buy. A saleswoman in Bonwit Teller's, on Fifth Avenue, cites to me as typical the case of a woman who adored a coat she tried on, and liked its price, but refused to buy it because, as she said to a friend who was with her, "What would I do for the rest of the day?"

Many women develop ailments of various sorts, ranging from insomnia or mysterious aches and pains to "female troubles" and symptoms of cancer. In considerable part, these are imaginary; some doctors estimate that close to half of all office visits by women are for complaints of psychogenic origin, and others put the figure still higher. "A shockingly large part of my practice, and of many a physician's practice, is made up of middle-aging women suffering from a general sense of pointlessness and worthlessness," a highly respected internist told me. "There is no organic basis for most of their symptoms. But they don't want us to tell them that. They don't want to hear the truth. They'd rather have a symptom to cling to." Some women go to psychotherapists and psychiatrists and struggle to understand the sources of their misery. Others flee into the internal retreat of mental ailments requiring hospitalization; "involutional psychosis," for instance, is generally known as a change-of-life mental disorder, related to the rapid shrinkage of satisfactions and consequent damage to the self, and appropriately enough, it is three times as frequent in women as in men.

At the opposite pole from the total accepter is the rejecting mother —the one who bears children only to find motherhood tedious, harassing, or emotionally exhausting, the one who struggles to love her children and manages to achieve only occasional fits of scalding tenderness, separated by long interludes of tight-lipped disapproval or snarling anger. There are many reasons for maternal rejection, according to the noted family-life psychoanalyst Dr. Nathan Ackerman: one woman may reject a child because she associates him with painful childbirth or with the loss of her own beauty; another may reject a child who was not of the sex she desperately wanted; still another because her child forces her to assume responsibilities she is not mature enough for; and yet another because he deprives her of things she prized highly, such as her intellectual life. These complaints all sound modern, yet there must have been many rejecting mothers throughout history; the wicked witches and cruel stepmothers of a hundred fairytales reflect the way countless thousands of men and women have seen their own mothers, and millions more have feared they might see them.

The rejecting mother is despised by nearly everyone, yet perhaps she deserves pity, for she carries a grievous burden: not only does society condemn her feelings, so that she cannot even ventilate them, but she hardly knows whether she most dislikes the friends who sold her on motherhood, the children that resulted, or herself for being a failure. The safest and easiest thing is to hate other parents for being successful and happy, and to misinterpret and malign their parental love. From Colorado a woman writes to say that she and her husband were childless for twelve years and ideally happy, but that friends and acquaintances constantly badgered them about it. Finally they had one child, and then a second—and now she says, "I know why the parents of normal, active demons thought we were terrible in being childless. Nobody who lives the constant, exhausting day-to-day existence with children could bear to see the dull, peaceful, happily ignorant life the childless people live." Another says she is revolted by a madonnalike look on her friends' faces as they gaze at their children and ask each other, "What did we ever do without them?" "I could tell them what *I* did," she writes, "—I *enjoyed* life."

But her children are closer at hand than other adults and are the immediate source of her discomfort. They bear the brunt of her dissatisfaction every day, in ways varying from "black looks" and smacks in the face to virtual abandonment. The mother, as much as one may dislike her for this, dislikes herself even more. A woman who lives in a lovely home in a placid suburb of Boston sat down to dash off some answers to my questionnaire, with dire results— and a most enlightening postscript:

> P.S.: I thought I was safe—the six-year-old was at school, and I had to control only the three-year-old. Only! While my back was turned for just moments, he managed to accomplish his main mission in life at present— to utterly turn his mother into a nasty screaming maniac. I just discovered that he burned out the transformer (I *think* that's what it is) to his brother's electric trains. That's only one of many mishaps that will occur today, making me, by day's end, irritable, tired, nervous—all in all, a monster, absolutely out of control. I'm sure my husband wonders what ever became of the sweet little girl he acquired eight years ago. Sometimes I wonder, too.

Such feelings, like a suppurating wound, are usually too hideous to look upon; consequently, they are rarely exposed in this fashion. But humor is a safe, decent covering which masks the wound and yet indicates its presence. In a joke or a story told with grim amusement, even hatred of children becomes socially permissible. No one, for instance, takes offense at the deplorable sentiments of that scapegrace alley cat, Mehitabel, when she tells how she feels about her kittens:

> it is not archy
> that i am shy on mother love
> god knows i care for
> the sweet little things
> curse them
> but am i never to be allowed
> to live my own life
>
> a tender heart is the cross i bear
> self sacrifice always and forever
> is my motto damn them

Similarly, humor is a permissible way for a mother to tell stories releasing pent-up angers. I recently received an extremely funny, but faintly hysterical, letter from a St. Louis woman with three small boys, aged four, two, and six months; in it she described a day in which her four-year-old upset a canister of flour on himself and the kitchen floor; the two-year-old pasted a dollar's worth of good stamps on the wall; the two boys then painted the baby's legs with nail polish and wrote "messages" on the mirror with her best lipstick; the four-year-old threw paper into the toilet and flooded the bathroom; and both boys, when at last in bed, unscrewed the stoppers on their hot-water bottles. As the finale to this trial-by-water, a childless friend came visiting that evening, elegant, bejeweled, and fresh-looking; she peeped in at the sleeping boys, cooed gently, and told their mother that they were absolute angels, and that she was a terribly lucky woman.

Some women find themselves too uncomfortable as full-time mothers to tolerate their own feelings, and manage to escape enough of the time via a job to function acceptably as mothers for the balance of the day. A handsome lady editor at a leading fashion magazine spoke with unusual frankness to a reporter for the *Barnard*

Alumnae Magazine a couple of years ago: after trying homemaking and motherhood for three years, she decided, "I'm not really very domestic and have no talent for children. I handed the baby to the maid, threw on my clothes, and came uptown" to win a beginning post at the fashion magazine, where she has stayed ever since without regrets or guilt feelings.

A considerably larger number of rejecting mothers, who either cannot or will not take this route of escape, endure their negative feelings by denying them to everyone, including themselves. From the outside, in fact, such women may look like excessively attentive and careful mothers; they are continually worried lest the two-year-old stumble and hit his eye against the corner of a table, the five-year-old fall from his bike and break a bone, or the ten-year-old drown while fishing in the local pond. In clinical studies it has been amply demonstrated that when a woman harbors aggressive feelings toward her child, her own fear of these feelings pushes the thought of them deep out of awareness; any situation which even remotely suggests that the hidden wish to be rid of him could be granted causes a wave of anxiety in her, and an overprotective attitude. She often becomes self-sacrificing in order to atone for her evil feelings: she gets up too early so the children may have freshly squeezed orange juice rather than frozen juice; sews, shops, and cooks more carefully and exhaustingly than anyone wants her to; rushes off to school with their galoshes in mid-morning, if a few flakes of snow start to fall; and stays up at night, pale and exhausted, to see the teenagers arrive safely home.

We looked at the drawbacks to total acceptance, but it is almost unnecessary to speak of those to rejection. Quite simply, maternal rejection is a disaster to the child, and a major cause of neurosis in him. Even when it is concealed and turned into self-sacrifice, it remains damaging—indeed, some psychiatrists consider it more serious than overt rejection. For it does not fool the child; he senses that he is unwanted, and reacts with provocative behavior, anger toward others, a general distrust and fearfulness of other people, or any one of many other serious maladies of the psyche, the most severe being schizophrenia. As for the mother herself, her rejecting feelings make her thoroughly wretched, and frequently self-punishing—and her punishment goes on and on long after the child has grown up and left home. His failures in life or his personal problems are a constant reproach to her over the years, and he himself may be cold and vindictive toward her at a time when she pathetically wants to be welcomed and allowed to play the role of benevolent grandmother. As the old saying has it, though the mills of God grind slowly, yet they grind exceeding small.

5 IN PRAISE OF THE NOT-QUITE-IDEAL MOTHER

The total accepters and the rejecters are both in the minority today; the majority of middle-class women have a distinctive, complex kind of maternalism characterized by mixed feelings. The love, the companionship, and the day-by-day excitement of giving her children new experiences and seeing them develop are interwoven with darker threads of regret for her lost chances, dislike of her entrapment in the home, alarm about the wasting away of her intellect, and sorrow for the diminished intimacy and intensity of the husband-wife relationship.

We have already heard women making many of these complaints —but their complaining does not mean that they fail to love and enjoy their children; it does mean that, being many-sided human beings with complicated sets of values and goals, they cannot take a simple, unalloyed delight in motherhood. But it is difficult to live continuously with openly mixed feelings. More often, the normal human being makes them tolerable by camouflaging the unacceptable half with rationalizations, or making it disappear altogether into the unconscious by the legerdemain of repression. Thus, many a woman who felt sharp discontents during the early years of motherhood says that she "got used to" her life, or "decided not to let myself feel frustrated," or made herself "think differently" about it all. Some of these "solutions" to the problem are really quite trivial; one woman says, for instance, "Whenever I start feeling sorry for me, I Count

My Blessings." But others are more profound: a second woman says, "I came to terms with the facts, and learned to accept life as it is." And still others sweeten their lot with syrupy sentimentality: a Detroit mother who keeps feeling a vagrant urge to get out into the world and Do Something with her college degree comforts herself with the treacly fantasy that a little voice whispers to her as follows:

> You are doing a real job here! Those warm cookies for after-school snacks are far more important than a stack of neatly-typed business letters! Your voice smoothing out a quarrel between brother and sister is much more important than your voice in front of a class. Your hands drying up little tears are much more important than your hands rapping a ruler for attention.

Rationalization and repression are useful, but they do not actually annihilate the negative emotion; it still exists, and is likely to keep untidily popping back into view. A young woman from Wheeling, West Virginia, describes her own conflicts after quitting her job and becoming a mother: after various struggles, including a guilt-ridden attempt to combine work and motherhood, she decided the only right thing to do was to stay at home, seek her satisfactions in her children, and add a dash of Sunday-school teaching for flavor. This decision, she says, has brought her peace; she now enjoys the children so much that "it seems a small sacrifice to have made." Yet, in concluding her letter, she lets the concealed truth slip out of the dark: "Two years have elapsed and I am reconciled to my role in society. I discuss with no one the fact that there is still a void in my life that household rituals, child rearing, and community work cannot fill."

Time and again, certain women are gripped by a nameless fear that they are not living life completely enough; others suffer the pangs of blocked ambition; and still others, despite being good mothers and homemakers, feel they have not served the world around them in any significant fashion. Writes a suburban mother who has "everything": "I wish I had just one outside activity in which I could feel I was making some worthwhile contribution to society."

A certain amount of discontent, however, spurs the human creature on to achievements—and potentially, thereby, to feelings of satisfaction deeper than those of mere placidity. If modern woman comes unprepared to motherhood and is distressed by her lack of skill in rearing children, her discomfort is often what impels her to read, talk, and learn about mothering. She is neither a "natural mother" nor free from mixed feelings about child care, but she compensates for this by her diligent, if bookish, efforts to understand and employ child psychology. It is easy to sneer at her ostentatious use of terms like "sibling rivalry," "attention getting," "fragile ego structure," and "task orientation," but something has to replace the vanishing traditional upbringing for motherhood, and it might as well be psychological knowledge.

Even more important, it is the discontent many mothers feel that drives some of them to make a little time for themselves during the busy years to paint, read, act, tutor, visit the city, attend lectures, or any of scores of other things which reawaken and stimulate both mind and soul, and make for a more self-sufficient as well as a more interesting human being. Other women with both drive and ingenuity manage, despite babies, formula, and diapers, to go trout fishing with their husbands, take night courses at college to restock their minds with thoughts, and squeeze in some volunteer work or a few meetings of the Junior Women's Club. A lesser number— only a few of whom are rejecting mothers—find that only a return to part-time or full-time work is sufficiently rewarding.

Obviously, these activities are not all of equal merit, but all of them do more or less serve the same purposes: they employ aspects of the total personality other than housewifery and motherhood, they decrease the negative feelings involved, and they keep alive some of the skills and functions the woman prized in herself. Many are only shallow and palliative; even so, they make her inwardly more content, and outwardly more satisfactory, as a wife, mother, and citizen.

Moreover, some of these activities form a foundation (even if not the most substantial) on which she can build further as her children start school, and grow into their teens; she becomes more and more involved in the outside world, makes increasing use of her abilities and resources, and multiplies her activities until they often seem to get out of hand and overwhelming. But most of the women who complain that they are "pulled in all directions" at once by community, church, school, family, and friends obviously love their involvements and are greatly stimulated by the busy, complicated life they lead. The mother of two teen-age girls in a commuters' town on Long Island writes:

Women are expected to be jacks-of-all-trades and often feel that they are masters of none, which can be depressing. There is terrific community pressure here that often pulls me out of my home, and I get so interested that I have to tear myself away to get back to house and family—and then I worry about not accomplishing enough in my outside activities. But children take an awful lot of time and thought, and you're given just one chance to bring them up. I'd like a thirty-hour day so that I could do everything I want to do for husband, children, and community. It's hard to keep a level head—but at least I'm never bored!

Other women, in increasing numbers, are choosing paid work when the busy-years period is over, rather than community and volunteer activities. Only about a tenth of middle-income wives work when they have children under six years old, but by the time the children are in school the figure more than doubles, and when they are all over seventeen it reaches almost 50 percent. And these women are beginning to think about it earlier in the mothering phase of life: a social anthropologist recently polled college-educated wives in Scarsdale, New York, all between twenty-five and thirty-five years old, and found that, although 62 percent are currently doing a little volunteer work, over 50 percent intend to work for pay starting anywhere from immediately to fifteen years hence, and many are already taking courses toward that end. In a later chapter, we will look more closely at this question.

This sort of modern woman thus falls far short of the imaginary ideal of motherhood, but does not run the risks of momism. She traps herself, to some extent, and feels painfully mingled feelings about her choice and about her family; yet her attitude allows her scope for at least some second-guessing and adjustment via additional roles. Such a woman frets about her problems and talks too much about them, but is capable of at least partially alleviating them; does not give totally of herself to her children, but loves them reasonably well and not too unwisely; and, though she falls far short of the person she belatedly wishes she had been, arrives at the menopause with too much to do—even if it is often trivial—rather than too little. Motherhood is a major part of her life, but not all of it; and so she finds life still worthwhile when motherhood is done.

1 THE COMPANION: OLD STYLE, NEW STYLE

Among the many curious features of modern woman's life is one that would have thoroughly offended St. Paul, bewildered Tristan, and amused Don Juan—namely, the fact that she is her husband's best friend and he is hers. Neither her education, her civil and legal powers, nor her equality in the marriage bed is a more radical innovation than this.

During most of man's million or so years on earth he lived in quite primitive societies in which, to judge by those that existed until our own time, the functions of the primitive male and the female were always kept quite distinct and separate. However masculinity and femininity may have been defined, the lives of men and women intersected rarely—at mealtime, bedtime, and a few other occasions—and whatever activities were considered suitable for men women did not encroach on, and vice versa. Accordingly, men and women have never had much in common except their economic and child-producing partnership; the real alliances of each sex were with those of their own kind.

Among the Dakota Indians, for example, a brave's closest emotional ties were with his "brothers," a term which referred to any full or half-brother and to all cross-cousins. The Dakota would say of such a brother, "He is a part of me," and if one of them seduced his wife, he would show no anger, saying quietly, "Take her, my brother, since she means more to you than our relationship." The Homeric Greeks felt much the same, the emotional bonds between fellow warriors or between father and son being far stronger than those between a man and a woman. Homeric verse is full of images like "—as a father greets his dear son who has come from a distant land in the tenth year—," but has none drawn from a husband's joy in his wife. In general, writes historian Moses Finley, "the meaningful social relationships and the strong personal attachments were sought and found among men"; and this was all so many centuries before the appearance of quasi-romantic Hellenic homosexuality.

The same is true of primitives of our own time. The Bemba husband and wife of Northern Rhodesia eat, work, talk, and joke with relatives of the same sex, but say little to each other and are alone together only when they go to bed. When one anthropologist queried the Bemba some years ago about closer forms of intimacy between man and wife, they were confused and inarticulate; finally they pointed out that one man, who used to sit on the veranda in the evening talking to his wife, was the butt of scoffing and criticism. Until recently, in many parts of the world, segregated eating and sleeping were customary, the men having their own huts or men's houses, the women and children theirs; as an extreme case, in one Colombian tribe a man and his wife would never meet face to face during their marriage except in their own garden, and then only to till the soil or to copulate.

Civilized Western man, during most of his history, has behaved a little in the same fashion. Though there are scattered examples of companionable husbands and wives, most men have felt that they could far better talk to, trust, and be understood by their male friends. The leisured warrior-gentlemen who were the glory of Athens in the time of Pericles had a fondness for music, sculpture, philosophy, poetry, and love, and shared these tastes with each other, but, as we saw earlier, their wives meanwhile stayed home, confined to the women's quarters of the house; a decent woman was dull, unlettered, and unworldly, and hence not fit company for men at the banquet table. The Athenian man spoke of woman as a *hetaera* (companion) only when referring to a courtesan.

With many a variation, the same general rule has held good for most of the intervening twenty-four hundred years. The early Christians regarded woman not only as an inferior being, but as a constant temptation to lust, even within the licensure of marriage; the desert anchorites and the monks merely expressed the ultimate form of preference for male company. Knightly troubadours played earnestly at love, but ladies were their inspirers and romantic tormenters, not their best friends; a baron might plan a battle, drain a swamp, build a castle, and make peace with his bishop or with God, but to his lady he talked only of love, manners, and chivalry. The gallants of the eighteenth century, though they spent a great deal of time in the pursuit and conquest of women, did so in a spirit epitomized by the aphorism of Chamfort: "The sympathies that exist between women and men are only skin deep, and do not touch the mind, the feelings, or the character." Even the sober middle-class man saw woman as a useful helper rather than as a friend. Dr. Johnson, though he had some friends among the Bluestockings, sometimes spoke as a bourgeois: "A man," he once said, "is better pleased when he has a good dinner upon his table than when his wife talks Greek."

Recent history has changed all this. The larger and more fluid our industrial society has become, the more the ancient loyalties to clan members, neighbors, and fellow townsmen have broken down, leaving stable relationships to be found only within the immediate family of procreation—the man, his wife, and their children. Individualism and the competition of the marketplace have weakened the abiding male friendships that were based on lifelong common purpose; but as woman became emancipated and educated, and emerged as a more complete human being, she at last became capable of being man's friend in the lifelong common venture of marriage.

And, in fact, almost his only friend. The mobility of modern society allows man to move up or down socially, as well as sideways geographically, at such a pace that he makes few lasting friends, and is held to them only by impermanent bonds. Whom, then, can he rely on? Why, of course, the woman who makes a home for him and goes to bed with him at night. And she, newly isolated in her privacy, and moving once every five years in accordance with the mores of the mobile society—to whom shall she turn for lasting friendship? Why, of course, to her husband, whom she needs now even more than he needs her.

An excellent answer? Perhaps, but not an easy one. How can a woman be her husband's friend when she accepts the tedious duties and the inglorious half of life, while he sallies forth into the world of achievement and rank? How can they be comrades when she is bored by the problems of business, and he recoils from her daily recital of bloody noses, burned rolls, and poison ivy? Friends respect one another; but suppose whenever she has an opinion on space travel, Sartre, or high fidelity he chuckles indulgently and under- takes to show her how little she understands? Friends accept and forgive each other's faults; but how shall she forgive adultery when it so directly hurts her, and how shall he forgive her overspending when it puts intolerable burdens on him?

Yet many social analysts believe that the role of friend offers modern woman the way to the most stable and wholesome relation- ship with her husband. Talcott Parsons maintains that the role of companion offers modern woman the greatest possibilities for a last- ingly satisfying relationship to her husband, and for some years Ernest Burgess and other sociologists studying family life have main- tained that middle-class marriage has already evolved into a form of companionship, and that individual marriages are likely to suc- ceed in proportion to the degree of companionship they involve. American women themselves, if asked to name the primary reason for marrying, almost always say "love," but this means many things; if the question is rephrased so as to separate the romantic-erotic functions from the functions of companionship, they answer quite differently. In the University of Michigan survey referred to earlier, wives were asked to say what was best about marriage, using this list: companionship, the husband's expression of love and affection, the husband's understanding of the wife's problems and feelings, mate- rial things (the standard of living), and the chance to have children. Companionship was head-and-shoulders winner; the husband's ex- pression of love and affection came in a poor fourth.*

---

* The chance to have children was second; the husband's understanding of the wife was third; and the standard of living was fifth.

Everyone knows that women are incurably romantic, that they regret that their husbands are not, and that they solace themselves with such synthetic fudge as daytime TV serials and novels by Edna Ferber. But all this is only a species of daydreaming; when women snap out of their reveries and speak realistically, they put the companionship and friendship of marriage far above all else. People marry because of love, and the romantic and erotic components of love are essential to give marriage its savor; but a large part of the daily emotional nourishment in it is derived from friendship.

2 THE BEST THING ABOUT MARRIAGE

Can we really make the foregoing distinction? Is it possible to precipitate and filter out for closer scrutiny the friendship that is dissolved within marital love, and there mingled with romantic and erotic feelings? The first step would be to define rigorously both love and friendship—a task outside the scope of this book, and on which, in any case, many scores of gifted men have spent their lives without final success. Despite all the existing knowledge about human behavior, there is still no agreement on the meaning of love, or even on the source of its power. Nor have the wise men of the past or present been able to agree about the meaning of, or reasons for, friendship; there are almost as many theories about it as there are schools of philosophy or psychology.

Any effort to distinguish between love and friendship would be further confounded by the fact that they resemble and even overlap each other in many ways. Friends, like lovers, admire each other, and lovers, like friends, do things for each other; friends and lovers both use special words, private jokes, favorite gestures; and so on. Yet a reading of history makes it clear that love and friendship do not necessarily coincide, and indeed have more usually been separated than joined. Legions of dead concubines are proof positive that erotic love need not be accompanied by friendship, and conversely in most eras strong same-sex friendships have not signified homosexuality. As for marriage, during most of Western history neither wives nor husbands expected to be friends to each other, let alone romantic lovers; they were partners, a quite different relationship in which they had no need to feel romantic love or friendship for each other, but only to trust each other, exchange services, and mate sexually.

Whatever love or friendship may be in a philosophic sense, they are not identical functions. To begin with, lovers need not be equals, though unequals can rarely be friends. The heights of romantic love were reached in eras when woman was still housebound, voteless, and legally a nonentity; Sancho Panza, however, was Don Quixote's loyal retainer rather than his friend. Lovers need not share ideas or care about the same subjects, being sufficiently absorbed in discussing their feelings about each other (one cannot picture Lancelot and Guinevere discussing the need for Old English spelling reform); friends, however, are most delighted when they are sharing some idea or interest outside themselves, whether it be a way to play the market, an abstract painting, or the best technique of reefing a mainsail in a hard blow.

Lovers are concerned with an act performed by two alone, and so never want to share their beloved with another; friends not only enjoy sharing each other, but persistently try to bring their friends together, hoping to enlarge the network of affection around themselves. Love can thrive despite little communication or contact, and an occasional man may, like Dante, be so enamored of the perfection he imagines in a woman that he never need speak a word to her; but friendship is a process of interaction in which the more things we do together or say to each other, the closer our relationship. Love is hushed and friendship noisy; lovers meet with whispered words, friends with glad cries; lovers may be playful, but friends make jokes.

When love and friendship are both absorbed into marriage, they undergo inevitable modifications, and coalesce in part; but since they continue to serve somewhat different ends, they still exist as distinct ingredients, each one of which must be present in due proportion. The simple labels "mature love," "conjugal love," or "companionship love," which many writers often use to lump together all of the aspects of the married relationship, only obscure the fact that a woman and a man play many different roles to each other, and that excellence in one or several roles does not make up for a deficiency in another. Even with romantic feelings, a good physical adjustment, and a successful division of duties within the home, a marriage lacking in companionship may still leave a man or woman frustrated and wretched.

From Rochester, New York, for instance, writes a woman who holds a master's degree in education and has a wide range of intellectual interests. A decade ago, when she was twenty-three, she met a handsome, taciturn management consultant and married him. But although he did, and still does, love her, he has never taken any interest in her as a friend and equal, and she has slowly come to a bitter conclusion about love:

> My husband cannot tolerate career women or working women; even community work annoys him so much that he makes insulting remarks to me if I try it. There is nearly a total lack of communication between us on philosophies of life, goals, personal dreams, etc. The only topics we discuss are the weather, the children's clothing, and the price of eggs at the supermarket. He does not even want me to meet or entertain his business associates. You asked me how my idea of love compares with the one I had when I was engaged. I can answer briefly—I now feel quite positive that "liking" is a far better basis for marriage than "loving."

The average woman's need for friendship in marriage is, indeed, greater than her need for erotic satisfaction. Although she may say that people should marry for love, she means by it an aggregation of emotions; when these are separately named, she recognizes that the thing she prizes the most in marriage is not the erotic, but the amical component of love. And though formerly this kind of friendship could hardly exist between husband and wife, today it not only can, but must, if they are to reckon their marriage as satisfying and successful.

Three-quarters of divorced people remarry within five years—an astonishingly high rate in so short a period, considering the pain and the psychological disturbance that marriage must have brought them. What drives them to try again? Not sex hunger: divorcees are not promiscuous, but they are a lot less timid and inhibited than single women.* Not romantic love: divorcees do fall in love, but they seek it gingerly, are wary of being fooled by it, and soberly weigh it in the balance. Not for economic reasons: some divorced women talk of looking for a richer man or a better provider the second time, but such words are often a pose of toughness to hide the sense of hurt.†

More than anything else, the divorcee is *lonely*. Of the friends who seemed so close before, some are loyal to her divorced mate rather than herself; others become uncomfortable in her presence or make her uncomfortable with their synthetic cheerfulness; still others appear, in new perspective, to be selfishly cloistered within their own marriages, emerging only once in a while to be friends to outsiders. She learns to dread her silent bedroom at night, and the bedtime hour when it is hardest to turn off the light or the TV and let loneliness wash over her. And so when she remarries, it may be in part for sex, or for money, or out of infatuation, or the need for a father for her children—but most of all she does so to be, once again, someone's friend, and to have him be hers.

3 THE WIFELY FRIEND: SOME CARICATURES

A woman cannot be almost a virgin, nor partly give birth to a baby; she either is or isn't, has or hasn't, without in-between degrees. She can, though, be more or less of a friend to her husband. In technical terms, friendship is a "segmental" relationship; it may exist in only one or two small compartments of the personality, extend to many of them, or include practically the whole of the being of the two friends.

* Three-quarters of them, according to the Institute for Sex Research, have at least some intercourse during their years as divorcees.

† In Locke's survey, for instance, only 4.5 percent of divorced women picked economic security as a reason for marrying. And see the footnote above, p. 202.

Perhaps the least rewarding type of friend she can be is the kind one might call Old Faithful—homebound, patient, loyal, and uncomprehending. She greets the sound of her Master's footsteps at night, smiling and gladsome; had she a tail, she would wag it furiously. She is a reliable caretaker, a good cook and mother, and a companion against the quiet hours, but incapable of understanding or caring about automobile maps, electrical wiring, or bank statements. She has only a hazy idea what her husband does all day or how he is making his way in the world. When he comes home, he pats her, talks in her words, and seems grateful for the comforts she provides, but once in a while she is uneasily aware that after many years of marriage he is still in many ways a stranger to her. A while ago, an advertisement in a major magazine showed a husband sunk in thought, seated near his knitting wife; the legend read, "Sometimes a man has moods his wife cannot understand." But his problem was neither waning potency nor the fear of death; he was worried about which pension plan to select for his employees, a subject which a man in his right mind simply does not bother to tell Old Faithful about.

Such friendship is exercised chiefly at home; the Master rarely takes her out with him, or, when he does, leaves her to talk to others of her kind. This relationship, quite common in Latin America or Italy, can often be seen among our own lower classes. As one young working-class woman told an interviewer:

> I don't like my husband to run off all the time and I nag about it. I've been downtown two times since we've been married [four years], and I took the kids with me then. One night last year my husband said he'd take me out. The lady next door said she'd watch the kids. We got down to the corner and my husband said he was too tired. He took me right back home. I never was so mad in all my life!

And it even still is occasionally to be found in the middle class. An attractive woman of thirty-five, married to an up-and-coming party politician in Boston, says she hungers for friendship but hates women's clubs; she would love to go out with her husband in the evening, or have people visit them at home, but he hardly ever takes her out, is reluctant to invite his associates to their home, and has almost never let her accompany him on business trips. "He is kind and loving, and a wonderful provider," she writes, "but I do not feel we have the mutual understanding I see in others. I try not to let it bother me because I am lucky to have all the things I do have."

As opposed to this type, some women are perennial Dates whose companionship with their husbands exists chiefly in their shared sorties outside the home in search of diversion. The prime exemplar of the type is the idle wife of the well-to-do big-city businessman. She lies abed until 11 A.M., while the help takes care of the house and the children. Rising at last, she spends an hour and a half erasing circles and lines with make-up, selecting the perfect dress, and deciding on the right perfume for the day; then she is off to the massage parlor, doctor, hair salon, department store, or matinee, until cocktail time. In the evening, having made herself a vision of painted, brilliantined, teased, lacquered, and bejeweled elegance, she is ready to go with her husband to the country club, night spot, or party. There she cha-cha-cha's beautifully with him on the dance floor, but is careful always to have friends at their table lest he and she be caught alone together with nothing to say. At a private party, in fact, she is most comfortable when congregating with the other women to talk female talk, leaving the men to bunch together happily at the other end of the room and talk their male talk.

Yet this friendship, however limited, is real. Her life is centered about these hours with him, and he, for his part, is incapable of going anywhere for pleasure without her and needs her for reassurance, for display, and for company. Theirs is a mutually helpful friendship, even though there is little communication in it. But Nature abounds in such oddities: the shark and the pilot fish benefit each other without eloquent discourse or sentiment, and so do the crocodile and the Egyptian plover, the moray eel and the California cleaning shrimp, and dozens of other strange pairs of symbiotic friends.

The third exhibit in this gallery of caricatures is the Hostess. Though she and her husband have a good deal in common, she conceives of her major function as making their home his little castle, in which he relaxes and to which he proudly invites business acquaintances and friends. She decorates it with his approval and for his benefit, and since she herself is a part of the décor, she tries to keep up not only her appearance, but a shallow knowledge of events. She will not accept him in grateful silence like Old Faithful; in fact she invariably seems to have something to say whenever he is absorbed by television or a book. She devotes many of her hours to their social life; each evening of entertaining takes careful planning and endless discussions with him in order to insure an impressive but manageable menu, touches of décor that will be original but not *outré*, and most important of all a group of guests who will have things to talk about but will not drift into heated or disturbing discussions. It is a lot of trouble, but it is worth it to her, for her husband is proudest of her as his companion when they achieve an evening which "goes well."

For some women, the part of Hostess is richly rewarding and the companionship it brings her is quite adequate. But others feel that something about this special kind of companionship is not altogether satisfying, though they cannot always identify the difficulty. Often, they think the problem is merely one of pace. "It's the whirling round of activities," complains the wife of a Chicago concert manager, "it's the many things we *do* together that keep us from *being* together. I love all the entertaining we must do, but sometimes I can't help longing for the old days when we had lots of time alone with each other to ramble on about everything in the world. Now sometimes weeks go by without our having a real talk." And sometimes, when the door closes on the last guest, such a woman will kick off her shoes and start emptying ashtrays, asking her husband meanwhile with feigned nonchalance whether he enjoyed himself; actually, she isn't certain, nor is she quite certain whether she enjoyed herself, because she so well managed an evening of smooth sociability that she left no room for the interactions of real friendship.

A fourth variety of wife-friend is the Silent Partner—not that she is speechless, but that she is an unseen assistant and collaborator. Her type has roots in the past: many a nineteenth-century woman tried to envision herself as the inspiration behind a man's accomplishments, and imagined herself the gentle counselor who subtly gave him the best advice and tendered him his most brilliant ideas. This much-admired, if largely imaginary, role was epitomized in the often-quoted line from Barrie's *What Every Woman Knows:* "Every man who is high up loves to think that he has done it all himself; and the wife smiles, and lets it go at that."

The contemporary Silent Partner, however, is much more like a same-sex friend in that she seldom tries cunningly to steer her husband, and does not need to solace herself with the fancy that she is the major source of his success. She listens to him, encourages him, discusses things with him openly, and helps him chiefly by being an adjunct mind and second self; the more he brings his thoughts and problems to her as to a real friend, the less she needs the false consolation that she is the reason for his achievement. Almost none of the women replying to my questionnaire, for example, claimed that they had helped their husbands in concrete or specific ways, but over a third felt that they *had* given their husbands emotional support or a sympathetic ear. From the wife of a clothing manufacturer: "My help is largely that of listener, and a reminder of past events which bring things into proper proportion." From the wife of a novelty distributor: "In the early years, when he was doing academic work, I helped by proofreading and by discussing his ideas with him. But ever since he has been in business, I can do nothing significant except be a good listener." From the wife of a biologist: "In the early years I helped by working while he finished school; ever since, I've been mostly a cheerleader."

Others are not so diffident; they recognize that such support can be distinctly valuable, and are greatly pleased at being able to give it and thereby to share their husband's other life. From the wife of a lawyer: "Hard to measure my help. He always wants to tell me about difficult or worrisome cases, and talk them over. I don't suppose my ideas play much part in the final result, but he needs me, and that means a lot." From the wife of a publisher: "He *says* I'm a big help, and he always discusses his business problems with me. Actually, he doesn't often take my advice. I guess I'm mostly a sounding board for him—but I love it!"

The Corporation Wife, a subspecies of the Silent Partner, is definitely important to her husband's success. According to reports made in *Fortune* by William H. Whyte, Jr., many companies carefully size up an executive's wife before hiring him; one major corporation rejects a fifth of otherwise acceptable trainee applicants because their wives fail to meet the specifications. The Corporation Wife must be a good mixer, hold reasonable middle-of-the-road views, and have good but not avant-garde taste. She must be friendly with other executives' wives but never form cliques, charming to other husbands but never flirtatious. She identifies herself so thoroughly with her husband and his career that she says things like, "The Company has been very good to us," or "The Company has done nicely by us." But her participation in her husband's life is one-sided, like the love affair between a movie fan and a star; executives are busy and get busier the higher they go, but a good Corporation Wife is always willing to let the Company be first in his heart, and to accept the leftovers of his companionship for herself.

These several species of friendship range from a very narrow base to a rather wide one, the latter being, of course, more deeply satisfying. But all of them exhibit to some degree what one correspondent of mine has called "the Ruth in every woman"—the fact that where he goes, she will go, whatever he does, she will do. It is a lovely antique sentiment, which sees woman not as man's *alter ego* but as his loyal follower, faithful servant, shadow, sycophant, and hanger-on. It is a gentler form of the philosophy behind a common-law doctrine dating from 1365, which held that a wife has no separate existence but is a part of the identity of her husband. The Supreme Court finally overturned this bit of common law in 1960 on the reasonable grounds that it no longer truly represented the ethos of our society.

Legally, psychologically, and socially, the Ruth concept of friendship is obsolescent, for even when such a wife is loyal, helpful, understanding, and intelligent, she remains somewhat the adoring follower rather than the loving independent equal he really needs.

There are always times when one longs for a protector, or enjoys giving protection, when one wants mothering or yearns to act like a mother, but the highest level of friendship goes beyond protection or dependency; it involves affection and interaction between people of equal stature and maturity. They may comfort or help each other at times, but above all they are able to offer each other mature understanding, vicarious experience, and the exchange of adult emotions and perceptions. A Complete Friend needs to be not only a sounding board, but a string vibrating a note of its own to the other's sounding board. As much as a man welcomes the friendship of the Old Faithful, Date, Hostess, and Silent Partner, or even all of them lumped together, he will still hunger and hunt for a friend who is challenging to be with, rather than merely comforting; stimulating and not only reassuring; demanding and not simply helpful; admirable and not just admiring.

4 FRIENDSHIP'S LIFE CYCLE

Husband-wife friendship thus varies along the dimension of extensiveness, that is, the number of segments of the two personalities that interact. But as is true of all forms of friendship, it also varies along the dimension of time. The curious and significant finding of several recent large-scale social-psychological studies is that the direction of change is the opposite of what nearly everyone supposes. Most people think that marriage is at first made up of passionate and romantic feelings, and then slowly evolves into a cooler but ever more complete and satisfying companionship; the actual curve of marital companionship is more complex and, for a good many years, is not one of growth but of decline.

The desire for companionship, let us recall, is a major force behind the going-steady pattern. Having someone to rely on and with whom to exchange innermost feelings is more gratifying to many girls than any other element of young love. The importance of companionship continues into the early phases of marriage; when a broad sample of wives is asked how satisfactory the companionship of marriage is, it gets the highest ratings from the honeymooners and the newly married. This is not by way of some confusion with physical delights of the honeymoon; widows and divorcees past fifty, when they remarry, are even more affirmative about the merits of the companionship they find in wedlock than are young women. Perhaps the older brides, having lived more, have a great deal more to say to their husbands, a great deal more to explore in them, a far greater potential enjoyment of that process of mutual disclosure and interweaving of the selves that has been called "the exchange of biographies."

Psychologist Samuel Deitcher, a member of a team of Cornell University researchers investigating marital communication, recently studied the conversational habits of 120 couples in upstate New York. To almost no one's surprise, he found that husbands and wives talk to each other more when they are newly married than at any other stage of married life. What was more interesting was his finding that the talk of the newly married is the kind close friends enjoy most—the subjective exploring and mutual revealing of beliefs, inner feelings, likes and dislikes, and the trading and comparing of ideas about sex, aesthetic subjects, and plans for the future. As other researchers have pointed out, along with this profusion of talk they also *do* more things together than they ever will again, taking their recreations together, cleaning house, cooking, and shopping as a twosome, and even finding it agreeable to share the counting of the dirty laundry.

But then it comes time to progress to the other meanings of marriage. Even though, like Peter Pan, most young men and women are reluctant to grow up, almost all of them do so anyhow: they rent a larger place or buy a home, have children, work harder, save money if possible and invest it, and accumulate possessions, duties, and community involvements. All of these cut down the amount of their companionship as well as the intensity of satisfaction it yields. Children, fulfillment, and maturity yield new satisfactions, but exact a price; yet if one does not purchase them, he later pays the still higher price of futile regret.

The house itself, to begin with, and the possessions accumulating within it, make inroads on companionship. As we already have seen, inefficient or compulsive housekeeping can absorb so much of a woman's time and attention as to reduce her adequacy and ability to function successfully as a lover and friend to her husband. Not many wives let housekeeping seriously impair the marital relationship, but with the expanding of the domain almost all of them do become somewhat distracted and less attentive to their husbands. One man's account of his triumph over a business rival is interrupted by the ding! of the timer on the kitchen stove, another one's explanation of the foreign situation is broken off by his wife in favor of loading the dishwasher or putting away the laundry, a third one is in a mood to take his wife dancing but has to defer to the priority of her Thursday night supermarket expedition.

But even such things are trifling compared to the impact of the children on companionship, as I noted earlier. Children have an uncanny ability to break into grown-up conversation, get into fights, or fall down the stairs, just when whoever is talking is coming to the crux of the matter; when he finally gets the child shushed, bandaged, and shooed off, he finds he has lost the thread of his argument or forgotten altogether what he was about to say. Even so, all this is of minor importance compared to the specialization and division of duties that children make necessary. As the woman becomes housebound and child-fixated, and her husband becomes money- and career-oriented, the gap steadily widens between their current funds of information, their daily experiences, their interests and thought processes. Where each once strove fully to understand and be understood, each now settles for an occasional sympathetic, half-distracted hearing, or even just a series of well-meaning grunts. The young women whom we previously heard fretting about "going to seed" and stagnating intellectually are, as we saw, suffering a loss of identity—but also, a loss of communication and mutual comprehension, of empathy and friendship. The exchanging of biographies that they once practiced with such delight has dwindled to the exchanging of unintelligible footnotes.

According to Dr. Deitcher's calculations, the average parents of preschool or school children talk to each other only about half as much per day as they did in the intimacy of their first years of marriage. And, the decrease in quantity may not be as painful as the change in quality. Talk about money problems, household matters, child rearing, and the like now shoulders out talk about books, music, personal relationships, and ideals. Husband and wife use the mundane words of business partners rather than the emotionally and intellectually richer ones of friends. In severe cases, this even feels not so much like a different order of communication as none at all. "Sometimes," one woman told a researcher on the Cornell project, "I daydream of meeting my husband in disguise on a train or boat or at a party, and staying up all night talking to him. I think if we could forget we were married and talk as two human beings, we could mean something to each other again."

The neo-traditional woman is apt to react to this situation by blaming her husband for the decrease in their interest in each other. "We're told that we must make stimulating conversation," writes an indignant housewife from South Dakota, "and that we must compete with all the charming and intelligent people he has seen during the day. Well, I wouldn't give two cents for the husband who is not eager to hear about his children and his household at the end of the day." The non-traditional woman, on the other hand, is more likely to find herself at fault, and to struggle to make herself more interesting and less parochial via any of the methods we glanced at earlier. But to do so she has to surmount some considerable obstacles, not the least of which is her acquired tendency—heightened by housewifely preoccupation—to ignore certain kinds of information dear to the masculine heart. The Gallup organization reports, for instance, that half of all men, but less than one-quarter of all women, know the U.S. population; 54 percent of men, but only 32 percent of women, know where the Suez Canal is; and only half as many women as men know what the initials "NATO" stand for.

That being the case, intellectual conversations are likely to begin hopefully, only to get derailed and end up nowhere. For instance:

SHE: We had the most fascinating lecturer at the club today. Sir Shawcross Framingham. Arthur, I'm talking to you!

HE *(coming up from the depths of a magazine):* Umph. Yes? What did he say?

SHE: He's just been all over Africa, and he says that in many places people only earn about $200 a year. Isn't that just ghastly?

HE: I'll say. That's why Communism has so powerful an appeal— what do such people care about freedom of speech, when they can hardly survive?

SHE: I think that's a terribly defeatist attitude.

HE: Oh, *really?* Well, just exactly what do you think can be done about it?

SHE: I think the UN ought to pass a minimum wage law for those countries. *(He chuckles, and she gets thin of lip.)* Just what is so funny? Was that a dumb remark, by any chance?

HE *(hastily):* Well, no, but, sweetie, you can't just pass a law to pay out money that doesn't exist. They're so underdeveloped and lacking in productive capacity that there *isn't* any money to be had. Anyway, the UN isn't—

SHE: We could lend them some. We're always lending money.

HE: It isn't money they need, it's industrial development.

SHE: But you just *said* they needed money, and now you're trying to back out!

HE: I'm *not* backing out. When I said there isn't any money, I meant there isn't money-making capacity.

SHE: They could print more; paper is cheap. Isn't that what you called fiat currency? It would be a start.

HE: No, no, *no*, that isn't—look here— Listen, you never did go for economics, so why get yourself all upset about it? *(He picks up his magazine.)*

SHE *(white around the nostrils):* You don't *like* my trying to have intelligent discussions with you. You can't stand it if a woman shows any brains!

HE: That's ridiculous. I just happen to recognize that there are some subjects you and I never seem to be able to discuss.

SHE: I'll bet you discuss them with that blonde assistant of yours. Blonde! I know where *her* blonde hair comes from!

HE: For Pete's sake, what has her hair got to do with the starving Africans?

SHE *(on the verge of tears):* You *never* want to talk to me any more the way you did when we were going together. *That's* what it has to do with the Africans!

HE: Aw, sweetie—come here and give us a kiss. Come on. . . . That's better. That's my girl!

Such garbling of communication increases with increasing sexual task specialization. Each primitive people, as we have seen, generally has its own rigid allocation of jobs and privileges to the sexes, and a correspondingly low level of communication and companionship between them. In primitive life, with its abundance of same-sex friendships and intimate communal living, this works out well enough. In modern American life, on the other hand, which offers few important adult relationships outside of marriage, the pattern of specialization can slowly cancel out the immensely rewarding mutuality of interests and understanding the couple began with.

As one woman told a Cornell sociologist, "Talking together used to make us feel so close. We told things about ourselves we'd never confided to anyone else. Sometimes we'd lie in bed and talk into the small hours of the morning. The whole world seemed to spread out for us to explore together. Now we have so little to say. Something wonderful seems to have gone out of our marriage." In extreme cases the marriage actually disintegrates as each partner finds it essential to satisfy his emotional need for friendship elsewhere. A surgeon who was on the point of leaving his wife for another woman told a marriage counselor at Dr. Paul Popenoe's American

Institute of Family Relations, "My moments of greatest happiness in life come at the conclusion of a difficult surgical episode when I peel off my gloves, knowing the patient will survive and benefit from my skill. Several months ago I went home to describe such a triumph to Lynn, but before I got the words out she launched on a tale of woe concerning the misdeeds of our third son that lasted until the dinner hour." As a result of many such episodes, he would retreat, as soon as he came home, to the greenhouse where he raised orchids, or into the study where he built ship models. Even on those occasions when his wife was receptive or cheerful, he was thus neither available nor interested. The other woman in his life was neither prettier nor sexier than his wife, but she would listen to his talk about his surgery with appreciation and genuine under-standing, and had an unending supply of interests in many things, partly derived from her work in a bookstore, that made her worth listening to and exciting to be with.

Even those husbands and wives who continue to have a great deal in common, and are able both to confide in and be confidants to each other, often must fight for time in which to do so. One woman may feed the children early so as to have a late dinner, alone with her husband; another finds the evening so crammed with duties like check writing and laundry folding that she waits for the privacy and relaxation of the before-bedtime bath; a third says she communicates well only when she and her husband go out alone to dinner, leaving children, phone, dog, and responsibilities behind; and one seem-ingly fragile Southern girl has forced herself to endure the bugs, cold water, and night noises of camping-out in order to find time for companionship with her husband.

Though such devices work for some people, the average amount of conversation husbands and wives have with each other and the degree of their satisfaction with each other's companionship con-tinue to decrease during married life until the children are on the verge of leaving home or have actually left. This does not mean that parenthood makes men and women dissatisfied with marriage *in toto;* their relationships with their children cut down on compan-ionship, but supply equivalent or even greater joys. Nor does it mean that they necessarily become dissatisfied with life in general; the husband's growing career, his and her pride in their children, and her gradual involvement in outside interests may provide each with new sources of satisfaction. But the disagreeable fact remains that their marital friendship does fade and shrink over a period of years.

And then, for some couples, it surprisingly takes on new life and color. Once the children are all launched, the practical problems and distractions of family life greatly diminish. Husband and wife have much more free time for each other; their conversation veers back toward cultural topics, discussions of friends and acquaintances, shared experiences; and once again they are interested in going out together, doing things jointly, talking everything over, understanding each other.

But for the unfortunate ones, the gap has become too wide; there is neither the impetus to bridge it nor any bridge-building material on hand. Some couples who have apparently had a solid, smooth-functioning marriage astonish and mystify their friends by abruptly separating or seeking divorce in middle age. Yet there is no mystery about it; they had simply been too busy to notice that they were no longer friends, until their aloneness made it obvious.

Almost every marriage starts as a linkage of two people who are both lovers and friends. The later addition of mateship, property ownership, parenthood, and community life obscure to some extent the original basis of attraction. When, in due time, the latter functions are partly concluded and much of their paraphernalia dismantled, the two people may be revealed as having lost their original connections. They are no longer intensely passionate, but what is more crucial, they have nothing much in common, little to be friends about, and no reason to remain married.

And so some couples break up; but many others, whose relationships are equally moribund, are too ashamed or lazy to take formal action. Instead, man and wife practice the invisible divorce, living under one roof and sleeping in the same bed, but withdrawn from each other into the fastnesses of the personality. It is anyone's guess which kind of divorce is the more painful.

5 THE GROWTH OF PERSONS AND FRIENDSHIPS

The middle of life and the launching of the children may thus signify for women either a period of newly intensified friendship with their husbands, replacing the lost satisfactions of motherhood, or it may mean the virtual end of the emotional life and the onset of an atrophy that slowly turns them into gnarled, juiceless old women.

What accounts for the difference? The most common answer has long been that people who do not achieve lasting marital adjustment probably were not well-matched to begin with, and had no real basis for a close relationship. Recently, however, several thoughtful students of family life have called this a static picture which fails to take into account the lifelong processes of change and growth. Sociologist Nelson Foote, a long-time researcher in family problems, says that many well-matched newlyweds become *un-matched* with the passage of time, due to major differences in their personal growth and development. Even though most divorces occur within the first few years of marriage, others happen much later on, the average duration of all broken marriages being on the order of eight to ten years. Merely because a marriage has long endured does not mean that it has survived all obstacles; at the end of the tenth year, for instance, a marriage still has a one-in-nine chance of ending in divorce in the future. There is, in fact, no time in our lives when our marriages become absolutely secure.

A prime value in American culture is "progress"; in terms of the individual this means a continuing effort to increase his status, wealth, achievement, and knowledge. But the assigning of the career exclusively to the husband, and of homemaking and motherhood exclusively to the wife, gives the husband by far the greater chance at all this. Between his twenties and his forties, he spends about five thousand working days dealing with other human beings, acquiring knowledge in his field, experiencing something of the larger world he lives in, and attaining a measure of personal and professional stature. His wife, meanwhile, spends those same years with her children, her housekeeping, and her fellow homemakers; she is very likely to emerge from motherhood in her forties with little more than the talents and stature she had in girlhood, somewhat faded from disuse.* To be sure, she acquired many skills in running a busy household, and maturity and emotional competence in dealing with children and neighbors, but these are no longer of much use; she is freed of her duties and thereby stripped of much of her value. She becomes unemployed at a time when her husband is more absorbed in his work than ever, and is nearly useless at a time when he is at his most productive. Perhaps he and she never were equals in an absolute sense, but they surely were *equivalents;* now the scales are badly tipped.

Indeed, the imbalance may appear even before the children leave home. According to William H. Whyte, Jr., many fast-rising corporation executives begin to find their wives an embarrassment and a hindrance after about fifteen years of marriage. The wife is not up to the husband's rapidly achieved rank, and neither graces him sufficiently outside the home nor complements him within it. For many such men, writes Mr. Whyte, "the office becomes the spiritual home, the house merely a base of operations, and the wife somebody to be kept in the background lest one's style be cramped." The same disparity appears in other areas of American life; it has been said, for instance, that Washington, D.C., is full of brilliant men and the women they unfortunately married in their youth.

A special aspect of this unmatching process is that, as the husband outstrips his wife intellectually, she is less and less able to function as his confidante. The average top-level executive talks less to his wife about business than he did as a junior executive, not only because they spend less time together, but because she has fallen too far behind him to be an adequate listener. The same is true of men in most branches of science. Some wives try to fake interest: "He

---

* Her children, if they have turned out well, are of course a great achievement, but to live the next thirty years on that accomplishment is to be a little like the middle-aged former war hero, pathetically recalling the glories of his time of greatness.

loves his work and continually talks about it," confides the wife of
an organic chemist. "I listen dutifully and pretend to be very interested, but I'm bored and often can't even understand what he is
talking about." Few men are fooled or satisfied by such listening;
as the surgeon whose case was cited earlier told his marriage counselor, "Lynn prefers to smile pleasantly and echo my remarks. A
steady diet of conciliation and agreement can be deadly. Margaret
[the other woman] and I argue and wrangle. We can talk about anything and everything. I feel alive in Margaret's company." Despite
all the cartoons about dumb voluptuous blondes sitting on the boss's
lap, what makes many a man suppose himself in love with his secretary or female business associate is her sympathetic understanding
of his triumphs and failures, and her ability to respond with equivalent ones of her own.

Yet the wife's need of a friend may be far greater than her husband's. The hunger for friendship, like the yearning to fall in love,
is keenest when the self has few sources of satisfaction and pride;
hence love is never so intense nor friendship so fierce as in youth.
We observed that a disparity exists even in the teens, when love and
companionship are more important to the girl than to the boy. And
when the boy becomes a man and makes his place in the world, the
gap widens further. The girl, meanwhile, continues to derive the
larger part of her satisfactions and her identity from being his wife;
and since his love and friendship are not inner resources of her own,
she continually needs reassurance that they still exist. He knows
that she loves him, even without hearing her say so, but she must
have him say that *he* loves *her,* day after day and year after year.
Many of her worries and moods arise from no real problem but
from her lack of self-esteem. In "typically feminine" fashion, she
does not want him to reason with her or assist with some difficulty,
but simply to say he adores her; for him this solves nothing, but for
her it solves everything.

The disparity grows with the years and reaches a critical point
in middle age when his employment is yielding him maximum
satisfaction, but hers is ending. More than ever, she needs some

buoyant friend to cling to, lest she drown in the sea of her own un-importance; yet the greater her need of him, the less he is apt to find her the kind of companion he now wants.

In contrast, the woman who has managed to grow along with her husband has a far better chance of renewing and intensifying her friendship with him at the mid-point of life. Her husband continues to communicate with her not only because she is a willing and comprehending listener, but because she has things of value to give him in return. She is no drowning swimmer, clutching him around the neck, but as buoyant a soul as he. Even when she does turn to him for support, she is asking for a mature kind that he delights in giving: the University of Michigan survey reports, for instance, that wives who work discuss their problems with their husbands more than nonworking wives, and by and large get a more sympathetic and helpful response than do homemakers. Similarly, when a woman has some special competence or valuable knowledge of any prized sort, or holds a particularly important post in the community, she is more likely to share the decision making at home with her husband, and to be deeply satisfied with her husband as a companion. And although college-educated women are among the most likely to exhibit the "trapped-housewife" syndrome, they are also among the most likely to try to develop outside interests—and, significantly, they rate their marriages, and their lives in general, as happier than do women of equal economic status but less education.

But what is the emotional meaning of the statistics that show a correlation between equality and companionship? What is the human import of such abstract terms as "comparable personal growth" and "the matching process"? Listen to one woman, who, despite some complaints from her husband, taught school part-time when her children were small, and who, now that they are teenagers, has just begun a full-time schedule again:

You ask what I consider best about my present life. The answer: almost everything. The main thing is the feeling of growth in my relationship with Jules, with our boys, and to a lesser extent with friends. I feel free in many ways, less hemmed in than in some earlier times in my life; I am better able to love with less need to control others, I force fewer of my needs on them, I have a greater willingness to let others, especially Jules, be themselves. Maybe this is all just illusion—maybe I'm just feeling good today.

In the last sentence, one may assume, she is just knocking on wood, lest her boasting cause the gods to take back her good fortune. But it was no gift from them in the first place; it was something she herself was largely responsible for.

1 THE BATTLE OF THE SEXES

In A.D. 585 a group of learned bishops at the Council of Macon, after soberly debating the proposition that woman does not have a mortal soul, magnanimously concluded that she does. Since she might thus turn up in heaven, some Fathers of the Church were thereafter able to face the prospect of eternal bliss only by assuming that at the last trump, when this corruptible puts on incorruption, the risen would don a sexless modification of their old selves and spend eternity in decorous neutrality. It was a reassuring idea: not only did it rule out the possibility that voluptuous desires might manifest themselves among the blessed, but it promised that heaven would be peaceful. For, judging by the evidence here on earth, as long as we are differentiated into male and female we are compelled not only to love and lust after each other, but to engage forever in hand-to-hand combat in an unending Battle of the Sexes.

Modern woman is often castigated for the aggressiveness and rivalry she displays toward man, and her critics speak as though such behavior in her were new and abnormal. But it is an old story; time out of mind, man has been outraged by feelings in woman which he finds quite permissible in himself. Because he has almost always been the master, her hostility has usually seemed to be lèse-majesté, not to say treason. Many primitive men have lived in continual fear—allayed only by the defensive barricades of taboo—that women might cause them to lose their strength, virility, hunting skills, or prowess as warriors. A Marquesan man, for instance, might kill his wife if she endangered him by eating from his gourd. An Arapesh man of New Guinea would at certain times avoid sleeping with his wife for fear she was an *unuk* (female demon) in disguise, enticing him to copulate in order to bring about his death by means of teeth hidden in her vulva.

The early men of our own civilization felt much the same way. Though they saw woman as the fertile, homemaking, mothering half of humanity, they also envisioned her as a malevolent sorceress and vindictive enemy. Recall a few of the myths that deal with vindictive or man-hating females: the beautiful warlike Amazons, who tried to conquer men and overthrow their rule; Circe, the sorceress, who lured men with her beauty only to transform them into pigs; Medea, the magic worker, who poisoned her ex-husband's new bride and father-in-law, and murdered her own two sons by him. Judeo-Christian tradition, too, has its full measure of wicked women—Eve, Lilith, Delilah, Jezebel, and all that host of imagined sirens, hags, beldames, witches and assorted minions of Satan who have ruined the sleep of so many generations of Christian men.

Parallel to all these mythical or semi-legendary harpies have been the real women of whose vindictiveness and hostility men have complained, age after age: Xanthippe, archetype of the eternal shrew, belaboring Socrates in the marketplace; Theodora, exemplar of the domineering woman, running Justinian and the Empire with a strong hand; Elizabeth I, model of the frigid competitor of man, fishing with herself as bait but never marrying; Carry Nation, epitome of the rabid feminist, battering down the enclaves of masculine privacy with her hatchet.

In the past several generations, men have been alarmed by the unprecedented rivalry offered them by female free-love exponents, cigar-smoking poetesses, lady tennis champions, big-game huntresses, channel swimmers, and existential philosophers; but it was the forms of rivalry that were new, and not the basic drive. Many contemporary critics worriedly ascribe the Decline of Masculinity to the unwonted aggressiveness of modern women, but the plaint is of ancient provenance: practically every fault modern woman is accused of can be found in the writings of Juvenal, who lived eighteen centuries ago, or even Hesiod, who lived twenty-eight centuries ago.

All the while, however, men have continued to fall in love with women, and women with men; each sex, despite all it hears against the other, supposes that in its generation love will at last prove to be perfect and pure; each is astonished to find that it is, after all, strangely alloyed with irritation, quarreling, and strife. Countless men and women have discovered for themselves what countless others have previously learned. One of my correspondents, married eight years, writes with some astonishment, "I never used to think— nor would I have believed—that I could be supremely exasperated by somebody and still love him," but human beings have been making the same astonished comment for thousands of years. Aristophanes long ago quoted what was even in his time an old saying, probably uttered by wives as often as by husbands: "It's impossible to live with the tormentors, impossible to live without them."

Yet it is not only between man and woman that this curious amalgam of emotions exists. Mothers adore their children, but often think them pestiferous and tormenting. Soldiers forever gripe about their officers, but are fiercely loyal to them in battle. And even dear friends have somewhat the same mixture of feelings for each other; as La Rochefoucauld cruelly put it, "In the misfortune of our best friends we find something not wholly displeasing."

It is, in sum, characteristic of the human animal to feel comforted, yet annoyed, by those of his fellows with whom he huddles close for solace and mutual defense; all his life he struggles to love them well enough not to fight with them. Some decades ago the sociologist William Graham Sumner pointed out that every human group from the smallest to the largest manifests the quality of "antagonistic cooperation." More specifically, the contemporary sociologist John Sirjamaki, writing about the tiny two-person society of man and wife, stated that "cooperation and conflict characterize every marital relationship; paired together, husband and wife can live and love more effectively than when single, but they chafe, also, from the complications which arise from their coresidence."

Ambivalence, is, of course, the technical name of this coexistence of opposite feelings; it is at once a normal and universal phenomenon, yet also a potential source of severe emotional illness. In his later years, Freud postulated a dualistic instinct theory which would explain its universality. The human being, he held, is motivated by two fundamental forces—a positive drive or love instinct, and a negative drive or death instinct, the former accounting for our ability to love and live together, the latter for our aggressive impulses and our ability to fight whatever hinders our desires. Since we must forgo at least some of our selfish desires in order to live together with other human beings, we inevitably feel negative emotions toward them along with the positive ones caused by the benefits we derive from them.

Not all psychologists and psychiatrists accept the theory of the death instinct; in practice, however, they frequently speak of something very much like it. In studying child development, for instance, psychologists describe the child as loving the parents who protect him and gratify his childish desires, and, at the same time, being angered and frustrated by the demands and limitations they put on him as he grows up. The normal child, because of his love for his parents, learns not to release his angers at them but at other objects, particularly in the form of play; later he even converts his aggressive energy into constructive efforts to master his environment. As he grows up, he continues to displace some aggressive energy into games in which he "lets off steam," but more importantly he "sublimates" the bulk of it into activities with a positive social value. "The little criminal becomes the G-man," writes Dr. Karl Menninger in *Love Against Hate*. "The jealous sister becomes the protective nurse. The boy who wanted to chop off his little brother's head becomes a surgeon."*

For the most part, however, this darker side of our feelings re-

---

* Sublimation is still popularly thought to be the substituting of a nonsexual activity for a sexual one, but this is a leftover bit of Victorian morality. As Dr. Menninger and others have pointed out, the unacceptable and aggressive drives are the ones which require sublimation, rather than the love instinct.

mains concealed or transformed; lovers, parents, friends, and patriots are often unaware of any flaw in their love, or are unwilling to admit its existence. But sometimes circumstances prevent sublimation, or make the proportion of love to hate insufficient; then the mixture of feelings produces anything from vague anxiety to outright revolution. Absolute dominion, for instance, will frequently make those who are dominated passionately love—and passionately hate—their rulers: the many heresies against the medieval church, or the defections and factional fights of Communists, are examples. A lack of any useful way to expend aggressions leaves a person with undischarged angers which may be vented on those he or she should be kindest to: the vicious squabbling among prisoners of war is a case in point. A sense of personal worth makes a subjugated person capable of turning his angers to account against his oppressor, rather than passively submitting to domination: the colonial peoples of the nineteenth-century world were hardly able to hate Westerners or cast them out, but today the belief of such peoples that they are as good as the Westerners is perhaps the strongest weapon in their arsenal.

All in all, despite the hullabaloo about the damage done by modern woman's rivalry toward man, perhaps her hostility is less virulent, even if more visible and audible, than it was of yore. At least, there are good grounds for thinking that it *could* be so; but just how antagonistic any woman actually is, or whether her rivalry takes a beneficent or malevolent form, depends on how she sees herself, how she is seen by her husband, and how she plays the rest of the roles which add up to her total being.

2 *ALL FOR LOVE, OR THE WORLD WELL LOST*

In the days of suffragette agitation, it seemed as though the Battle of the Sexes was a struggle of the legal Have-nots against the Haves, with the disenfranchised on the warpath to fight for equality. Feminist propagandists of that period claimed that inequality was the primary cause of sexual strife, and that when it was wiped out men and women would live in a wondrous new harmony. Many males, however, feared a real revolution in which women would come to dominate them legally and socially; from Shaw's Jack Tanner, pursued and exhausted into submission, to the varied bitchy and man-eating women portrayed by Faulkner, Hemingway, Wylie, and O'Hara, there has been a considerable literature showing the predatory female becoming all-powerful in an age of triumphant feminism.

Neither side's prediction has come true. Women have possessed practically all the major legal rights since 1920, and although a handful of inequities remain (most of which regulate working conditions), few American women are aware of them or feel any keen sense of injustice in their continued existence; yet no wondrous new harmony has suffused the land. On the other hand, as we saw earlier, the reports of modern matriarchalism and the subjugation of the hapless male have been something less than accurate. It is a rare middle-class husband who beats his wife, indulges in marital rape, or issues absolute edicts about her spending, her clothes, or her coming and going outside the house, but it is an even rarer one who is told by his wife how to run his career, what he may spend on the car or on himself, or when he must take charge of the kitchen and the children.

Indeed, for many a middle-class woman the hostility she feels (often without recognizing it) toward her husband stems from the fact that all her life she has accepted a lesser stature and traded away part of herself in return for his love. She both adores and is angered by man for dealing with her on these terms; she both admires and detests herself for being so willing to make the bargain. The very forms of politeness and gallantry in man that please and flatter her most are symbolic of the frailty and inferiority she acquiesces in; when he takes her arm, holds her coat, orders the dinner, or pays the bill, she feels a pleasant little triumph in being taken care of, yet the triumph is gained only by accepting the tradition of her own passivity and weakness. And these minor courtesies and manners only symbolize the larger truth: though she has come a long way from the demure Victorian maiden who waited with down-cast eyes to be chosen (praying not to be passed by and left to become a spinster), it is still true that in order to win her man she gives up a large part of the brave new world that lies before her.

It is of great psychological import that she still takes the man's name in marriage; it signifies that his identity is the larger, the productive, the money-earning one. The rabid feminists of earlier generations regarded the change of name as a real grievance, and fought against it, continuing to use their maiden names after marriage; some of them even insisted on having their passports made out in that fashion. But it came to nothing; most women still intend to be dependent on their husbands, and never question the custom of name changing. Indeed, the new bride is flushed and delighted with her new name, and properly so, for it symbolizes the unity between herself and her husband. But so, too, does it symbolize the difference between them, namely that he will be the leader and the primary source of his family's food and shelter, while she will be a follower and a part of his entourage.

This means that she must accept the lesser prestige and status that go with such a position. In an industrial society, what a man does is far more highly valued than what a housewife does; the status of the whole family, the pride or shame of each of its members, is therefore derived from his work and his achievements. Whether the woman makes a good mother or a bad mom, a fine housekeeper or a sloven, a loving mate or a shrew, she has no effect on the family status; dignity, position, reward, respect, all come from him, and though she shares in them, she does so only vicariously, and not in her own right. Thus, though she lives in a democratic and equalitarian society, she is denied real partnership with her husband in the pursuit of success and status, and is left with only a pseudo-occupation and a second-hand sense of worth.

All this is bound to cause resentment along with gratitude, fears of abandonment along with trust, and, most painful of all, envy and rivalry along with pride, particularly if she once wanted to do things comparable to the interesting and prestigeful things he is doing. Often the form it takes is harmless and merely pathetic. I recall meeting a noted historian at a party recently, who was being lionized by a number of people; his wife, a handsome woman of about forty, was standing nearby, ignored and pouting. I decided to chat with her, and asked her what she did; she replied, a little too off-hand-edly, that she was a "literature major," but when I tactlessly inquired further, it turned out that some twenty years earlier she had studied literature in college, and ever since had vaguely thought of doing something more with it.

Other times, envy and rivalry may be deeply disturbing. A Midwestern correspondent, for instance, writes that she found herself severely depressed and almost unable to function for several days after her husband, an automation engineer, had jubilantly told her of his latest promotion and raise; finally she recognized the reason for her feelings:

> We started out as equals—both intelligent, both well educated, both working in scientific research. Then we became parents of three children. Wonderful children—but why aren't they his all day as well as mine? Nowadays for his forty hours of work he gets honors, applause, a new title, his name in the journals; I put in eighty hours a week and am lucky if anyone says dinner wasn't bad. I am nothing but one person's wife, and three persons' mother. There is no Violet any more, but just a useful possession of other people.

The neo-traditionalist assures woman that she can find happiness by abandoning all these shoddy envies and vaporous daydreams—indeed, he claims that the abdication of her individuality is *good* for her, and signifies true womanhood. Helene Deutsch writes, for instance, that the ideal, and ideally happy, woman feels, "He is wonderful and I am part of him," and adds that a mature woman should be completely willing to renounce her own achievements in favor of the man's without feeling that she is sacrificing anything. Such advice inevitably calls to mind the belief of some Southerners that the Negro was never so happy as in the days of slavery. History, however, has provided the Negro with an awareness of his own potentialities, and hence with a conception of happiness that matches the white man's; even if he sought to regain the happiness of the slave—assuming it is no myth—he could not fool himself that he felt it.

It is much the same with women. In giving up the outside world and a part of themselves for love and marriage, they seem to know what kind of bargain they are getting, and to be all in favor of it; only later do many of them discover that history has tricked them by making them desire and need a larger sense of participation and feeling of fulfillment. The neo-conservative suggestion that they immerse themselves in traditional female activities and do by hand a great deal of the old-fashioned sort of woman's work is an answer of sorts—it might, indeed, absorb some of the aggressive energy they have no good way of using up; but what is unnecessary and archaic is not really satisfying, because it does not match the realistic image they have of their own capacities and of the values of the world around them.

"I enjoy being a girl!" sings the exuberant Linda Low in *Flower Drum Song,* and like her most women enjoy being women—only not terribly much. Between a fifth and a third of them, according to different surveys, admit that if they could be born over again they would prefer to be men; probably a large number of others unconsciously feel that way but refuse to let the thought rise up out of the depths into recognition. (By way of contrast, only 3 percent of men say they would switch sexes if they could.) Modern woman is well aware that in many ways she has a far better life than her grandmother or than most women in the past; yet, since her net satisfaction in life is determined by her own standards rather than theirs, she still feels like a Have-not. And in the classic fashion of the Have-not, she cannot help resenting the Have—particularly since it is for him that she more or less voluntarily accepted second place in life.

3 *THE TYRANNY OF THE WEAK*

What is the woman to do with her basic fund of aggressiveness? If she sublimates it via a career, she is called unfeminine; if she vents it on housework, she is a drudge (and the foe, in any case, seems unworthy) ; if she expends it on her children, she is a mom; and if she directs it against her husband, she is a castrating wife and very likely a future divorcee. At least, these appear to be the unpromising alternatives. One conservative solution has been to deny that any problem exists: woman is sweet, mild, loving and gentle by nature, and has neither any aggressions nor any feeling of rivalry toward anyone. It is not a very credible belief, but it *is* an answer of sorts for some women who are too inhibited to tolerate the sight of their own feelings, or who have married men unable to tolerate any form of rivalry from them, even if playful or good-natured.

It can, for instance, take the righteously noble form of a claim by the woman that she has no right or wish to assert herself in any way; she is a dedicated and selfless worshiper of her husband, seeing in him no fault or wrong, and in herself no frustration or anger. Certain women's magazines administer this type of analgesic to their readers now and again, though how easily it is swallowed is not known. A superior specimen is an article that appeared in *Ladies' Home Journal* a few years ago (written by Marlene Dietrich, of all people), which began with the impassioned advice, "Love him. Unconditionally and with devotion. You chose him. He must be wonderful." Specifically, Miss Dietrich recommended that the wife adapt herself completely to her husband's needs and whims, pampering and comforting him, and never for an instant questioning any of his wishes or voicing any objections And some women really do manage to make this work. A woman in her mid-thirties writes from Worth, Illinois, to say that she and her husband, married twelve years, are still ardently in love and do none of the marital dueling she hears so much about; they have simply followed the directions of Paul (in Ephesians, Chapter 5) who called for unquestioning obedience by the wife. She explains:

The modern man should have Granddad's authority, despite new customs. His wife shares the bank account (but doesn't spend money contrary to his wishes), drives the car as well as he (but never turns the key if he doesn't want her to take it out), and even earns a living (but not unless he wants her to). Whenever they differ, she should give in. This is agony at first, but becomes quite painless with practice.

Sometimes a woman's denial of her own competitive drive is required of her by circumstances: William H. Whyte, Jr., reports that in some corporations an executive's success is contingent upon having a wife who is uncomplaining, acquiescent, and distinctly antifeminist. And sometimes the major circumstance is her husband himself, who, to her astonishment, proves unable to tolerate anything but humility and obedience in her. "This is my second marriage," writes a highly cultivated New England woman, "and I shall try to avoid divorce if at all possible—but the man I married has no sense of compromise in any way. He wishes me to confine myself to his comforts, and to stay 'in my place.' I dare not compete with him in any part of our life; even intellectual discussions are ruled out. He *must* feel superior at all times, and I must remain silent." A woman musician who retired to take care of her children, ostensibly out of pure maternal feeling, says elsewhere in her questionnaire that her husband is a musician too, who "flatly states that no woman worth her salt has to compete with a man for her ego satisfactions, and no man wants a woman—and especially not his wife—competing with him in work or play beyond tick-tack-toe. So there you have it, right from the horse's mouth."

But the human soul is not a steel tank, and things contained in it under pressure do not rest in harmless equilibrium. Repressed aggressive energy will find a way out, in one form or another. For the woman who represses even benign forms of rivalry with her husband, the safest alternative targets are herself and others of her sex. As Gunnar Myrdal and others have pointed out, woman shows scorn and contempt for her own kind just as do "marginal men"—Negroes, Jews, immigrants, or other persons who live on the margin between two cultures, vainly longing to be admitted to the dominant one, and venting their angers on each other.

Like other marginal persons, woman has legal equality but remains on the periphery of the dominant group, her outsideness justified by men in almost the same terms they use about the Negro ("childish," "emotional," "less intelligent," and "all right in her place"). And like the Negro, whose transition is made particularly difficult by physical traits, she sometimes accommodates herself to her marginal status by overemphasizing her differences: distinctive clothing, a special vocabulary and inflection of voice, a flattering or pleading manner with the rulers, a craftiness and cunning in getting around them by improper means. In a brief, she Uncle Toms it.

But as with the Negro, she pays for these accommodations with self-contempt. No one derides kinky hair and dark skin more bitterly than the Negro; only a woman refers savagely to the menses as "the curse." She defers to man's opinions, sometimes by way of deceiving him, but more often because she thinks so little of her own judgment; despite the dire predictions of the antisuffragists of half a century ago, there has never been a "woman's vote" in the United States, for women by and large adopt the political preferences of their husbands.*

Women dislike all manner of things about womankind in general, and about each other and themselves in particular. "However bad the things a man may think about women," Chamfort slyly observed, "there is no woman who does not think worse of them than he." Though millions of women join women's clubs, many millions of others can't stand the sight of a large room full of their own kind or endure the high strident cacophony of their chatter. And even those who can may secretly dislike them. From Scarsdale, the president of the local chapter of a woman's organization writes, "Most of the women I know best are spoiled, selfish, insufficiently enlightened, insufficiently interested in being part of the world, disinterested in

* Woman's low estimate of her own opinions has been clinically demonstrated. At the University of Texas, psychologist Robert R. Blake set up five isolation booths in which subjects would hear and count the ticks of a metronome via earphones, and report their counts to each other on an intercom hookup. Actually, all but one were empty; the single live subject heard only a tape recording of the metronome and voices, but was unaware of the fact. He might, typically, hear and count twenty-four ticks, followed by four voices all claiming to have counted twenty-seven. Two-thirds of the men tested clung to their own count and said what they really heard; less than half the women did so, the rest changing their minds to conform to the fictitious majority.

politics, world events, or scientific progress." In a moment of honesty, a female patient of Theodore Reik summed it up in a single sentence: "I don't like any of my best friends."

For most homemaking women, however, contempt of self and kind is an unsatisfying and inadequate release of their feelings; part of these feelings are, therefore, directed toward the husband, but with that same care for deception, cunning, and tricky maneuvering which many colored people find themselves forced to use, and in which they take a perverse pride. As a Negro remarks in *Purlie Victorious,* a Broadway play of the 1961-62 season, "Man, some of the best pretendin' in the worl' is done in front of white folks!" Countless generations of slaves, servants, laboring men, and wives have filched a bit of the master's money, laughed at his jokes, smiled sheepishly at his jibes, played the fool to flatter him, dropped hints in seemingly accidental fashion, and smirked behind his back when they got their way about something. Yet man, the oligarch, has greatly exaggerated the extent to which he has been put upon in this fashion by his underlings, and especially by his wife. "The history of woman," wrote Oscar Wilde, who did not care much for the female sex, "is the history of the worst form of tyranny the world has ever known, the tyranny of the weak over the strong." There is some truth in that, but only some.

That nub of truth was formally stated by the sociologist W. I. Thomas: "In general," he wrote, "people become more cunning when they are oppressed, or do not participate on an equal footing in their society. . . . The 'racial' cunning of the Jew has the same origin as the particular cunning of women." It is not irrelevant that the woman doctor quoted in Chapter Two, who revels in her noncompetitive retirement, says that the main secret of wives might be called How to Soften Up Your Husband Without His Recognizing It. She illustrates:

One wouldn't dare announce to him *ever:* "I know the way you tick— a good breakfast, a smile, a touch, a chance to read the paper without interruption from the kids, and you'll agree to a skiing trip this weekend." Blackmail? Trickery? No. One loves him; the smile and touch are for him, and not just for the trip. But he recognizes only the part that's for him, and doesn't tie it in with the request for the trip.

Slightly more overt than such wordless artifices is woman's use of language to wheedle, cajole, and pester, with the aim of getting a more equal footing. As we saw earlier, she is superior in language abilities from babyhood on, and, in fact, verbal aggression is her favorite form—but it is often subtle and low-keyed, rather than loud and angry. Popular mythology makes much of the wife as a yammering scold, but much of the time middle-class woman is likely to use gentle, friendly, insistent talking to break down a man's defenses. "Where once woman shook man," wrote James Thurber, "or struck him with a rock, or at least screamed imprecations at him, when he sat down to draw pictures on the walls of the cave, she now contents herself with talking to him when he is reading." Or let the men at the party become absorbed in a discussion of politics, and like a mother bird distracting the hunter, some feminine woman who would never dream of contradicting them will flutter in and deflect the conversation to prattle, banter, gossip, or topics like natural childbirth—all in all, as competitive an act as arguing, but a good deal less honest. If she does, however, get into discussions on topics the men care about, she carefully stops short of displaying unfeminine vigor or logic. At home, on the other hand, she will disagree with her husband as forcefully as he will stand for, but because of her poor opinion of her own opinions she is likely to listen to him respectfully on any subject of substance, and speak out vigorously about matters of no importance.

Although husbands and wives do argue about important matters, often the subject itself is only a blind and the quarrel merely a vehicle for the expression of hostility. Money, for instance, is the most frequent subject of quarrels, but many agencies affiliated with the Family Service Association of America have found that in the present era of sustained prosperity it is often a substitute for other problems which the husband and wife do not dare put into words. Typically, a frigid wife may do her part sexually for her husband's sake, not even admitting to herself that she resents it—and then even the score by overspending, forgetting to write check stubs, and lashing out angrily as soon as her husband starts to lecture her on her ways. Or again, a man may hate female extravagances but tolerate them as long as he doesn't have to hear about them, yet his wife may insist on flaunting or hinting at her foolish spending, thus bringing about a row; she does this because, being unsure of her own power over her husband, she would like him openly to accept and approve of everything she does.

The conjugal quarrel is therefore often less an effort to arrive at some sound conclusion than to vent aggression verbally. The quarrelsome wife is a stereotype—behind which is the fact that the homemaker has less opportunity to sublimate aggressive energies than her mate, and coincidentally a slight average edge in verbal prowess. Like a teen-age gang member, she accumulates a charge of inner tensions, and almost revels in the explosive discharge of combat, even if, figuratively, she is bruised and bleeding afterward. She would sometimes rather indulge in a pointless scrap in which neither one wins than pursue a discussion dispassionately and logically to an end in which she is proven wrong. As the wife of a brilliant business economist writes:

> In private I often argue hard about ideas or personal matters. But he enjoys discussions, being impartially argumentative by nature and not associating arguments with bad feeling. Not me—I get all wound up. And I hate to lose. Sometimes I even hear myself being deliberately unfair and mean in order to get him angry, since I know that if he remains calm he'll win the argument. This gambit is very successful—it always leads to a terrible fight and a stalemate in which neither wins. It is a cheap rotten thing for me to do, and I hope to be able to stop it some day.

Not quite so overt, but even more unpleasant, is a wife's expression of hostility in the form of competition for the love of the children. A woman may not realize that this is what she is doing when she offers her children bribes and indulgences that are to be kept secret from the father ("You can have an ice cream soda, but don't tell your father—he thinks you're eating too many sweet things already"), or when she makes herself out to be the kinder and more tolerant of the two parents ("I understand, darling, but don't say things like that in front of Daddy"). Nor is she always aware that casting her husband in the role of instrument of wrath ("Just you wait till your father comes home and hears about this") is part of such a contest. But in more severe cases the competitiveness is openly avowed; few children are as unlucky as the one whose parents vie with each other in giving him presents or showering him with favors, for he recognizes with his very glands and fine-spun nerve fibers that something is amiss. He is likely to be spoiled, dissatisfied, and disgruntled in the midst of his riches, for the present he needs is not a thing or a favor at all, but the gift of harmony between his parents.

Love-making is another area in which woman can subtly express rivalry or vent hostility against her husband. As we saw earlier, the better-educated and upper-status American man has, in general, become sensitive and responsive to his wife's emotional readiness for sexual relations, and either restrains himself or loses his urge when she indicates disinterest. This gives her great power; in her hostile moods she is tempted to use it with devastating effect. If for some reason she is feeling vindictive, she may prepare for bed, all smiles, and then just happen to remember something he did or said at a party last week; as gently as any sucking dove, she tells him about it, ostensibly in order to help him, but an ice-cold shower would be no more magically detumescent. In extreme cases, a wife's repeated ridicule or criticism can render a man as impotent (with her, at least) as if he had been castrated. She thereby evens the score for what Nature gave him and denied her; though she cannot become a man, she can at least make him no better than a woman.

Such overt and repulsive expression of hostility is rather uncommon; more often its translation into sexual terms is apt to be disguised and unrecognized even by the woman herself. Adultery, as we observed, sometimes represents rivalry or even revenge, though this is not always apparent to the adulteress. Frigidity, in addition to having neurotic origins, can also be a woman's way of refusing to yield; she may accept the invading male, make the appropriate

sounds and movements, and yet unconsciously assert her own independence by not being carried away, and by refusing to be transported and ravished. Such women, unless they seek counseling or
psychotherapy, are usually unaware of the reason for their difficulty;
a few, however, not only employ frigidity deliberately, but on occasion will admit it. One woman, who had been normally responsive
at the outset of her marriage, and slowly become frigid over a number of years, complained at length to a marriage counselor of her
husband's dictatorial domination; then, as though giving voice to
an afterthought, she said that about the only thing she did control
was her own orgasm, explaining, "Maybe I don't want to give him
that much satisfaction."

As with frigidity—a physical symptom which is almost always of
psychological rather than organic origin—women may unconsciously
"choose" any one of a number of other ailments to express resentment or rivalry. Menstrual pain, for example, is in many cases the
result of emotional factors rather than physical ones. What, indeed,
could be more simple and justifiable than menstrual pain, and at
the same time better calculated to humble the male a little? Not
only does he have to sympathize, but he must relinquish some of his
male prerogatives. It is he who gets out of bed to bring her a pill,
makes her hot tea, and takes care of the baby at 3 A.M. She can act
cross, lose her temper, and be more than usually illogical and im-
pulsive; if at last he objects or bridles, she effectively crushes him
with a single sentence: *"You* should have it just once!"

Many other female ailments, likewise, represent foolproof ways of
getting even with a man, or with life in general. Migraine head-
aches, insomnia, hives, acne, colitis, respiratory difficulties, genito-
urinary irritations, and arthritis are only a few of the many diseases
that may have a real organic basis—or may be the result of personal
dissatisfaction or long-lasting emotional conflict. Visits to specialists,
new medicines, bed rest, mid-winter trips to the Caribbean, and
regular costly psychotherapy sessions are all effective, though temporary, ways in which a woman can make herself feel important and
penalize her husband without leaving him room for a counter-

attack. Such ailments are socially irreproachable and, best of all, when unconsciously assumed, are guilt-free; no wonder that the doctor has so little chance of freeing the woman from what Dr. Flanders Dunbar has called the "beloved symptom."

Some of the preceding forms of hostility lie too close to the forbidden and the shameful to be recognized by the woman herself for what they are. But the classic and best-known form is also the most overt and unabashed: it is the outright vocal and physical violence of the Battleaxe, who bullies and dominates her husband by means of sneers and slurs, shrill nagging, cascades of abuse and invective, sharp nails and flailing fists, flying crockery and the deadly rolling pin, and before whose assaults the poor man ignominiously flees or sues for peace. It is an ancient tradition, but we hear about it primarily from a prejudiced source—men. One of the choicest specimens of the breed was the Wife of Bath, who used up and outlived five husbands, cheerfully describing how she drove several of them so hard that "many a nyght they songen 'weilawey!'" ["Woe is me"] and scolded them so unmercifully that they would bring her presents whenever she relented a little. The portrait is so vivid and her despicable sentiments so unforgettable that one easily forgets she was not real, but a satirical fancy created by Geoffrey Chaucer, Justice of the Peace, Member of Parliament, and man.

Battleaxes represent what men fear women might be; actually, they are probably much rarer than men like to pretend. Some months ago I hailed a cab and told the driver to hurry me to the Lunt-Fontanne Theater to meet my wife, whom I did not wish to keep waiting. "Aha!" he said knowingly, "orders from the War Department, eh?" I chuckled politely; then I decided to pursue the point, and asked him whether he felt that most wives really bulldoze their husbands and keep them jumping. "Ah, naw," he said grudgingly. "Anyway I don't feel that way about *my* wife. But people kind of expect you to talk like that." It is an old American tradition; Founding Father John Adams, for instance, wrote as follows in 1776, to his wife Abigail, who had suggested that as part of the Revolution men cease being masters of their wives and become their equals: "In practice, you know we have only the names of masters, and rather than give this up which would completely subject us to the despotism of the petticoat, I hope General Washington and all our brave heroes would fight."

In his survey of 909 Michigan wives, Robert Blood found that less than one half of one percent of them have complete control over family decision-making, and only 24 percent usually win out over their husbands when there is a difference of opinion; in a larger number of the cases, the wives are the ones who usually give in, and in the largest number, husbands and wives give in equally often. The henpecked man, according to Professor Blood, turns out to be far rarer than humor indicates, and is unlikely to be middle- or upper-class, well-educated, or successful. The men who submit to domination by harsh wives are usually those who earn less, know less, and have less success and status than other men in their segment of society; by reason of race, class, or personal shortcomings, they are already beaten, and thus are passive targets as well as sources of annoyance to their wives.

Bossy or sadistic wives in the middle and upper classes are, however, much more likely to use a battery of less-violent methods. These include quiet managership and not-so-quiet nagging, occasional favors and frequent arguments, the overt arranging of the family's social life and the covert control of finances, and a great many others. A few will boss their husbands around or openly belittle them in public, but most recognize that this is as socially ruinous for a woman as smoking a cigar. The real tragedy of the weak man with a strong wife is not that she crushes him in public, but that she publicly restrains herself and allows him to feel almost manly in front of other people; then, as they get in the car to go home, she punctures his self-image by lightly reminding him of some *gaffe* he made, or telling him of her decision as to what to do about the oil burner, or sweetly asking whether he wouldn't like, as a Christmas present from her, a year's membership in a downtown

athletic club, which, she feels, would do him a lot of good; it occurred to her, she adds, when she saw him standing next to several
of the other men.

4 CEASE-FIRE

If it is human nature to be not only cooperative but competitive,
and to have not only loving instincts but aggressive ones, it would
be wise not to expect total sweetness and light in marriage; the better course would be to recognize that both man and woman have
aggressive energies and to plan to use them up as beneficially as
possible. The major avenues via which woman has always used hers
up, overcoming them with love and so transmuting them into creative or useful work, have been her homemaking, her motherhood,
and her sexual relations with her husband. Yet in modern life, for
many reasons, these traditional female activities frequently provide
insufficient outlet for them. Moreover, many of the needs and desires
created in her by her education and emancipation are frustrated by
total domesticity, and this only adds to her surplus of aggressive
feelings; the result is, as we have just seen, that homemaking, mothering, and the sex life may become discolored and poisoned, and use
up aggressiveness in a malign rather than benign way. The answer,
it would seem, is for woman not to deny the existence of her aggressive energies or to play-act the passive female of a by-gone century,
but for her and her husband to allow for other forms of outlet
through which she can use up these energies safely or even pro-
ductively.

Games and gamelike activities, for example, are one of the safe
(though unproductive) forms of outlet for competitive or aggressive
drives not disposed of elsewhere.* "Since I stopped working and
devoted myself to the household and the children," writes a woman
who had been a journalist in the early years of her marriage, "I find

---

* So say psychologists of modern vintage—and also wise men of ancient times;
Aristotle, for one, stated that in play the emotions "become purified of a great
deal of the distasteful and dangerous properties which adhere to them."

I love all sorts of games and sports, and do my best to win against my husband. He doesn't need to have anybody boost his ego by faking, I'm glad to say, and whether I win or lose, it does *mine* good to be a serious challenge to him. It's much more fun for both of us, for instance, to bet on who can land the biggest bass; he's way ahead at the moment, but just wait till next summer. . . ."

Playing together can provide not only a "harmless discharge of aggressions," to use Dr. Menninger's words, but yield an actual enhancement of love via shared pleasures. Yet one must choose wisely; not all forms of joint recreation serve the refreshing function of friendly rivalry equally well. One of the most curious scraps of information in a major study of divorced women by sociologist William J. Goode is his finding that the major recreations the divorcees had shared with their ex-husbands were going to the movies, going dancing, or drinking together socially in bars. Goode believes that couples who choose such activities have a greater chance of breaking up because these diversions feature little "sharing" and hence have little cohesive value. But on a different level the explanation may be that they fail to allow for the playful and healthful expending of competitive drives, as do games, sports, and many hobbies.

Moreover, games succeed only to the extent that they do not seriously threaten either partner. Many a man cannot tolerate the challenge made by his wife in play; his superiority is too shaky or too important to permit even a symbolic defeat. And some women feel uneasy about direct rivalry with their husbands, since a victory seems to demean that image of the protective male which time and social change have already so much diminished. Such a one may want to prove herself against her husband, yet contrarily wish that he would gently but masterfully defeat her. As one woman writes, in apparent seriousness, "I greatly enjoy playing chess with my husband, except that I hate losing to him—and feel just terrible when I beat him."

Sophisticates often josh at the slick-magazine ideal of "togetherness," but it, too, can offer a healthful means of using up competitive impulses. The major peaceful outlet for aggression in civilized society is, of course, work. But the emotional value of any form of work is proportional to the challenge it offers and to the value society accords it. Scrubbing the floor and folding the linen, therefore, may exhaust a woman without letting off enough of her inner pressures. Some of the things a man and wife can work on together, however, have greater value; and even when they are doing something no more complicated than painting a wall or making dinner together, there is a curious and precious satisfaction in measuring themselves against each other, in seeking to outdo each other in helpfulness and accomplishment. So does competition assume the form of cooperation, and a skirmish turn into an amiable truce.

The value of shared duties thus stems in considerable part from the fact that they involve work of a kind which enables aggressive impulses to be sublimated and turned to kindly ends. The same is true even more so of club and volunteer activities. One often hears of the hostile woman who uses community or club activities as a weapon against her family, letting her children go unbathed and her husband unfed while she runs a meeting somewhere on better garbage collection. But this is only the extreme and unhealthy case; more typically, the activity itself absorbs and ennobles a woman's aggressive drive, and yields satisfactions of a positive kind. The woman who labors diligently to round up signatures on a petition for a better traffic-light system, or who makes endless phone calls and addresses hundreds of envelopes to help raise money for a new hospital wing, does so not by the force of native kindness and altruism but because her devotion to the good cause is powered by the same high-octane energy the careerist possesses.

Only now and then does this show through, as, for instance, when the officers of a club fall into unseemly struggles for prestige and honors, and one sees whence came the energy they lavished on the organization. And sometimes good works are done by women whose real aim is social success; Lucy Kavaler, in a study of high society, reports that she was told any number of times that "if a woman comes to a strange city where she knows nobody, and wants to become a member of society quickly, all she needs to do is head for the nearest hospital and work like hell."

Yet whatever the source of the energy, the results are admirable in many ways. The aggressions, to begin with, are channeled away from the home, thus decreasing the need for rivalry with the husband. Furthermore, they are not merely ventilated, as is the case with games and sports, but are genuinely sublimated and made an important and rewarding part of the psychological economy. Finally, society itself benefits; indeed, it is a commonplace among sociologists that American women are largely responsible for the cultural and aesthetic aspects of American life. For it is primarily they who visit the schools and do the work of the P.-T.A.'s; it is they who play the major role in supporting community theaters and agitating for better hospitals; it is they who do the bulk of fund soliciting for health and medical-research organizations, and who operate church and welfare groups. For many of them, the work remains at the level of stuffing envelopes and decorating ballrooms; yet the goal is always a good one, and the work yields genuine satisfactions.

The very women who protest that they are caught up in too many outside activities and bear too heavy a burden of duties actually seem to cherish them and to feel vigorously alive rather than fatigued and torn apart by their multiple responsibilities. They get caught up in a round of meetings, program arrangements, and committee work; they make reports and speeches to their fellow members, meet leaders of the community and visiting celebrities, and become genuinely and seriously involved in the goals for which their group is working. A woman from Rochester writes that she left her job as a technician at Eastman Kodak and remained at home with her three daughters for a dozen years; then, about three years ago, she began to be active in a local chapter of a national welfare organization, and threw herself into it so vigorously that she is now vice-president of the chapter. She explains what it means to her as follows:

Nothing can be as important in my life as my family. But I was missing something terribly vital for all these years, and never knew it. I work my

head off for the organization, and next year when I'm president I'll probably be on the phone or at my desk half of every day. But it's marvelous.
It gives me a terrific feeling of accomplishment to program a fund-raising
art show or a formal dance and really make it succeed—and then turn over
the proceeds to a truly worthy cause. It has brought me a sense of value
and pride in myself that I was missing and I am much more contented than
I have been for a long while.

For just such reasons, club and volunteer activities have a very
broad appeal, and enlist a huge number of American women. About
five million of them belong to clubs affiliated with the General
Federation of Women's Clubs, and millions of others belong to clubs
with other affiliations. Perhaps ten to fifteen million women do volunteer work for various community agencies, their contributions
ranging from bedpan duty in a hospital to masterminding a city-wide
campaign to support the local orchestra.

Yet the vast numbers mean less than they seem to; except for the
few women who achieve top rank in clubs and agencies, these activities fail to give certain crucial rewards, or to serve as adequate means
of altruistic competitiveness. Since American society accords status
and prestige primarily on the basis of paid positions which involve
skill, rank, earned income, the chance of advancement and the risk
of being fired, club and volunteer activities, lacking these characteristics, often fail to be highly valued or compelling.

Many clubwomen do little more than come to a meeting once a
month. Any woman who has been a committee head or officer of a
club will attest that except where a crisis or self-interest is directly
involved, the average club member is full of excuses when she is
asked to accept an assignment, and negligent or inert if she takes it
on. The women who wrest a full measure of satisfaction and find
thorough outlet in club activities are those who devote the kind of
time and unremitting attention to them that they would to a paying
job; and, not illogically, many of these women are today deciding
in favor of the job, and leaving the clubs to get along as best they
can.

Much the same is true of volunteer work. The ranks of the volunteers are huge, but on the average they do very little individually; officials of a major national volunteer organization estimate that the average woman volunteer works only about forty hours a year. Many volunteer duties are tedious, low-level work; while women will stuff envelopes or ring doorbells once, they quickly develop a resistance to it, and many clubs and volunteer organizations therefore have a high turnover. The wife of an architect told me that she was quite enthusiastic when she first began pushing a cigarette cart around the wards of a hospital, but that she quit after two months; by that time, her husband and children had heard all they wanted to hear about it—and she herself was finding it a bore.

The net result is that all of these various answers to the Battle of the Sexes yield a truce rather than a permanent peace. Only the rare or lucky woman can keep such a truce for a lifetime, for, as we have seen, even if she achieves balance early in her marriage, she arrives all too soon at a time when her major duties begin to fall away from her and her equilibrium is upset. At best, the roles of wife, mother, and woman of the house are not as valued or as satisfactory as those of husband, father, and man of the world; at best, the truce she achieves by one makeshift means or another is apt to be broken by this fundamental source of grievance. And this is how it apparently must be—unless, of course, there are other ways to fulfill her needs and employ her restless energies.

CHAPTER ELEVEN

THE MORE-OR-LESS

CAREER WIFE

1 THE MEANING OF WORK

Women have always been creatures of paradox, but never more so than today. At a time when they are accused of being masculine and acting like men, they have taken to three-inch spike heels, sheath skirts, green eye shadow, and other paraphernalia of impractical girlishness; in an era when they have painlessly achieved almost all the goals the feminists fought for, they seem to hold these unimportant in comparison to the search for "real femininity."

And yet there is one greater paradox: despite their seeming desire to recapture certain traditional aspects of womanliness, they have not actually lost their interest in the larger world nor ceased trying to be part of it. Few of them show any hard-driving careerism, but more wives than ever before would like to work, more actually do work both before and after rearing their children, and more work even while their children are young.

But woman's interest in work has become muted and subordinated to finding a mate and making a family life. "Young women today think much less often in terms of career *versus* marriage," says Dr. Emily Mudd, Professor of Family Study in Psychiatry at the University of Pennsylvania. "Today marriage comes first in their minds— but most of them take it for granted that they will also work during their married lives, though probably not continuously." As a result, more than half of the twenty-four million women now working part-time or full-time are wives, and seven million of these have children under eighteen. The percentage of wives who work has been increasing for decades and has doubled just since 1940; if the trend continues, in another generation or two the majority of American women will combine work and marriage throughout the larger part of their lives.

A number of single women, widows, divorcees and desertees must work to support themselves, but these are the minority; why do all the others do so? For work is pain; does not the dream of Paradise involve blessed idleness, and did not a wrathful Lord say to a sinning Adam, "In the sweat of thy face shalt thou eat bread"? Yet, oddly enough, men have also long considered work precious, health-giving, and the source of their sense of purpose; as Thomas Carlyle put it, "Work is the grand cure for all the maladies and miseries that ever beset mankind."

The inconsistency exists for good reason. A certain amount of dismal, grubbing *labor* is essential to the survival of men; it is necessary, but always disagreeable. When, however, a society manages to get this much done efficiently and so creates some leisure, its privileged classes nearly always turn to *work*. They become inventive, acquisitive, deliberative, constructive, and artistic; they exert themselves to advance their culture beyond the subsistence level; they accomplish things that have no relation to survival per se, and are thus in a sense unnecessary. An arrow flies no straighter for being decorated; men live no longer for listening to a symphony; and no one, even today, really needs to go to the moon. Men offer themselves many reasons for working—moral, artistic, creative, and so on—but underneath them all is the fact that work fills a major psychological and social need: it absorbs the supply of aggressive energy and diverts it from destructive and hostile acts into deeds and objects of value, thus at one and the same time serving the economy of society and the individual psyche.

Housewives too once enjoyed challenging and productive work along with their more tedious labors, but modern life has changed things. Except during the children's preschool years, the housewife no longer has urgent and highly valuable tasks to occupy her all day. She may fill up the vacuum by multiplying those household

chores still left to her, but this gives her little deep satisfaction; or
she may manage her homemaking efficiently enough to have leisure,
but if she fails to put it to use, it only makes her feel bored and
profoundly uneasy.

The talented and highly motivated woman feels this most keenly
and, if she does nothing but homemaking, is the most likely to
suffer from her own unused aggressive energies. A physician who is
the mother of two small girls writes: "Every normal woman wants
to go through the wonderful experience of having children and raising them. But to a person who is used to working and being mentally active, motherhood is only partially fulfilling; her very mental
health depends on her ability to combine motherhood, wifehood,
and career." An opera singer from San Francisco confides, "Being a
mother has been immensely important to me, but it would be *deadly*
to be only that. If I suddenly had to give up singing I'd be nothing.
Or at least I'd feel like nothing, and I'd probably take it out on
everyone at home." A young actress writes that she gave up her acting career when her first baby was born, and that concurrently
she and her husband began to get along rather badly and quarrel a
good deal; for a while, she even entertained thoughts about a separation. Now that her children are six and two, however, she has
again begun to do a little part-time work in television, and things
are much smoother at home. "Right now," she writes, "this year,
today, I feel good enough about myself not to have to prove that
I'm better than he is in order to feel good about myself, if you
follow me."

These examples show, in extreme form, what many middle-class
women feel about work even though they have no blazing talent or
major career goals. Where lower-class women see their jobs as *labor*
and value them for the money they yield, middle- and upper-class
women see their jobs as *work* and value them not only for the money
but the job satisfactions they afford. So said more than half a group
of young working mothers surveyed by the *Ladies' Home Journal* a
few years ago; and of the nonworking mothers in the same survey, a
considerable number admitted that they would actually be willing to

take jobs in which they would merely break even after all expenses for help, and extra taxes.

Work thus has many meanings for modern woman: it is a source of money, identity, achievement, status, personal pride, inner joy, and for many a woman, whether she realizes it or not, a means of achieving a lasting peace rather than a cease-fire within marriage. For aggressive energies can take the form of open hostility and personal competition with one's husband—but they can also take the form of generalized, impersonal competition in the world of work. A career need not mean a way for a woman to triumph over her husband, but a way to keep her marriage free of rivalry and to filter the hostilities out of her love, leaving it more nearly pure and unclouded.

2 THE TROUBLE WITH WOMEN WORKERS

But this grand desideratum will not be achieved easily and automatically. The mechanism of modern woman has many outmoded and archaic parts, and runs haltingly toward its future. A major difficulty, for instance, is woman's—and her employer's—poor opinion of her capacity. Everyone knows that aside from the occasional great women of history, the female sex has simply never amounted to much outside the home. James Cattell, an experimental psychologist, once calculated that of all persons who had ever become eminent only 3.2 percent had been women; even in our own emancipated age, only 6 percent of the celebrities in *Who's Who in America* are women. No matter that woman has had exceedingly little opportunity for achievement of the sorts recorded by history; the record stands, and convinces both sexes that she is not very good at man's kind of work.

Many beliefs and notions crystallize around this tradition. Some concern woman's physical limitations: she is frail and easily fatigued; noise, dirt, and drafts bother her unduly; she has to visit the washroom frequently; and five days per month she can't do anything right. These clichés are one part truth and nine parts nonsense, but are as tough as crabgrass; they survive all applications of disproof, including the examples of the pioneer women of our own frontier days, and the women of the Israel *kibbutzim* who work as long and hard as their men in the fields; the findings of the War Department that women war workers had no greater susceptibility to occupational diseases than men; the data of physiologists that show no significant impairment of mental or physical ability due to the menstrual cycle; and so on. A Detroit auto maker quoted in *Fortune* defends the exclusion of women from his industry with the explanation that "women aren't able to stand up to the stress and strain of the business," though the evidence all around him indicates that men, rather than women, succumb to ulcers and heart attacks. Indeed, as we saw in Chapter Two, there are genetic grounds for thinking that women might stand up to the strain of the auto business, or nearly any other, rather better than men; but what male executive could believe such a thing and still charge manfully into the fray each weekday morning?

Even more important are women's emotional defects as a worker. According to many businessmen, professionals, and college faculty members, their female colleagues are overemotional, disloyal, hypersensitive, and difficult to handle; they are easily offended in conferences or discussions, incapable of discussing differences rationally and argumentatively, and prone to take everything in a very personal fashion without even realizing it. As an old joke puts it:

HE: The trouble with women is that they always take everything so personally.
SHE: That's absurd. I never do.

Woman's emotional qualities might actually be very desirable; there is room and need in almost every human endeavor for a variety of attitudes, including an infusion of the gentler and more sensitive touch. But that is not the whole difference woman manifests in her emotional behavior at work; she has behind her thousands of years of not being accepted, and as a new arrival she is chronically unsure, touchy, and always on the lookout for offense or condescension. Once again, the analogy between woman and the Negro seems fitting.

Her uncertainties and sensitivity are, curiously enough, aggravated by the very observances of sexual manners which seem so important to her female ego. For while she wants to be spoken to and noticed as a woman, she sometimes recognizes that this helps maintain a barrier between coworkers of different sexes—and that she is on the wrong side of it. A woman public relations executive tells me that she is always secretly jealous when she hears men addressing each other with hearty, brusque directness. "I learned a long while ago," she says, "that a woman can never be really part of things in the business world. When the men pass my office in the morning, or come in to discuss something with me, it's 'Good morning, Mrs. R——, how are you today?' But then I hear them going in to each other's offices and saying in an easy, friendly, confidential way, 'Hi, Jack, how's it going?' or 'Hey, you old booze hound, let's have a few together at five today, whaddya say?' They talk to each other in a completely different way, they go out to lunch together or for cocktails after hours, or they golf together on Saturdays, and that's where they really get close and clinch the deals. I can never be in on that—I can't be their buddy, and no woman can. It took me a long while to be able to accept that."

The trouble is that women want to keep their feminine advantages, but not the concomitant disadvantages. As some wit has put it, they want to rest their foot on the bar rail without ever saying, "Next round is on me." Pamela Hansford Johnson recently wrote a testy complaint against discrimination in the literary world as exemplified by the practice of referring to "lady novelists," a term she finds condescending and courteously demeaning. But at the same time, she says that females, by accepting the male right to exclude them, retain most of those feminine privileges which she herself would hate to give up. "As a novelist," she says, "I shall always have the instinct to sit modestly and speak softly in the presence of a writing male, even if I know that his work is only one half as good as mine and that he is a blazing ass anyway. I am so conditioned. As a woman, I have not the slightest objection. As an artist, I know I am harmed by it."

The most potent part of the tradition concerning women and work is, of course, the firm belief in their mental limitations. They are thought to be generally illogical, incapable of reasoning things through, inept at handling figures and calculations, and too literal-minded to see things in broad perspectives or theoretical terms. Men formerly treated women who were attempting intellectual work with simple scorn or offered them kindly advice to tend to their knitting; today they are more tactful and less forthright, without having abandoned the same essential prejudice. Psychologists Marie Jahoda and Joan Havel, for instance, noted recently that when they began a psychological study of modern women their male colleagues treated their efforts with bantering, gentle joshing, mild amusement—or exaggerated seriousness, which signifies much the same thing. It is the way one would treat a gifted child or precocious aborigine, who is doing work that is beyond him but who is making a respectable try, all things considered. In the case of the female, men say that she is doing a wonderful job—for a woman. But if she proves to do a wonderful job for anyone, the man still has two last resorts: either he can say that her feminine traits happen to be useful in that particular situation, or he can say with admiration that she "thinks like a man"—in other words, that she is, after all, not really a woman.

Men still believe this sort of thing, and it is not altogether their fault, for women continue to play the part in which they have been cast. They are supposed to be poor at financial matters, and so they shun business, commerce and economics courses in college and avoid financial careers: only 3 percent of U.S. insurance agents, very few of Wall Street's executives, and none of the members of the New York Stock Exchange are women. It is all the more peculiar, therefore, that women handle the bills and money by themselves in 38 percent of U.S. families, and do so jointly with their husbands in another 31 percent, according to a survey made for the U.S. Treasury; apparently they are stupid about such things only when men find it disagreeable for them to be smart.*

Yet despite the survival of the tradition, the definition of femi-

* The same contradiction exists, as we saw earlier, between the abilities girls demonstrate in school and their avoidance of "unfeminine" professions; see above, pages 35, 38.

ninity is changing; like smoking, many of the skills and occupations that once seemed unfeminine are slowly becoming sexually neutral. Even though women have lost ground in some of the more demanding professions, they have been pushing into others of a technical nature for which the training is briefer, and which therefore are easier to combine with marriage. In 1910 only 1 percent of draftsmen were women, but in 1950 7 percent were; and as recently as 1940 only 3 percent of chemists and 2 percent of radio operators were women, but by 1950 the figures were 10 percent and 9 percent respectively. Women may still be considered unsuited for financial management, yet between 1940 and 1950 the number of women accountants and auditors tripled.*

Many other similar inconsistencies exist which indicate the piecemeal erosion of the traditional beliefs about woman's work abilities. There is almost no resistance, for example, to a widow's taking over her husband's business, or entering a supposedly masculine line of work; she is not thought to be aggressive or unfeminine for doing so, nor presumed to be incompetent—these conventional ideas are reserved chiefly for unmarried careerists or working wives, rather than widows. Representative Coya Knutson of Minnesota lost her fight for re-election in 1958 in large part because of the pathetic appeals her husband made for her to return home, but in Oregon in 1960 Maurine Neuberger solidly captured her late husband's seat in the U.S. Senate, a body notably tough for women to gain entry to.

The effect of the lingering tradition, however, is to make women uncertain of themselves in any but routine low-level jobs. Although it is widely believed that women executives are aggressive and hard-driving, sociologist Margaret Cussler reports in her study, *The Woman Executive,* that she found a great many more of them afraid of the stigma of unfeminine conduct, and hence not aggressive enough to push their way upward or to handle situations calling for overtly domineering qualities. The successful ones often have to make their way by personal charm, subtle manipulation, fake naïveté, and other techniques which an admirer might call "the

* Comparable figures based on the 1960 Census had not yet been released as of this writing (April, 1962).

human touch," and a detractor might call deceit. "A woman should not try to go ahead of the men at any time," a female department store executive told Dr. Cussler. "They'll only buck her and give her trouble, but if you will work with them and sort of take the attitude that he who is humble shall be exalted and so forth, you'll make out much better."

Similarly, one hears a great many complaints to the effect that women are difficult and domineering bosses, but time and again Dr. Cussler got men to name all the faults of women executives only to have them add that their own female boss was "different." The real trouble, it seems, often lies not so much in the personality of female bosses as in the lingering tradition that makes the whole idea of working for a woman unsettling to the manly male.

A choice example of this reaction was observed some years ago by sociologist William F. Whyte in the course of a study of restaurants. In one of them he found no friction between waitresses and counter-men, although in most of the others there was a great deal of it. The difference, it turned out, was that in the peaceful case waitresses wrote out slips and put them on spindles on a counter so high that few of them could see the countermen face to face; in the other restaurants, as an articulate counterman told Whyte, there was no such barrier and the girls called in their orders directly. He stressed the word "orders," and termed this "an ordeal to which no man should be subjected." Perhaps a woman *could* be president of General Motors, or United States Steel, or even the United States, if she would only remain out of sight and send her orders out via a male vice-president.

3 THE NEW COOL MOOD

There is a modicum of truth, nonetheless, in the charges that career women are aggressive, domineering, and hostile to men; historically a number of them were all of that, and even today a small number of women are anachronistic holdovers of the type. In the era of embattled feminism, when women were struggling against heavy odds to obtain wider privileges, the active fighters among them often angrily regarded man (both as an individual and as a genus) as the oppressor and the enemy. It seemed only logical to them to blow up the patriarchal marriage system at the same time that they stormed the ramparts of business and the professions. Indeed, they themselves used just such metaphors. "We mean treason," cried Victoria Woodhull, the firebrand advocate of feminism and free love, "we mean secession, and on a thousand times greater scale than was that of the South. We are plotting revolution."

Feminism thus came to be linked both with the rejection of marriage and children, and with the effort to compete against men for success, directly and on exactly equal terms. In the nineteenth century, some extremists adopted mannish behavior and clothing—George Sand, Rosa Bonheur, and Amy Lowell are the often-cited examples—and right up to the 1920's, writes Agnes Rogers in *Women Are Here to Stay*, "many women felt they must look as much as possible like men to succeed in a profession dominated by men." Women lawyers, scientists, and professors pulled their hair back tight, wore four-button man-tailored suits, and scrupulously avoided make-up, perfume, and jewelry. For some of them this pseudo-masculinity symbolized a real rejection of their own feminine biology; they shunned marriage and love because to be "possessed" by a man seemed the continuation of inferiority and subjugation. Some of these women were able to choose activities which served as a substitute for love and offered a way of sublimating their aggressions into altruism; they became humanitarians, crusaders for social reform, and the like. Others, however, in whom the supply of love had remained deficient, or whose aboriginal childish hatreds were excessive, chose activities which were socially permissible ways to compete with and conquer part of their world of imagined enemies; they became the hard-driving, relentless, ice-cold careerists.

But all that was decades ago; the dust and smoke of battle have long since blown away, the revolutionaries are old, retired, or dead, and the inheritors of their victories face the conflicts in a far different and milder form. Some observers even speak as though the older style of careerist were already extinct. "One of the striking changes that have occurred in the present century," writes an economist in the *American Journal of Orthopsychiatry,* "is the almost complete disappearance of the old-style career woman. History marked her for extermination by letting her win."

This is perhaps a trifle premature; though career women today are more likely to wear flowered hats and smart dresses than bowlers and man-tailored suits, some of them are still driving and possessed personalities whose burning desire for achievement and prestige withers and kills the possibility of normal love or home life. But the great majority of today's so-called "career girls" in our major cities are only having a brief fling before marrying and settling down, while most of the older women who work are spinsters or widows who have to do so, or married women who work for the "extras" they can buy or for the interest and variety involved in getting outside the home.

The old-style careerist's scorching ambition and hostility toward men are now passé; they have been very largely supplanted by a temporizing and peace-seeking attitude which sees no necessary conflict between work and marriage, and finds no cause for crusades or battles. With rare exceptions, today's young women regard love as the sine qua non of successful life, and marriage as their primary goal; but at the same time ever more of them also consider work valuable and important. They no longer consider marriage and career as alternatives, but as activities to be combined whenever possible, the career taking second place whenever there is conflict.

There still are many women, to be sure, who have no interest in working, but the figures cited earlier show that they are on the way to becoming the minority. This does not contradict the previous statements about woman's partial retreat from certain high-level professions. The overall number and percentage of women who work has grown greatly, but the proportion of girls who are motivated strongly enough to fight their way into high-level careers has decreased.* Publicists like to point out that in the 1960 Census for

* E.g., in 1930 women comprised 32.5 percent of college faculty members, but in 1959-60 only 22 percent.

the first time women were represented in every one of the 446 occupations listed by the Bureau; there are women blacksmiths, bank
presidents, boilermakers and sailors, among others. But these are
only minor curiosa; the important fact is that the vast growth of
female employment in the past two decades has been in clerical
work, which, with service work (waitresses, practical nurses, and the
like) and sales work, accounts for twelve million jobs, or roughly half
of all female employment. Not surprisingly, although women form
one-third of the entire United States labor force, they take home only
one-fifth of the total pay. Even though there has also been a notable
growth of professional employment, professional women by and
large lag well behind professional men in status and pay; for instance, three-fourths of all public-school teachers, but only one-fifth
of college and university teachers, are women.

In part, woman's lower level of achievement is due to resistance
on the part of employers and of institutions that offer training for
the higher-level occupations; almost all graduate schools of medicine, business, and law, for instance, have unacknowledged quotas
for women of 5 to 10 percent. These and similar discriminations
sometimes seem unbearably cruel to the dedicated and gifted woman.
I have at hand a bitter note from a young Ph.D. in English literature who says:

> I am sick and tired of the difficulties put in the way of women in all the
> more desirable vocational areas. Currently what has me steaming is that
> I've just been punished for my pregnancy by being deprived of my tenure
> at The City University. The Board of Higher Education of New York City
> has a bylaw that pregnant women may not work, and another bylaw that
> one cannot get tenure without six consecutive semesters of teaching. I am
> being forced out on maternity leave (even though my baby isn't expected
> until summer), and my five accumulated semesters of credit toward tenure
> have just disappeared. Everyone is sympathetic—but accepts the status quo.
> I'm so furious I haven't been able to do any research work for two months.

But in their own defense, the schools and employers can offer certain justifications for their actions. Few women, they say, have the
drive and interest to achieve the heights; they are willing to settle
for the easier job and the lesser accomplishment. College administrators have been claiming for a decade that the real reason they do

not hire many female instructors or professors is that they cannot find good enough ones, even though they want and need them. Moreover, they say, no matter what time and effort they invest in a female student, she will, for the sake of love or motherhood, abandon her career with bland unconcern. "You are a perfect example of why we should never admit women to a medical school," a professor of surgery told one young woman who quit medicine just after her residency to become a homemaker and mother. "You were a complete waste of our precious space and time and energy; we made a physician and you threw her away." In industry the complaint is succinctly put by an employer quoted in *Business Week:* "If she's unmarried, she gets married. If she's married, she gets pregnant. If she's divorced, she remarries." Of the young women who spend four or more years to become schoolteachers, more than two-thirds leave teaching fairly soon for homemaking; some never return, and most do so only many years later. Similarly, the majority of registered nurses, after two to four years of training, work only a few years and then disappear from the hospitals, most of them for good. The dream job for the average American girl is that of airline hostess, chic, glamorous, and on the loose; such girls draw pay while being trained, earn anywhere up to $465 a month—and drop out after an average of only 27 months in the business.

These female practices concerning work are all more or less justifiable from the woman's viewpoint, even if hard on the colleges and employers; but many women will quit their employers for unimportant and even frivolous reasons. If the boss won't grant them leave to take a midwinter trip, they simply give notice; they switch jobs because they want a change of scene; and they go out on sick leave over twice as often as male employees, not because they are more prone to sickness but because they stay home on account of minor illnesses men would ignore.

In the managerial and administrative sides of business, most young career girls today shun the appearance of real ambition or eagerness, regarding it as unfeminine, unnatural, and unwanted. Russell Lynes says that to the average young career girl today a job means a way to meet interesting people, keep amused, continue her education, and maybe make her way to Europe for a year or two—but it must not be allowed to become all-absorbing, for that might defeat the other ends. Her attitude toward participating in the creative or decision-making part of business is epitomized in a remark made by one Madison Avenue girl: "I like to sit in on meetings and just listen. It's fascinating. They don't want to hear my ideas anyway."

This lack of intensity about her work is modern woman's major adaptation to the problems and conflicts involved in combining a career with marriage and motherhood. Rather than be buffeted between them, or risk spoiling her chance at love and motherhood, she deliberately lowers her sights on achievement—and yet is more likely than ever to seek work, particularly in those periods when she is not totally occupied or satisfied by homemaking and motherhood.

And since motherhood today occupies only half or less of her adult years, the American woman's working life has recently been assuming a distinct new two-phase form. Women work until they become pregnant; then most of them quit for some years; then some of them begin part-time or full-time work again, the number increasing until in middle life even more of them work than did during their youth. The curve hits its first peak at about age nineteen (when 48 percent work), its valley at age thirty (when 35 percent work), and its second peak at fifty (when 49 percent work). This is strikingly different from all the curves of female employment prior to fifteen years ago; until then, the percentage of women who worked dwindled slowly and steadily from youth toward age.

The circumstances of modern woman's life and the complexity of her needs have produced this radical innovation, which can be called the "split career" or the "before-and-after" career. Either term, of course, stretches the meaning of the word "career" almost to the breaking point. The split career minimizes conflicts and makes the best of both worlds, but it is rarely a real career at all. Usually it means leaving a position and a life of the intellect just when one has a good grip on it, remaining at home while others forge on ahead, and then coming back fifteen or twenty years later, without rank, skill, or accomplishments; hence the degree of achievement it involves would be deeply disappointing were modern woman not so cool and nonchalant.

Many women, nevertheless, think of the split career as a fine compromise and a good kind of adjustment to reality. The executive assistant to the publisher of a major national magazine, now in her forties and the mother of one child, says, "It is utterly unrealistic to teach girls, as they do at some of better women's colleges, that they're going to go out and *be* something and make a big mark in the world. The girls graduate all starry-eyed and then find, as I did, that they're really unwanted and unwelcome; besides, they discover that they can't be something important and also have time for marriage and children. It's a slow and awful disillusionment. But *not* to train them for work, or not to teach them to plan on it, is just as bad. Women who have nothing to do from forty on except to worry about themselves and go shopping become nothing but adult delinquents."

But the split career is not really a simple or sure plan of action. For one thing, certain careers must be practiced when one is young, or later on they cannot be practiced at all; music, theater, and sports are some of the fields where this is true. For another thing, homemaking and leisure are habit forming, and after fifteen years or so a woman may feel as sluggish about going back to work as a torpid sunbather does about leaping up and flinging himself into a cold ocean. A former newswoman, now thirty-six, writes, "I could go back to work, now that our daughter is in high school, but I'm so lazy and spend so much of my free time reading that I can't seem to buckle down and recover the old ambition that made me certain I was Dorothy Thompson II. Each day I tell myself, Okay, I'll do something about it tomorrow—but tomorrow never comes." Other women can't force themselves to undertake the extended training they would need before being able to do work they would enjoy. A quite intelligent woman of thirty-nine, a former fashion model who had no college or business training, explains that she can't get anything better than a receptionist's or switchboard operator's job now, neither of which would interest her in the slightest. More than anything else, she'd like to work in the field of clinical psychology, but can't face the thought of five years of study in college, at her age, to gain a master's degree. "There isn't that much *time!*" she says in a tone of desperation. "I want to do something *now.*"

The married woman who seeks work in her late thirties or early forties is not primarily interested in putting in forty hours a week and collecting her paycheck; she wants stimulation, challenge, fulfillment, and position; to use the terms with which this chapter began, she does not want to labor, but to work. But neither industry nor the academic world is glad to see her. *Business Week,* in a nation-wide round-up on working women in 1961, reported that the married woman of thirty-five or more, frequently college-edcuated, is becoming a familiar figure in placement agencies and personnel offices, but that more often than not industry turns her down or offers her only low-level clerical work that she doesn't want.

Some educators argue that for this very reason general liberal education for college girls should be replaced by specialized occupational training so that they won't be mere beginners at thirty-five or forty. But the specialized woman who has not worked for ten or twenty years has forgotten a great deal, is out of practice, and is simply not a good prospect for any employer at the job level she wants. Marion Sanders, writing on this very problem in *Harper's,* cites the case of a friend of hers, a college graduate with a social-work degree, who was having trouble getting back into her field. The family agency to which she first applied told her to go back to school first. "They were quite right," she admitted. "My M.A. has been in mothballs for eleven years and I wouldn't dare face a client [i.e., a case-work subject] all alone. I'm really unemployable without a refresher course, and there don't seem to be any."

It is much the same in the academic world. A woman who graduated from Vassar with honors twenty years ago recently wrote to the school's president, Sarah Blanding, to state her problem:

I once hoped to teach history at the college level and, foolish as it may seem, that is again my dream [but] everywhere I turn it is forced upon me that my Phi Beta Kappa key must have tarnished and my diploma grown moldy. There are of course no college jobs or even secondary school jobs for elderly holders of A.B. degrees. The universities aren't enthusiastic about doddering graduate students of forty-one. I will shave my ambitions to reality and prepare for teaching at the secondary school level, although I yearn for "the company of scholars." I hope that my two daughters will not have to settle for less than their potentialities.

In fields other than the humanities, the difficulties are still greater: a physicist, chemist, or mathematician who has neither worked nor kept abreast of new developments for fifteen or twenty years finds herself, when she tries to re-enter her field, a kind of intellectual Rip Van Winkle, her skills rusted and her information hopelessly out of date.

There are signs that the schools are beginning to recognize the need of these women for a way to renew their skills and update their knowledge. Radcliffe, Mount Holyoke, Douglas, Smith, and Sarah Lawrence colleges, and the Universities of Wisconsin, Kansas City, and Minnesota have all started or soon will start experimental programs of postgraduate education for married women who need help in order to make the split-career plan work. But so far these are only token or pilot-stage efforts. As for industry, it has shown little willingness to set up special training programs for the intelligent but fortyish woman who would like a late-blooming, but important, occupation.

The cool mood and the split career are thus a major answer, but not one that can satisfy all intelligent or talented women. It is quite satisfactory for those who want to stay at home for a decade or two and are content to do part-time or low-level work afterward; moreover, it works well for at least one kind of professional—the public-school teacher, for whom the return to part-time work in her latter thirties, and to full-time teaching later on, is feasible. But women without college degrees, or those who do not want to teach in a public school, may not find it a good answer at all, and may prefer community activities at a high level to jobs at a low level. Nor will the split career satisfy that minority of women who, although they

very much want a normal family life, have a powerful career drive
that makes them feel trapped and harmed by full-time homemaking;
for such women, there is no easy or pat answer, though a difficult
one is now being found by a growing contingent of dogged pioneers.
Let us see what it is and how well it works.

4 THE CAREER WOMAN, NEW STYLE

The answer that is more difficult than the split career, but more
capable of fulfilling all the life aims of the talented and career-
minded woman, is the combination of marriage and motherhood
with a continuing, lifelong career in which the interruptions for
childbearing and infant rearing are reduced to a kind of sabbatical
of one to several years, bridged over by continued reading, studying,
and professional contacts. And not only does this offer personal fulfillment to a growing number of middle-class women, but it prom-
ises to help alleviate the nation's serious shortages of highly trained
professional personnel.

Most neo-traditionalists are certain that any such combination of
roles is harmful to the womanly functions, and will dry up a wife's
femininity, damage her husband's masculinity, deprive her children
of proper mother love, make her resent the demands of her family or
make her guilty and oversolicitous, and inevitably turn her into a
vicious, neurotic, unloving monster.

This portrait, however, is not the likeness of today's career wives,
but of part of the earlier generation of feminists and career women.
Some of those bristling, driven women did marry, only to engage in
lifelong guerrilla warfare with their husbands, their children, and
themselves. The new-style career woman is a different breed; though
she is more bent on achievement than the split-career woman, she
inherited the gains of feminism painlessly, and is accordingly less
hostile and less personally aggressive. She uses her drives in a general and diffused fashion, rather than in the form of highly individual competitiveness; this permits her to place a high value on
her marriage, to succeed in her womanly functions, and yet to enjoy

the satisfactions of a career—even if it is interrupted and somewhat hindered.

This combination of roles is difficult, complicated and trying; indeed, it is almost impossible for a woman with several children, unless she has money to spare and access to highly qualified help. And even with these aids, some women find it simply too fatiguing to carry on a career at a time when they want to give a great deal of themselves to their children. Yet for other women of talent, ambition, and energy the combination of roles is proving to be less difficult than any simpler alternative. Such women feel that work has great meaning and that the strain of combining it with home life is worth enduring. "It is not easy to be a devoted wife and mother and a first-class artist," writes Agnes de Mille, herself all three of these things, "[but] it is impossible to be a good wife or a wise mother, embittered, balked, and devoured by inner energies." In her book *And Promenade Home,* Miss de Mille says that during the war she daydreamed that when her husband came home she would quit the theater in favor of normal home life—yet in her heart she knew she really intended to do nothing of the kind. "I wanted wifehood, motherhood, and work," she says. "I had drunk the Milk of Paradise. . . . I could not think to give this up. I could forfeit my life, and my comfort, riches, and convenience, for love—but not the magic release of work! This was my identity."

Miss de Mille is, to be sure, an extraordinarily talented human being. Most of the women currently making a go of the wife-mother-careerist combination lack her gifts, and wisely content themselves with a limited amount of success. Marriage and motherhood make a top-level career all but impossible, particularly for people of less than dazzling endowments; yet new-style career women do not therefore choose spinsterhood or infertility in order to advance their careers, but prefer a whole way of life, even though it means a somewhat restricted achievement in their work.

Many careful students of American family life feel that in this direction lies one of the major solutions to the conflicts and role confusion of American women. Professor Mirra Komarovsky advocates a plan of schooling and work, with a brief retirement to the home during the children's babyhood, an early return to part-time work and later the resumption of full-time work; and Ray Baber, Clifford Kirkpatrick, and a number of other sociologists have come to the conclusion that marriage and motherhood, plus part-time work (rather than a lengthy split in the work history), would satisfy the desires and resolve the role conflicts of a great many modern women.

Though relatively few American women have gone all-out for such a life, millions of them are already moving toward it. The gap in the split-career pattern is gradually narrowing; currently almost three million wives stop working for only a brief time during and after pregnancy, although four out of five of these work only part-time as long as their children are preschoolers. Formerly this was true only of laboring-class women, but the Census category "Professional, technical and kindred workers, female," which nearly doubled in size between 1940 and 1960 and stands now at nearly three million, includes 352,000 women who are married and have children under six years of age.

Not very many of them will admit, except in confidential or anonymous interviews, what their motives are. Nearly all of them say they are working primarily for the money, so as to help support their families or raise their living standard, and at the lower economic and job levels this is probably true. Elsewhere, however, it is camouflage. The report of the National Manpower Council's 1957 conference on womanpower states that after reviewing the evidence, the conferees generally agreed that the reasons many women give for working are remote from the real ones, and that they are reluctant to admit motives other than those their social group approves of.

The woman who works although she does not need the money is a thorn in the flesh of her friends. As Pearl Buck puts it, "If she tries tentatively to do something a little more serious than her fellows are doing they cry at her, 'My dear, aren't you *wonderful!*' meaning, 'Why on earth do you do it?' meaning, 'Aren't you queer!'

meaning, 'You think you're smart!'" And so she hedges about her reasons; nine out of ten working young mothers in the *Ladies' Home Journal* survey claimed that finances were the major reason they worked, but in response to a later question, 58 percent gave themselves away by admitting that they would rather work than stay home full-time. In a broader survey, the Survey Research Center of the University of Michigan found that three-quarters of all working women said they would continue working even if they inherited enough money to live comfortably. Work, in other words, is not a burden the modern woman shoulders unwillingly, but a privileged activity that she undertakes with pride.

The chief impediments in her way are, as I have said, her own guilt feelings, and social disapproval, both of which stem from her violation of the classic mother image. In severe cases, the warfare of her own emotions can, of itself, make her seriously ill and block her from succeeding in any of her functions. A woman novelist has described in a medical magazine her own experience of such inner conflict. When her baby girl was born, she confidently put a full-time nurse in charge of her in order to continue writing, but as the months passed, she slowly grew both guilt-ridden and terribly jealous of the nurse—and at the same time terrified that the nurse might leave. She suffered a series of crippling gall-bladder attacks, and for over a year could do little writing and less mothering. Finally the doctor ordered her to let the baby nurse go and take over the whole job herself. She did so fearfully, but soon found her whole being much more tranquil, despite her ignorance of child-care technique; gradually the gall-bladder attacks began to diminish, and in a while she found herself able to do at least as much writing on a part-time basis (while a college student took charge of the child) as she had in her pain-filled former freedom. Her doctor informed her at this point that she had pulled through without surgery, and, moreover, that she had pulled through without unduly damaging either side of her life.

Some women, unfortunately, are too severely plagued by guilt feelings to achieve equilibrium in this kind of compromise. A gifted advertising woman of my acquaintance has oscillated between home and part-time work for years; she will work for a while, slowly building up guilt and worry until she breaks off and flings herself into domesticity with a sense of discovery and relief; then, after several months, she begins to grow uneasy, morbid, and self-deprecating, until, with her husband's encouragement, she timidly but hopefully ventures forth again to try to find a modus vivendi.

Such women have, to their own harm, accepted the neo-traditional claim that a woman who works, except in case of dire need, is betraying a neurotic personality, the rejection of her own femininity, and a disastrous lack of love for her children. But many of the observations on which these charges are based date from the ebb tide of the feminist era, and have been contradicted by broader and more recent studies. It has been said again and again, for instance, that the working mother is tense, rejecting, and unloving toward her children, but sociologist Lois Hoffman of the University of Michigan studied eighty-eight working mothers and eighty-eight comparable nonworking ones, and found that, on the whole, the working mothers were warmer toward their children, more helpful, milder as disciplinarians, and more supportive. Again, it has often been said that working mothers are maladjusted and neurotic, but sociologist F. Ivan Nye has reported that mothers of adolescents who work part-time prove to have better psychological adjustment than those who work full-time—or than those who do not work at all. A generation ago, certain studies indicated that working mothers were more likely to produce problem children and juvenile delinquents than were nonworking mothers, but more recently the Detroit Police Department and social scientists of Wayne University analyzed twenty thousand cases of juvenile delinquency and found that the percentage of those with working mothers is *lower* than it is in the population at large.

Dr. Lois M. Stolz, a psychologist at Stanford University, last year completed a thorough review and evaluation of the existing research on this subject, and concluded that many of the contradictions in the findings were more apparent than real; if only data gathered since World War II are considered, and the factors of money, social background, and size of family are carefully kept in mind while making comparisons, there is no statistically significant relation between maternal employment and delinquency, adolescent adjustment, school marks in high school, or dependent-independent behavior of preschool children. Dr. Stolz cautiously concluded that "it looks as if the fact of the mother being employed or staying at home is not such an important factor in determining the behavior of the child as we have been led to think."

What does seem an important factor, however, is the woman's overall attitude toward *both* her work and her children. A distraught and frustrated woman can forgo work, but treat her children the worse for it; a happy woman may work, and mother her children excellently even in a limited amount of time. Dr. Lauretta Bender, formerly senior child psychiatrist at Bellevue Hospital in New York, says that it is not the quantity of maternal attention that matters but its quality, not workaday absences that do harm but the lack of love. Elizabeth Herzog of the Children's Bureau states, "There is a strong and growing conviction among psychiatrists and social workers that some women are better mothers if their mothering activities are part time rather than full time; and that their children may suffer adverse effects if the mother is constrained *not* to work."

A young woman who went to college and had dreams of a literary career writes that after she gave up her aspirations to concentrate on her three children, she found herself becoming dejected, exhausted, angry, and full of aches, pains, and obscure ailments. After her doctor had seen altogether too much of her, he firmly directed her to get herself a job. She found a part-time position as a hotel cashier; though it is a long way below her former daydreams, and though occasionally she feels guilty and defensive about leaving her children with a baby sitter, she believes that it has made her a warmer, more relaxed mother and homemaker. "If I can spend a few hours away from the children," she explains, "I can enjoy them and allow them to enjoy me for the rest of the day. If I can find time to write this, then I don't resent the pile of ironing. If somehow for a few hours each week I can have the sense of participation in the adult world . . . my house is a home instead of the place I once dubbed my 'chintz prison.' "

Besides the potential conflict between work and motherhood, the new-style career woman faces possible difficulties in her relationship with her husband. Traditionalist men detested the old-style career woman half a century ago, and today dislike even the new, milder variety. "I've never known a successful career woman who was a *real* woman," one businessman told me, "or whose husband wasn't either a zero or a hanger-on." Without being nearly that hard-shelled, many another man still interprets his wife's career as a form of personal hostility, and her success as his own defeat, though she means them to be nothing of the sort.

A noted Broadway actress confides that for nearly all the sixteen years of her marriage, her husband—a television producer—has disliked her acting and rarely been willing even to congratulate her in her moments of triumph. "It's been absolutely heartbreaking," she says. "Why on earth did he fall in love with me in the first place, if he didn't like what I am? I've never understood it. Well, thank God, he has really come into his own in the last few years, and he's beginning to like and respect my work. I don't think I've gotten better—I think he just isn't embarrassed any more to have me the celebrity, and himself the man they mistakenly call by my name."

For similar reasons, a number of career wives find it wise to modulate their manner from office to home. An interior decorator whose husband is a dynamic, fast-talking plastics salesman says, "My career doesn't make any trouble because at home I always let him be the live wire. I like it that way—it's the way we were when we first met. At the office I have to talk up, take charge of things, and deal authoritatively with suppliers and contractors, but when I come home I switch over. By day I'm a businesswoman, but at home I'm my husband's wife."

Somewhat trickier to handle is the fact that scores of nontraditional decisions must be made in such a family as to who does what. If husband and wife both have important evening meetings and the baby sitter has the grippe, which one will have to come home? If both have had an exhausting day, which one will put the children to bed, leaving the other to do the dishes? If both have brief cases full of weekend work to be done, which one will get up Saturday morning and shop, and which one will get the house ready for company? Some husbands find the sharing of household chores or child care unmanly, degrading, and demeaning; at the opposite pole, a few weak and dependent men seem actually to like taking over the traditionally feminine tasks; and the median, well-adjusted men take it all in masculine stride, regarding them simply as jobs to be done, and neither detestable nor delightful. If such a man has any complaint, it is only that the duties press upon his and her time; as one such man told his wife with wry humor, "What both of us need is a good wife."

Obviously, if a man's image of himself is that of the leonine but gentle *pater familias,* dozing at his ease, occasionally brushing aside his noisy cubs with a flick of his mighty paw, coming to dinner when it is ready for him and going off afterward as he pleases, he is bound to present insurmountable problems to a career woman; either her career or their union will be torn to pieces between his vision of marriage and her opposing one. But what may be equally painful is the situation in which both husband and wife favor her having a career until his future and hers suddenly call them in opposite directions. If a man's wife has spent five years building up her own travel agency, say, or her medical practice, the evening on which her husband comes home with news of a marvelous promotion to a key spot halfway across the country is apt to be both memorable and horrible. As things stand today, in such a dilemma it is usually the woman who must yield, and gamely try to start all over again in the new city. Her career is tailored more to her husband's needs than her own; the result is not a perfect fit, but at least it is wearable and comforting.

In the earlier decades of female careerism, when women often were driven by sharper, more personal hostilities than now, these several sources of conflict had a malign effect on marriage, and psychologist Katharine Davis, in a classic study of 2,200 women published in 1929, found that working wives were, on the average, less happy in their marriages than nonworking ones. But more than a generation has passed since then, and the changing pattern has already shown up in survey statistics: Locke, in 1951, and Blood, in 1960, both reported that working women were just as happy in their marriages as nonworking ones, and the consensus of other recent studies is that the wife's career is not, of itself, the cause of marital conflict, but only a peg on which conflict can be hung. Some authorities go still further: from her series of cases, Professor Komarovsky concluded that certain emotionally secure and normally masculine men accept and take genuine pride in their wives' accomplishments, and that adjustment in these marriages seems distinctly better than average.

For the present, the combination of career, wifehood, and motherhood requires an unusually favorable combination of circumstances and attitudes—all those that I have just mentioned, plus a tolerant social milieu, nearby employment opportunities, and, above all, competent available hands (hired, familial, or community-provided) to assist the career wife with some of the homemaking or child rearing, or both. Even so, the career wife and her husband will have half a dozen or more years during which their way of life will call for the scheduling talent of an efficiency expert, the tactical flexibility of an infantry platoon leader, and the stamina of an Alpine guide.

A typical specimen of such a life is that of young Mr. and Mrs. Pritchard (as I shall call them), both of whom hold Ph.D.'s and teach at a fine Eastern college; he is an associate professor of history, she an instructor in English. They have two children, a girl of three and a boy of a year and a half, which means that there are no hours of the day when the household can lie at anchor; some hand must always be at the tiller. At their college, to be sure, each staff member teaches only three days a week, but this does not make things as simple as one would expect; the in-between days are solidly filled with preparing lectures, reading papers, advising students on theses, attending to other college duties, and, when they can, doing research of their own.

To run this relatively small household and their two careers therefore takes close and effective planning. Mrs. Pritchard relies heavily on prepared and frozen foods, electrical gadgets, and short cuts of every sort to keep her housework and cooking to a minimum. A baby sitter arrives each morning as the Pritchards and their children are getting through breakfast and takes over for half a day, and a cleaning woman comes in two afternoons a week; in addition, other baby sitters come in certain evenings when the Pritchards are going out to a lecture or some college event. Most days, both Pritchards devote the latter end of the afternoon to their children, to puttering around the house and garden, and to getting dinner and seeing the children to bed.

They rarely give cocktail parties or go to them because they simply can't. "Our social life," Mrs. Pritchard observes dryly, "is curiously 'efficient,' even disciplined." Of necessity, their entertaining is simple and limited; they have people in to dinner once a week, and Mrs. Pritchard does all the work herself. For the most part, they try to preserve their evenings for work and for household duties. The remaining unfinished chores, correspondence, bill paying, and shopping must be crammed in at odd hours and quiet moments, when both children are napping. In so tight a schedule, many minor pleasures—particularly if they are time-consuming—must be sacrificed for the good of the major ones; both Pritchards, for instance, like chess and playing the recorder, but have given them up for the present and the foreseeable future.

At best, such a way of life is only possible with good help, and is only as stable as the help allows it to be. Let the regular morning woman fall ill or be delayed by snow, the cleaning woman move away, or both children get the mumps, and the beautiful machinery creaks ominously and threatens to grind to a complete halt. But by

heroic measures the Pritchards somehow always keep it going. The
question to be asked, of course, is whether it is all worth it. Even
if Mrs. Pritchard's job meant increased income (which it doesn't,
since nearly all of her salary goes to pay the help and other costs),
it would not seem worthwhile to many other women. But to her it
definitely does; he and she both lead a life of the intellect, stimulated
by their work, their colleagues, their students—and each other. Like
many an upperbrow, Mrs. Pritchard is reserved in her statements
about the net satisfaction of her way of life; she says, simply, "We
both work most of the time, my husband and I. Yet we love our
work—our work is also our hobby." But neither she nor her husband would change their way of life for any other they know of.

As busy and complicated as such a pattern of living is, a full-time
nine-to-five job for the woman would involve even greater strains
and complexities, and most contemporary career women therefore
settle for part-time work when their children are small. Teaching
in the public schools is particularly popular with college graduate
women for the very reason that it allows either part-time work (as a
substitute) or "full-time" work ending by 3 or 4 P.M. Women who
are free-lance artists and writers, or self-employed professionals (such
as doctors and architects) can limit their own hours, though it takes
strength of character to do so. At the lower job levels, too, there is
a slowly increasing market for part-time workers of many sorts. The
structure of the career wife's life is, in sum, not ready-made, but
materials are at hand if she wants to assemble them.

And if her career is a matter of choice rather than hard economic
necessity, the working wife is apt to treasure it despite its rigors,
and to consider that it has made her entire life far richer. This is
how one very articulate scholar, devoted wife, and mother of three
children explains it in words that might almost have been borrowed
from some neo-platonizing Renaissance lady:

All too many women in our culture still view their lives as a series of
pieces, and live them that way—first a period of this, then of that, never a
complete or rounded life. I'd like to see more emphasis on the whole
human being, an integrated, developing organism from cradle to grave,

changing her emphasis from time to time but keeping every aspect of herself functioning as fully as possible. I've tried to live that way, because I feel that all potentialities of every individual should be lived out to the fullest extent. Bill and I needed years to work out all the subtleties involved in this. There were many times when we were mad at each other and tried to hurt each other, but we have learned how to really live and work together in what has become a wonderful amalgam of our lives, rather than just a jigsaw puzzle. Love, I have slowly come to feel over a twenty-year period, is a lot better and more encompassing than I ever realized, even though I had some pretty large notions about it when I was young. And I think that developing the ability to love and express love in all its ramifications and with all one's capacities is the finest end to which men and women can direct their lives.

But how do the husbands feel about it? Many ways, of course, ranging from the truculence of the threatened male to the fatuous pride of the nonentity who basks in his wife's glory. But these are peripheral species; more usually the husband of the new-style career woman seems to accept her career because it is one expression of the particular human being he fell in love with, and an essential part of the wife whom he finds sometimes difficult but more often delightful, occasionally exasperating but continuously interesting. Such a man, in an unusually communicative mood, explained his attitude to me recently in these candid words:

I didn't meet Rosalie until I was twenty-eight, and had been running around a lot, all through law school and after. I'd known plenty of girls, some nice and some not so nice, and had even been more or less engaged a couple of times, but I always had the feeling they were trying to *land* me, one way or another, and I wriggled off the hook each time in a cold sweat. Then I went off to Fire Island one summer weekend and saw this tall good-looking blonde on the beach, studying Anderson's textbook of pathology, of all things. It amused the hell out of me. She was pretty cool at first, but I was persistent in a nice sort of way. She told me, finally, that she was a medical student, and it didn't take me long to realize that she wasn't just playing at it either. Her Dad was a fine orthopedist, and she was really bent on becoming one also. She was the first girl I'd ever met who had some goal in mind besides finding a guy. What struck me about her wasn't just that she and I had so very much to talk about—we did, of course—but that she was such a good-looking girl outside and so much of a *person* inside. It just bowled me over. I had never felt that way about the girls I had known, or been so proud when they liked me.

Anyway, it didn't take us very long to know that we were right for each other. We got married that winter. My practice was growing fast and I could have afforded a nice place, but in order to save her travel time I moved in with her into her little dormitory room. For a year and a half, I'd come back to that little place after a long day in court, take her out for a quick dinner, and then help her study until late at night, or help her relax sometimes by telling her stories about my cases, or hobnobbing with the other med students. I got to be the best midnight scrambled-egg cook on an illegal electric burner that you ever heard of. It was a grind, but I really loved the whole atmosphere—it was almost like being on some kind of wartime mission.

Then she graduated and became an intern, and we set up a nice apartment near the hospital where she could come in her off-duty time. After a year of internship and several of residency she went into practice, and four years later we had our first boy, and three years later our younger one. I guess it's *always* been somewhat like a wartime mission—a busy, urgent kind of life, with servants coming and going, kids getting sick and then well again, me having an important evening conference just when she has an emergency operation during the maid's night off, and all that. There have been periods when for days at a time we met each other only in bed. There were times during her residency when I thought that if her phone rang once more at night at just the wrong moment, I'd rip the goddamned thing off the wall and throw it out the window. And nowadays she often worries because she can't spend more time with the kids, but they're turning out to be wonderful boys and I don't think they could possibly love her any more, even if she did.

There *are* times when I think how much simpler it all was for my father—he would just come home and take his ease, and let everybody fuss over him. He was the one who counted, and everything was arranged to suit him. Sometimes I wish it were that way with me. But then Rosalie and I go out to dinner and I see people our own age sitting opposite each other but staring around sideways or looking at their food, and not having anything at all to say to each other. *We're* still like each other's dates—after eighteen years. We always find each other interesting, and it's amazing to see how she really looks especially pretty and full of bounce after she's just pulled off a tricky operation and is still all excited and pleased by it even though she's really dead-tired. I can't be sure how all this would have worked out if I weren't pretty successful in my own field, but I am. She has great respect for what I do and she has even come to court a few times to hear me. She's very much a woman with me, but once in a while, if she tries to take over a little too much, I call her "Doctor" very respectfully, and she gets nettled for a minute, and then laughs and turns it off.

I don't know how things are with other men and their wives—nobody ever *really* knows about anybody else, do they?—but as for myself, I wouldn't want it any way but this. It isn't ever simple, and sometimes things are pretty rough, but all in all it's a damned sight more satisfying to me than any other kind of life I could have had.

CONCLUSION

What will make a woman happy? The answers range from the vulgar to the sublime, and include a multitude of possible roles and functions; indeed, to some present-day critics it seems that woman's major problem lies precisely in this variety of possibilities, and in the temptation to sample them all. They sternly urge her instead to narrow her choices, pare away the unessential and the new-fangled, and recapture simplicity; only thus will she find genuine contentment.

This, of course, is a classic approach to the problems brought about by social change. In nearly every sophisticated age, when civilized men grow weary or bewildered they frequently fall to thinking that the secret of ultimate happiness must lie in the peasant or animal way of life, geared to the sun, the weather, and the body's biological functions, and innocent of possessions, ambitions, and pride. As Walt Whitman put it:

I think I could turn and live with animals, they're so placid and self-
    contain'd,
I stand and look at them long and long.

They do not sweat and whine about their condition,
They do not lie awake in the dark and weep for their sins . . .
Not one is dissatisfied, not one is demented with the mania of owning
    things. . . .
Not one is respectable or unhappy over the whole earth.

Philosophers have long argued for and against this viewpoint, irrationalists like Rousseau claiming that the noble savage was a better and happier man than the civilized one, and rationalists like John Stuart Mill replying that mere contentment is no criterion of happiness, and that it is better to be a human being dissatisfied than a pig satisfied. One can still enjoy such a debate, but its very terms have been made somewhat archaic; contemporary social scientists have made controlled observations of the emotional state of groups of people under varying conditions, and found that happiness is less the product of any given condition of life than of the expectations and aims of the person in that condition. In an important wartime study of soldier morale, for instance, a team of sociologists led by Dr. Samuel Stouffer of Harvard found, among other things, that northern Negro soldiers stationed in southern Army camps generally made a surprisingly good adjustment and manifested better morale than they did up North; the reason, it appeared, was that they compared themselves to the southern Negroes all around them, and felt so much better off as to be relatively happy. People, in other words, are happier or unhappier according to how far they have succeeded in being like their "reference group"—the people to whom they have learned, or feel the right, to compare themselves.

A century ago, most primitives and peoples in underdeveloped societies neither admired the ways of white man nor were dissatisfied with their own. But with prolonged contact and the gradual absorption of technological knowledge, these same people have begun to envision themselves living like Western man; recently, therefore, we have been witnessing that astounding "revolution of rising expectations" in which the impoverished decide that they have not been so happy after all, and start making vigorous and radical efforts to abandon their ancient ways for those of industrialized societies. In moments of nostalgia, we can wish they had never lost their old tranquillity and quaintness, but in good conscience we cannot really wish them the continuance of disease, hunger, poverty, and a thirty-five-year life expectancy; the only decent feeling is the wish that all human beings should have as healthful, as fulfilling, and as good a life as human intelligence can make possible.

The sociological principle of the reference group applies also to woman and her ways of life. Some generations ago, most women in remote polygamous cultures found the thought of monogamy disgusting or even funny, but as they have come to consider more developed cultures preferable to their own, they have begun favoring monogamous marriage and even harboring notions of romantic love. At the same time, having learned about vacuum cleaners, gas stoves, anesthesia, and antibiotics, and ceased to regard these as suitable only for their rulers or for foreigners, they desire them and will not believe anyone who assures them they are happier with their twig brooms, wood fires, childbirth agonies, and early death.

So it is, in a more specialized way, with modern American woman. For a score of social and economic reasons, her reference group today is not, and cannot be, women of the frontier or the Victorian era. She is educated alongside man, is legally and intellectually capable of doing most of what he does, and therefore develops most of the same social values. Yet at the same time she is as much repelled as she is attracted by the image of the highly successful, glamorous career woman with no home life, or a tenuous or broken one; and though she sometimes envies the idle wife of the rich man, the childless glamour-girl wife of the older man, or the self-indulgent kept woman, she finds all their lives impossible to consider for herself in a serious way. Her trouble is that her principal reference group consists of men, and the attempt to sell her some other model—some one-dimensional female pattern that worked in the past—conflicts with the realities of her situation and her civilization. Such models still work for some women, to be sure; but increasingly woman's better chance at happiness lies in the pioneering and venturesome effort to construct for herself a complex way of life from among the manifold roles and activities available to her.

As opposed to all those who plead for narrow and simple answers, certain careful and realistic analysts of woman's life urge the acceptance of complexity. As sociologist Ruth Hill Useem writes, "I think the question needs to be turned inside out—not how can we relieve the pressures on today's college girls and women, but how can they be socialized to live with existing pressures? For I do not see how these are likely to be decreased." Margaret Mead has pithily remarked that the problem will not be solved by a return to "naturalness," but by an increase in "unnaturalness"—that is, the elaboration of new and more sophisticated relationships suitable to the present era.

Today's complex woman is often harried and fretful about the complications of her way of life and its potential difficulties; the simple woman is not. Yet, Walt Whitman notwithstanding, the simplicity of one's life is not a good index of happiness, at least not in the modern environment. Most married women obviously lead a more complicated life than single women, yet they are generally happier, according to a large-scale mental-health survey by the Michigan Survey Research Center published in 1960. Similarly, many other surveys show the complex woman to be, on the average, happier than the unmarried careerist, the divorced woman, or the traditional homebody, all of whose patterns of life have fewer roles or role conflicts.*

But since successful marriage is, beyond question, more highly valued by American women than any other single goal in life, let us now use that as a touchstone by which to test the merits of the multi-role pattern of femininity. Throughout this book I have drawn upon the major studies of marital success or failure made by Hamilton, Locke, Burgess, Terman, Blood, and many others; in these studies, there are persistent correlations between marital happiness and such factors as an approximate balance of power between husband and wife, approximate equality of education, sexual and emotional sensitivity and empathy, intimacy of association and closeness of companionship, joint participation in outside interests, the sharing of friends, a more-or-less-equal enjoyment of love-making, the rating of self as equal to, rather than superior to, one's mate, a high level of communication and understanding, and many more. Please note that each of these factors associated with greater marital

---

* And similarly, the complex mother is almost certainly happier than the simpler childless woman, although as we saw on page 184, the survey data on this are inconsistent and inconclusive.

happiness is also associated with subtle, flexible definitions of male-female roles, with an increased complexity of the female personality and the marital relationship, and with a general movement away from the well-defined, specialized woman toward the not yet clearly defined all-purpose woman. The women on whom these findings are based were far from being the end product of this development, but they already show the way; it is for women of the present and the next generation to travel further along the route.

Those who argue against the concept of the many-sided woman often say that her complicated desires and activities produce marital quarrels, needless hostilities, and open rivalry with her husband. Actually, the very opposite seems to be true nowadays. To judge by separation and divorce rates, the destructive quarreling and bickering that often lead to marital breakdown are far more frequent among the lower classes and the less-educated, whose women are still cast in the classic mold, than among the upper and educated classes, most of whose women have evolved part way toward the new and multi-sided pattern. Moreover, as we saw in the previous two chapters, an analysis of the sources of rivalry and its sublimation in constructive activities indicates plainly enough why man, as he becomes acclimated to today's changing sexual roles, may find many-sided woman the least hostile and the most loving kind of wife.

Yet there *are* home-loving women who are neither immature nor unduly hostile, and who find the domestic, maternal, and wifely pattern of life good, deeply satisfying, and quite sufficient. Such women are apt to get indignant at any presentation of the case for the many-sided woman. "Let me alone!" writes one of them in anger. "What are you trying to do—make me feel guilty that I am a contented cow? Well, that's what I am, and I defy anybody to tell me I would be happier rushing around, doing a hundred idiotic things I don't care about, when what I really adore is staying in my lovely home with my beautiful children, and being a woman—*all* woman." No; no one should try to make you guilty, or to change you; if you are happy, and your husband loves you as you are and is contented with you, it would be both a cruel and foolish effort. But your sort of answer, though it may still work for you, is becoming obsolescent; for an increasing number of intelligent women it will mean more frustration, potential boredom, and risk to marriage than the more intricate and many-sided ways of life that are now available.

For modern society is vast, swift-changed, and friendless, and each of us, to use Riesman's familiar term, is a member of a lonely crowd. Families, group loyalties, personal friendships, all are far weaker and less emotionally reassuring than they used to be in smaller, more stable societies. The love of man for woman and the ties of marriage therefore have an emotional importance today far greater than in the ages when love was more a delightful game, and marriage primarily an economic partnership. Only in each other can a man and woman today find (and hope always to find) all the many traits each of them needs in another human being—the opposite and yet the likeness of oneself; the lover and the friend; the parent and the child; the assistant and the adviser; the sober ally and the playmate. And for this nearly total interaction of the selves to take place, man and woman must be of generally equal stature and inner completeness—not identical with each other, but complementary in all possible aspects of the being, not deprived of distinctive masculinity and femininity, but distinctively masculine and feminine in every facet of their personalities.

But can things really develop in this fashion? If woman's life is presently marked by abrupt discontinuities, conflicts, and inner uncertainties—to say nothing of suburban isolation and the maid shortage —is it reasonable to suppose that she will continue to evolve toward the more complicated way of life and at the same time find it more satisfying? I believe it *is* reasonable; these suppositions are conservatively based on the totality of circumstances of woman's life today, and on the overall directions of change of the past century or two. The evolution of the complex woman may proceed faster or slower than any specific guess I might hazard, and it may wobble a trifle or veer to one side or the other for a decade at a time; but in larger perspective there is a grand logic and progression to the history of woman that seems sure to surmount cultural obstacles, and to produce solutions to her merely mechanical problems.

Many factors exist today which will aid the progress of this evolution. For one thing, the present crop of small girls more than ever includes daughters of mothers who have important activities, or paid employment, outside the home; these girls are absorbing not the conventional image of woman from their mothers, but a rather more complicated one. They are therefore learning to envision femininity and themselves in terms that include but go beyond household and mothering roles; as young women, they will probably be less pulled to and fro by seemingly irreconcilable alternatives, and more capable of planning to combine them and of actually doing so without psychological distress.

The schools, too, are having a similar influence today. Two generations ago, most female schoolteachers were spinsters; today, most are married women, two-thirds of whom have children. As important models of the female adult, they typify for schoolgirls one way in which a woman can pursue an intellectual vocation without losing any of her essential femininity. Still more important, perhaps, is the change in public education since Sputnik I was shot into orbit in 1957. This startling event touched off a series of curriculum reforms and a general shift in favor of educational achievement rather than mere social adjustment; excellence has once again become fashionable. Inevitably, this will influence girls as well as boys, reinforcing in them their interest in a life that includes mental activity and vocational achievement.

The schools are, moreover, beginning to help offset the negative factor of early marriage, which prematurely defines and sharply limits the woman's role. Teen-age marriage in particular often irrevocably freezes the personality when it has only begun to expand and to sense its own possibilities. It is not surprising that such marriages have an extremely high rate of maladjustment and divorce, part of which is surely due to the dissatisfactions which the narrow and stereotyped role fairly soon generates in the girl. A certain number of high schools (including all of those in California) have already set up courses in marital problems which are serving to educate the young in the weaknesses of teen-age marriage and in the realities of married life. Such education should help teen-age boys and girls decide in favor of dates and continuing education or employment, postponing plans for marriage until they have genuinely discovered themselves. The extension of such training to many more high schools and to clubs and churches can be expected, and is surely to be encouraged.

Even so the present trend toward going steady and early engagement will frequently seem to force girls to choose between marriage and continued studies, or between marriage and the long pull up the career ladder. Marriage will usually win: it is immediately available and very delightful, while the college degree or the heights of the career are a long way off and involve years of hard work. Yet, if the seeming need for a choice could be avoided, girls might not choose at all—or rather they might choose both rather than one. A few colleges make this possible by offering "earn while you learn" plans, which give girls a chance to try out the work role early enough to feel some real satisfaction and commitment to it, and a large number of hospitals let young girls get a taste of nursing life by acting as volunteers before they have begun to study for cap and pin. Similarly, many more girls might decide to become teachers if the programs of teachers' aides, now in use in a number of school systems, were expanded to include them and give them a feeling for teaching.

College women often drop out in order to work while their husbands study, or because housekeeping and mothering are too difficult or too expensive to combine with a full-time class schedule. Some few colleges have made it unnecessary for them to do this, by offering them part-time programs and extended-time curricula; most colleges, however, have been unwilling to permit such arrangements. Yet the future of such girls is importantly influenced by their dropping out; the Women's Bureau reports, for example, that 43 percent of wives who completed college are in the labor force, as against only 32 percent of those who did not, and it is a fair guess that much the same difference exists at the more important levels of community and volunteer positions.

Perhaps it is naïve to think that the institutions of graduate education will unbend far enough to follow the same course; nearly all medical schools, for instance, are quite rigid in their adherence to the four-year curriculum. But if the profession were sincere about its ostensible alarm concerning doctor shortages, the medical schools could institute special programs of study for women on a part-time or even interrupted basis, so that they might combine it with marriage and motherhood. Even if such women were not ready to practice medicine part-time until they were in their mid-thirties, and full-time by forty, they would still have the greater part of their working lives in which to enjoy their profession and be of value to their society. The same would apply all the more so, and with greater ease, to almost every other field of graduate study.

Industry and a few state legislatures have begun to make some concessions to the complex woman in the form of maternity leave and part-time work. Neither practice is yet widespread, though unionized and factory women get these benefits more often than office and clerical women. Employers still find it cheaper, at the lower clerical levels, to drop employees who leave on account of pregnancy, and to hire and train new ones, but six states and a number of unions have guaranteed a woman's right to have a child without losing her position, and the practice will undoubtedly spread in the years to come.

From the woman's viewpoint, if not the employer's, her guaranteed return—particularly to part-time work—would be an almost ideal answer. David Riesman and many others have suggested that the institution of a four-hour day for women would be a major breakthrough in solving their existing problems and making the manifold life possible. But even if this does not come about by design or legislation, it may do so by inadvertence; workdays for all workers are getting shorter, and automation may in a generation bring the standard workday close to manageable limits for mothers of young children.

The right and opportunity to work, however, is not the only issue;

many young women who have no desire to hold a job urgently need part-time freedom in order to avoid the stifling aspects of total domesticity and to experience some of those adult contacts and forms of personal enrichment that lie outside the home. Presently, middle-class mothers have quite inadequate resources; they turn to hired help when they can, or to relatives or friends, voluntary "sitting pools" of mothers, and other make-shift arrangements. But there is a genuine need for the expansion of organized high-quality child-care facilities such as cooperative play groups and nurseries, privately operated day nurseries and camps, and the like.*

Finally, some women neither need nor will seek important outside commitments until their children reach their teens, yet will want at that point to return to adult intellectual life or to an interrupted career. For them, there are straws in the wind in the form of the first few experimental college programs for mature women, which, as I mentioned earlier, retrain them or reawaken their capacities for nondomestic activity. At the lower occupational levels, a number of public schools and a handful of industries throughout the country offer training and retraining programs; there are far too few of them as yet, but according to the Women's Bureau they have already proven that women nearing or at the empty-nest stage are quite teachable, and, with retraining, are much more employable than they would otherwise be. Many middle-class women will probably continue to prefer club and community activities to clerical or other modest jobs; for them there will continue to exist a vast array of clubs and organizations, some of which have excellent training programs such as that offered by the Red Cross for nurses' aides, or by a few school systems for teachers' aides.

My thesis has been that when woman envisions herself as a whole person and harmoniously combines all the roles needful to her in

---

* These would only extend to middle-class women the advantages working-class women will shortly have in the form of a federally financed expansion of state day-care facilities.

modern life, she has the best chance of being enduringly feminine in a civilized, sophisticated sense, functioning well as a homemaker and as a mother to her children, proving a good mistress and friend to her husband, and being not only a valuable asset to her society, but a reasonably happy, fulfilled, and self-approving human being.

All of which, of course, is either worthy or unworthy, according to one's notion of the purpose of human life. And perhaps, therefore, we should for one final moment examine the assumption underlying the whole argument of this book. The very phrase "the purpose of human life" may seem stodgy and out of date in an era when it is fashionable to talk of the absurdity of human life, and to dismiss all goals other than day-by-day existential living. Yet all societies except those in dissolution have had their cherished goals, and one can only hope that the theory of absurdity is a symptom of a transient depressive phase rather than of hopeless disease.

Philosophies can be classified and evaluated in various ways, one of the most useful of which is according to their fundamental attitude toward intelligence. Along this dimension, the extremes are the two poles of the irrational and the rational, or, if you prefer, the instinctual and the intelligent, or the mystical and the scientific, or the unconscious and the conscious. Plato, in his day, was rather closer to the former pole, and Aristotle to the latter; St. Francis was closer to the former, and St. Thomas Aquinas to the latter; Rousseau was nearly at the one extreme, and Voltaire at the other. In our own time, the bipolarity is expressed in many areas, including politics, art, and the intellectual life; certain existentialists represent the one end, and scientists the other, of the spectrum.

Let us place in this dimension men's conceptions of woman's proper place in the world. At one extreme is the view of woman as the nourisher and life giver, the flowing breast and the fertile womb. Her proper activities are held to be those which are spontaneous, natural, instinctive, and biological; by virtue of being so they are right and healthful and good; and therefore all else in her life should either be subordinated or, better yet, forgotten. Clearly, then, this view is more of the irrational side than the rational; indeed, it rests on an assumption that the human purpose is the same as the un-reasoned animal purpose—survival by nourishment and reproduc-tion. But of course in the animal these are not *purposes* at all; they are only instinctive drives which result in eating, fighting, copulat-ing, and suckling, without intellection or conscious intent. In such natural phenomena there is no evil purpose nor any good one, but only a kind of natural law, neither more moral nor immoral than gravitation.

At the other extreme is the view that human beings are not like other animals: they think, consider the future, construct systems of right and wrong, and use their intelligence to control both their environment and their own conduct. The specific goals of individual men and women may range from the teaching of proper English to the investigation of the nucleus of the atom, from the writing of a string quartet to the curing of cancer; but each is part of the larger notion that man's purpose is the attainment of control over his own life and his world through knowledge, comprehension, and acquired skills.

Applying this view to woman, it would appear that since she is the child-bearing half of the human race, her fertility is the sine qua non of human life; but this is not the same as being its goal. It is an immense, sublime, all-pervasive *fact* of her life; but it is still a fact and not a reason for living. Child-bearing is what she does with her biology, as insemination is what man does with his; her share of the task is vastly larger than his, but for all that it is still the natural law of her body, and not her moral end.

The irrationalists and the rationalists agree on one thing: life must continue itself, or be a self-terminating contradiction. But to the rationalist, the continuance of life through marriage and child-bearing is an *a priori* condition rather than the real end. And that end, though it may seem to take any one of a hundred or a thousand forms, is subsumed under the general concept of man as a special animal who should strive not merely to continue living, but to im-prove the quality of life; who should aim to survive not just by multiplying, but by achieving greater mastery of the world and himself; who should seek his morality not in the instincts he shares with the lesser animals, but in the intelligence that he alone possesses.

Despite the charges of irrational men against rationality, it does not degrade or despise the instincts and the emotions, nor force man to be arid, loveless, infertile, or cold. Rather, it employs the intelligence to recognize the harm or the good of each specific instinct and emotion, and tries to control those that hinder, and accentuate those that help, man in his effort to live a healthier, more beautiful, more loving, and more fulfilling life.

This, then, is the assumption underlying my advocacy of the complex life for modern woman, and my optimism concerning the very trends which neo-traditionalists deplore. For above all I believe in modern man as a thinking creature, whose purposes transcend those of the oyster or even the noble savage; and by man, of course, I mean mankind; and therefore I mean woman.

For those who may wish to look further into the subjects covered in this book, I cite below certain of the major works on which I drew. I also cite minor sources, particularly if obscure, for points which are controversial and for data which are little-known or surprising; in general, however, minor and ephemeral sources are not cited, and when there are multiple authorities for a point, usually only one is named. Direct quotations from individual persons are identified in these notes only if drawn from published sources; all others are from my own files of correspondence, questionnaire replies, and interviews.

Most citations are given in abbreviated style; complete identification of each is given in the Bibliography following these notes.

INTRODUCTION

P. 5: Margaret Mead's estimate of the incidence of female discontent is from "What Women Want," in Bragdon, ed., p. 67.

P. 6: Kluckhohn (1953). Parsons, p. 246. Data on female doctors come from Bureau of the Census *Stat. Abst., 1961,* and the Central Statistical Board of the U.S.S.R., as quoted in CEW Newsletter, Dec., 1958.

CHAPTER ONE · THE MANY FACES OF WOMAN

P. 14-15: The portrait of the medieval lady is pieced together from Painter, Coulton, Kelly, Andreas, and others.

P. 16: On Augustus and Julia, see Suetonius *The Lives of the Twelve Caesars*; Tacitus *Annals* iii; Seneca *De beneficiis* vi; Macrobius *Saturnalia* ii.

Pp. 16-17: Aristotle *De generatione animalium* iv, 6. For Greek upper-class attitudes toward women, and source notes on same, see Hunt (1959), pp. 20-28, 401-2. On Thomas More, see Klein, p. 178.

Pp. 17-18: Governor Winthrop's diagnosis of Goodie Hopkins' illness is in his *History,* II, 216, 225. Lord Chesterfield's opinions are in his letter to his son dated Sept. 5 (O.S.), 1748. Tennyson, *In Memoriam,* xcvii. The female Pythagoreans are cited in Beard, p. 313. The curious details about Epicurus and Socrates come from Athenaeus *The Deipnosophists* xiii, and Plato *Symposium.*

P. 19: Intellectual Roman women are described viciously by their contemporary, Juvenal, in his Sixth Satire, and more dispassionately by Donaldson, Beard, and Carcopino, among others. Beard is a good source of information in intellectual ladies of the Renaissance; for additional details, see Maulde, Kelso, and Castiglione. Burckhardt, pp. 389 ff.

P. 22: Details on women's legal rights and obligations are in Woman's Bureau Bulletin 157.

CHAPTER TWO • THE MYTH OF THE FEMININE CHARACTER

Pp. 26-27: For Pope Pius' speech, see newspapers of Sept. 30, 1957. Gov. Hatfield's views are in *Coronet,* June, 1960.

Freud's apothegm is in Freud (1927). His general theory of the feminine character can be found in the same and in Freud (1933); a good brief résumé of these papers is in Klein, pp. 72-78.

P. 28: Deutsch, I, 274. Stekel is quoted in Klein, p. 81. De Beauvoir, p. 385.

P. 29: Details about animal sexuality come from Briffault, I, 442; Deutsch, I, 219-20; W. C. Allee, *The Social Life of Animals* (N. Y.: W. W. Norton & Co., [1938]), p. 168; Ford, pp. 102-3; and William Kephart, *The Family, Society, and the Individual* (Boston: Houghton Mifflin, 1961), p. 37. The viewpoint that in some cultures the Oedipus complex is all but imperceptible, or has little of its wonted power, is stated by Mead, (1955), pp. 95-96; Kardiner (1939), chap. vi; and Danielsson, pp. 85-86.

Pp. 30-31: The biological superiority of the female and the genetic reasons therefore are superbly set forth by Scheinfeld (1944) and (1958). On heart disease, see *Amer. Jour. Med.,* Jan., 1958, pp. 80 ff., and *Jour. Natl. Med. Assn.,* May, 1958, p. 184. On the Catholic Brothers and Sisters, see Madigan, *passim.* On arithmetic of woman's genetic superiority, see Leo Szilard in *Proc. Natl. Acad. Sci.,* Jan., 1959; and see also Bentley Glass, and C. H. Waddington.

P. 32: Relation between hormone output and behavior is discussed by Scheinfeld (1944); Wittkower and Wilson, in *Brit. Med. Jour.,* 1940 (Part I), 586-90; W. H. Masters, in *Geriatrics,* X (1955), 1-4; and many others.

P. 33: For data on mental health of women, see M. Greenblatt et al, eds., *The Patient and the Mental Hospital* (Glencoe, Ill.: The Free Press, 1957), pp. 147-48; Montagu (1953), pp. 92-93; and Scheinfeld (1944), p. 212.

Pp. 34-35: Concerning I.Q., see Komarovsky, pp. 19-22; Morgan, pp. 375-99; Scheinfeld (1944), pp. 84-85; and McNemar, *passim.*

Pp. 36-37: For the cigarette-butt problem and others, see Milton. Berry's summation is in P. C. Berry (1958).

P. 38: The amount of mathematics taken by girls is from *Background Factors and College-Going Plans Among High-Aptitude Public High School Seniors* (Washington: Natl. Sci. Fdn., 1956). Attitudes of New Jersey high-school seniors are reported in a study cited in CEW Newsletter, June, 1958. Figures on engineering talent in boys and girls are from Zapoleon, pp. 16-17, and the percentage of female engineering students is from CEW Newsletter, Dec., 1958.

P. 39: Re criminality, see Pollak, *passim;* intuitiveness, Scheinfeld (1944), p. 223; gossipiness, *ibid.,* p. 220; bank accounts, see Montagu (1953), pp. 109-110.

P. 40: Menninger (1942), p. 106. Mead (1955), pp. 117, 120, 176. On menstrual quarantine, see Westermarck (1908), p. 538.

Pp. 41-42: On M-F tests, see Terman (1936), esp. pp. 4, 76-78, 223. A brief discussion of the subject is in Klein, pp. 104-112. Replications of Terman's work are too numerous to cite here; consult *Psychological Abstracts.*

Pp. 43-44: Deutsch, II, 81, 277 (and cf. Bonaparte, *passim*). Biological and anthropological data contradicting Deutsch are from Ford, pp. 65, 260, and Kinsey (1953), p. 356.

P. 45: Dr. Anderson's statement is in "The Interpretation of Sex Differences," a paper read at the 1954 meeting of the CEW (q.v. in Bibliog.).

CHAPTER THREE • THE SEVEN DISCONNECTED AGES OF WOMAN

P. 47-48: Biological discontinuities in woman's life are discussed by Mead (1955), p. 139. Lack of female role-choice in simpler societies is referred to in Lerner, p. 546. Spiegel's statement is in N. Bell, ed. (1960), p. 364. Gesell (1950), p. 339.

Pp. 49-50: Gesell (1946), p. 313; Gesell (1956), p. 25. Komarovsky, pp. 54-66; quotations, *ibid.,* pp. 55-56.

Pp. 50-51: Acquisition of low opinion of femininity is dealt with in Gesell (1946); Hartley (1959); and Hartley (1960). See also *J. Genet Psychol.,* LIV (1939), 17-26. On the "It" study, see Brown, pp. 232-34.

P. 52: Sexual ignorance of and protection of girls are documented by Kinsey (1953); see esp. pp. 16, 173, 267, 487, 656-58. The disjunction of love and sex is well treated by Winch (1952), pp. 352-59.

Pp. 53-56: On puberty rites, see Menninger (1938), p. 258; Ellis, VI, 87 ff.; Westermarck (1908), p. 538; and Mead (1950), pp. 73-74. Behavior patterns and changing roles in this period of life are discussed by Gesell (1956), *passim;* Parsons, pp. 259-60; Matthews; Roff; Hacker.

Pp. 56-58: Problems of the "glamour" phase are discussed by Komarovsky, pp. 58-64; Ehrmann, *passim;* various contributors to Sanford, ed. (1956); and Sanford (1958). The Univ. of Calif. study is cited in CEW Newsletter, March, 1959.

P. 59: Rate of marriage after graduation is from a direct communication from the Bureau of the Census.

P. 60: J. T. Landis' study appeared in *Amer. Sociol. Rev.,* XI (1946), 666-77.

Need to make own folkways is indicated in Winch (1952), pp. 452-54, and Landis, *loc. cit.*

Pp. 62-64: Role-shifts and problems of empty-nest period are discussed by Blood (1960), Gurin, Kirkpatrick, and many others. See more detailed refs. to chapters viii, ix, x, below.

CHAPTER FOUR • THE RELUCTANT NYMPH

Pp. 70-71: The girl's conflicting moral codes are discussed by Ehrmann, pp. 216-17, 235.

Pp. 71-72: Dating as a novel form of mate-selection is discussed in every good study of the family; see, for instance, Burgess (1953a), Kirkpatrick, Baber, and Winch (1952). See also entries under Courting and Dating in Hunt (1959).

Pp. 72-73: Waller (1937); and cf. Gorer for a more recent reiteration of the view. Recent doubts about its validity are in Smith, Blood (1955), Blood (1956), and Lowrie.

Pp. 75-76: The college girl and the high-school junior are quoted from Bernard, ed. (1958), pp. 76, 72-73. Young love as a quest for identity is discussed by Winch (1952), chap. xiv; Erikson, p. 228; and many others. Komarovsky, pp. 77-80.

P. 77: The girl as the guardian of morality is discussed by Ehrmann, pp. 67, 78-79.

Pp. 77-78: Girls' and boys' divergent feelings about necking and petting are documented by Blood (1956); Ehrmann, *passim* (see esp. p. 316); Mead (1955), p. 216; and Kinsey (1953), pp. 250, 253-54, 263. The co-ed on p. 78 is quoted from Bernard, ed. (1958), p. 94. The estimate on going steady is from a 1960 survey made for *Seventeen,* and from R. Bell (1959). P. 79: Reasons for the going-steady trend are discussed by Winch (1952), Lerner, and Goode.

Pp. 79-80: The girl who wants to break off with Jim is quoted from Bernard (1958), pp. 160-61. The young man's quote, *ibid.,* pp. 58-60. Average age at marriage (p. 80n.) is from Gebhard, p. 33, n.6; divorce rate for teen-age and for older brides is derived from Bureau of the Census *Current Population Repts.,* Series P-20, No. 72 (Dec., 1956).

Pp. 80-81: Bud's girl friend is quoted from Bernard, ed. (1958), p. 57, George's girl friend from *ibid.,* pp. 206-7. Ehrmann, pp. 224, 316.

P. 82: The quotes are from Ehrmann, pp. 132, 311. On *amor purus,* see Hunt (1959), pp. 141-43.

P. 83: The quote concerning sexual confidences is from Johnson; the quote about saving oneself for one's husband is from Ehrmann, p. 312.

P. 84: Sexual responsibility of the "serious" boy is documented by Ehrmann, pp. 337, 343-45.

P. 85: On the value of the long engagement, see Burgess (1939), pp. 167-68; Locke, p. 91; Lerner, p. 588. Faults young women see in their fiancés are listed in Burgess (1953), pp. 132-34.

P. 86: Figures on premarital intercourse are drawn primarily from Kinsey (1953), pp. 286-87, 289, 292, 298-301, 310.

P. 88: The possible salutary effects of some premarital intercourse are indicated by the data of Burgess (1953), p. 185; Kinsey (1953), p. 318; and Locke, p. 134. For data on which I base the estimate of shotgun weddings, see Gebhard, pp. 45, 54, and 61. On women college drop-outs, see David, ed. (1959), pp. 14-15.

P. 89 and 89n.: Martinson's report is in *Am. Soc. Rev.*, XX (1955), 161-64. Locke, Table 15. Blood (1960), p. 150.

Pp. 89-90: The long letter is quoted from Bernard, ed. (1958), pp. 194-97.

CHAPTER FIVE • THE MARRIED MISTRESS

Pp. 94-95: Sociological depreciation of romantic love can be found in Magoun, Baber, Waller (1938), and many others. Sociological praise of conjugal love can be found in the same plus Mowrer, in Becker, ed.; Maslow, in Montagu, ed. (1953a); and Ernest van den Haag, "Love or Marriage," *Harper's*, May, 1962.

P. 96: The innovations and values of romantic love are discussed at length in Hunt (1959), chaps. v, vii, ix.

P. 97: Data on the infidelity rate for each age group are in Kinsey (1948), p. 587, and Kinsey (1953), p. 440.

Pp. 98-99: Happy wives' perception of faults in their husbands is discussed by Terman (1938), pp. 86-87, and by Burgess (1953), pp. 132-34.

P. 101: The bridal night quotation is from Bernard, ed. (1958), pp. 228-30.

P. 102n.: Similarities in male and female sexual anatomy are listed by Kinsey (1953), pp. 591-93, 640-41. Cultural variations in pre-coital play are cited by Ford, Mead (1955) and Ellis VI, 538-60. The lower-class American attitude on such play is given in Kinsey (1948), pp. 369, 572-73, and Kinsey (1953), pp. 361-62.

Pp. 103-104: Difference in erotic drive between men and women is a commonplace, but see Burgess (1953), p. 361, for data. Husbands' guilt-feelings, *ibid.*, pp. 12, 366. On woman's carnal nature (p. 103n), the Greek belief is cited by B. J. Rose, *Handbook of Greek Mythology;* on Sprenger and Kramer, see Hunt (1959); and on cultural variations in female arousability, see Ford, *passim*, and Ellis, III, 189-255.

P. 104: Statements by women on their methods of refusal come from Rainwater (1960), p. 113; Locke, p. 142; Hilliard (1960); and my own files.

Pp. 105-106: Data on refusal of husbands by wives, and vice versa, are from Terman (1938), pp. 290-93, and Locke, p. 146. Quotation about the apologetic bridegroom is in Lundberg, p. 286. Divorcees' failure to refuse is from Locke, p. 146. Statement about husbandly empathy in the middle class and lack of it in the lower class is based on Burgess (1953), Blood (1960), Rainwater (1959), Rainwater (1960), Koos, and others. Frigidity in lower-class women is discussed in Rainwater (1960), p. 121 f., and in Kinsey (1953), pp. 354, 356. For divorce rates by class, see Goode, chap. iv. The satisfactions of marriage, as reported by lower- and middle-class women, are treated in Blood (1960), p. 253, and Gurin, pp. 210, 222. Quotation by Levine and Stone is in Stone (1953).

P. 109: Maslow's comment on conjugal love is in Montagu, ed. (1953a), pp. 62, 65. Reik, pp. 92-3, 192.

P. 110: Seductive behavior of the modern wife is discussed in Terman (1938), pp. 282-83; activity of the female lover in other cultures is mentioned in Ford, p. 25 f.; and the 19th-century marriage manual is *The Philosophy of Love,* by Dr. Michael Ryan (orig. ed. 1839). Dr. Robinson's paean to inertness is on p. 217 of her book. Bonaparte (q.v.) expresses similar views.

Pp. 111-12: Pre-coital play of modern Americans is specified by Kinsey (1948), p. 575, and Kinsey (1953), pp. 361-65. Data on use of contraception (p. 112n.) can be found in Winch (1952), pp. 125, 187; Rainwater (1960), *passim;* R. Freedman (1959), pp. 11, 105, 403. See Hunt (1959), p. 348, for other sources.

Pp. 112-13: Mrs. Stopes' picture of the orgasm is in *Enduring Passion.* Lawrence is quoted by Stone (1952), p. 212, and Hamilton is cited in the same, p. 208. Dr. Farnham's explanation of frigidity is in Lundberg, pp. 269-70. Dr. Caprio's misleading statement is on p. 13 of his book.

P. 114-15: On enjoyment of sex relations by non-orgasmic women of other cultures, see Mead (1955), p. 108. Frequency with which women reach orgasm has been reported by many researchers; see esp. Terman (1938), pp. 300, 302; Kinsey (1953), pp. 354, 356, 375, 379, 402, 626; K. B. Davis (1929); Stone (1952), pp. 203, 208; and Locke, p. 145 and Table 22.

CHAPTER SIX • THE WOULD-BE ADULTERESS

P. 119: Statistics on actual, rather than fictional, adultery are given in Ford, pp. 116-27; Locke, p. 152; and many others; I rely chiefly on Kinsey (1953), chap. x.

P. 120: Frequency of the wish for extramarital intercourse is given in Ford, p. 117; Kinsey (1953), p. 431; Locke, p. 155 f.; and Burgess (1953), p. 362.

P. 121: Ford, p. 118. Lindner, p. 46.

Pp. 123-24: On the emotional meaning of flirtation, see de Beauvoir, pp. 547-48; on its dangers, see Mead (1955), p. 265.

Pp. 124-25: The Bergen County woman is from Gordon, pp. 120-27. Extramarital petting is mentioned in Kinsey (1953), p. 426, and in *Encyclopedia of Sexual Behavior,* A. Ellis and A. Abarbanel, eds. (New York: Hawthorn Books, [1961]).

Pp. 127-28: On American wives' plans or expectations of having extramarital intercourse, see Ford, p. 117. The French and Belgian women are discussed in Lanval; see esp. p. 123.

Pp. 129-30: Examples of the typical psychoanalytic view of adultery are Caprio, *passim,* and Bela Mittelman, in Eisenstein, ed.

P. 131: The relative harmlessness of a random episode of adultery, when encapsulated or confessed, is discussed by Lindner, p. 50.

P. 132: Adultery as part of the mores of "fast" groups is discussed by Menninger (1942), pp. 64-66. Nonfictional accounts of life in such groups have been given in many autobiographies, usually ruefully; see, for instance, those of Mary Astor and Diana Barrymore.

Pp. 133-34: The case of Louis and Sandra is in Mudd, ed. (1958), pp. 135-43.

P. 135: Data contradicting the notion that unappeased desire is the cause of adultery are to be found in Kinsey (1953), pp. 432-35, 530; C. Landis (1940), p. 172; and Seward, in Fishbein, ed., p. 96. De Beauvoir, p. 553. Adler is cited in the same, p. 548.

P. 136: The case is from Stone (1954).

P. 138: For the changing rate of infidelity by age, see Kinsey (1953), p. 440. Reasons for it are summarized by Bernard (1956), p. 277. Cf. Deutsch, II, 461-62.

CHAPTER SEVEN • THE LADY OF THE HOUSE

P. 144: Ithaca survey data in Williams. Kluckhohn (1953).

P. 146: For loyalty of women to their liberal education, see poll results in Friedan. On self-evaluation of own happiness by lower-class and middle-class women, see Gurin, pp. 46, 107, and Blood (1960), p. 252 and *passim*.

Pp. 146-47: Feminism's attitude toward homemaking is often mentioned in Mannin, de Beauvoir, Lundberg, and others.

P. 148: On the alleged cultural universality of the division of labor, see Zelditch, in N. Bell, ed. (1960), and Murdock, *ibid*. Professor Goldman's essay is in *Holiday*, May, 1961. Typical neo-conservative ideas on woman's education are expressed White, *passim*; Philip Burton, in *This Week* magazine, Feb. 9, 1958; and quoted (though not endorsed) by National Manpower Council (1957).

P. 149: On female doctors and teachers: Bureau of the Census *Stat. Abst. 1961* and *Hist. Statistics*.

P. 151: *Extracts from the Diary of Christopher Marshall* (Albany: W. Munsell, 1877), pp. 157-58.

P. 152: The Levittown mother is quoted from Rainwater (1959), p. 32. Descriptions of lower-class relationships are scattered through Koos, Goode, Rainwater (1959), Rainwater (1960), Kinsey (1948), Kinsey (1953), and many others. Murdock's data appear in *Social Forces*, XV (1937), 551.

P. 153: Figures on full-time housewives, including those who are college graduates, are derived from Bureau of the Census *Stat. Abst, 1961* and Women's Bureau Bulletin 275. Figures on national shortages in selected occupations are from National Manpower Council (1957); Winter; the Fund for Adult Education, and the American Psychiatric Association (the latter two by direct communication).

P. 155n.: On the high-school girls, see Douvan, in David, ed. (1959), pp. 24-25; on the Univ. of Minn. co-eds, see Rose (1951).

Pp. 156-57: Hours of extra work due to baby, from M. Wilson, in *Oregon Agricultural Experiment Station Bulletin 256* (1929). Komarovsky, however, cites

(p. 111) a different study which puts the increase at about 20 hours per week.

P. 158: For view that women do not allow labor-saving devices to free them from labor, see Meyer Nimkoff, "What Do Modern Inventions Do to Family Life?" *Annals of Am. Acad. Polit. and Social Sci.*, Nov., 1950; and Myrdal, p. 38. On housekeeping by farm wives and big-city wives, see Bryn Mawr.

Pp. 160-61: Fadiman, *Holiday* magazine, June, 1961.

P. 162: On the housewife's loss of productive usefulness, see Ogburn, *passim;* Smuts, pp. 608; or any major study of the family. The pay of houseworkers is from the Women's Bureau "Facts on Women Workers," July, 1961.

P. 164: *Wellesley Alumnae Magazine*, Nov., 1950, p. 4. *Fortune*, Aug., 1946, and direct communication from Amer. Inst. of Public Opinion concerning a Gallup poll of May, 1950. Dr. Jahoda's paper was an unpublished research memo submitted to the CEW.

CHAPTER EIGHT   •   THE NOT-QUITE-IDEAL MOTHER

P. 166: Fertility then and now, Bureau of the Census *Stat. Abst. 1961*, p. 52. On negative feelings of pregnant women, see note to pages 174-75 below.

P. 167: Newton's findings are in *Pediatrics*, V (1950), 869-75. Lerner, p. 567. High value placed by women on motherhood is documented by Blood (1960), pp. 117-19, 137, 140.

P. 168: The lyrical mother is quoted from *Wellesley Alumnae Magazine,* May, 1958, p. 228.

P. 169: The human lack of built-in instinctual mechanisms is discussed by Huxley, pp. 217-19, and La Barre, p. 77. Animal instincts gone awry are given in Huxley, p. 218, and Montagu (1955), p. 43.

Pp. 170-71: On natural childbirth see, of course, G. Dick-Read, *Childbirth Without Fear* (N. Y.: Harper & Brothers, 1944), pp. 5-6, 13, 19. The quote about Bushman or aboriginal women is from Montagu (1953), p. 32. For objections to natural childbirth, see Natalie Gittelson, "The Case Against Natural Childbirth," *Harper's Bazaar*, Feb., 1961; and Fielding, *passim*.

P. 172: The pros and cons of breast-feeding and bottle-feeding are in Spock, pp. 63-67, and Guttmacher, p. 237. The quote about suckling is from La Barre, p. 105, who, though usually very thorough, offers no evidence for this assertion. On the whole matter of the conflicts between leftover biological mechanisms and a civilized life, see Cobb, *passim*.

Pp. 173-74: Strecker (1956), p. 29. Wylie, letter in *Redbook*, Feb., 1961.

Pp. 174-75: Caplan (1957) and Caplan (n.d.). For a sound popular résumé of similar studies elsewhere, see V. Cadden, "How Women Really Feel About Pregnancy," *Redbook*, Nov., 1958.

Pp. 175-77: For a popular résumé of clinical studies on the changes in husband-wife relations, see Hunt (1959a). The Mich. State survey was by Poffenberger and Poffenberger, and appeared in *Amer. Sociol. Rev.*, Dec., 1950. On equalitarian character of modern marriage, see Hill, in Becker, ed.; Blood (1960), chap. ii; or Burgess (1953a). Loss of control in familial decision-making, generally and by social class and location, is from Blood (1960), pp. 28, 36-37, 40-41, 43.

P. 178: Hilliard (1957), p. 21.

Pp. 182-83: Decreasing interaction between husband and wife is discussed by Blood (1960), pp. 23-24, 70, and elsewhere; Feldman, *passim;* Deitcher, pp. 145-59.
P. 182n.: Locke, pp. 169-70.

P. 183: The woman from Arizona is requoted from Hunt (1961). On loss of sexual desire, see Caplan (1957), and E. B. Easly, in *North Carolina Med. Jour.,* Feb., 1961, pp. 63-71.

Pp. 183-84: Blood (1960), pp. 156, 265-66. On lack of proven correlation between parenthood and happiness, see Nimkoff, p. 496, and Winch (1952), pp. 205-6.

P. 186: The statement by the woman who isn't "Doing anything" is slightly digested from the *Wellesley Alumnae Magazine,* May, 1960, pp. 220-21.

P. 187: Mead, in *Am. J. Orthopsychiatry,* XXIV (1954), 471-83. On the locus of momism, see Isidore Portnoy, in Arieti, ed., I, 314.

Pp. 187-88: The three quotes by "total-accepters" come, respectively, from the *Wellesley Alumnae Magazine,* Nov., 1960, p. 4; my own files; and the *Barnard Alumnae Magazine,* Nov., 1959, p. 14.

Pp. 188-190: On the growing incompatibility of many middle-aging couples, see Useem (1960), and W. H. Whyte (1951). For "change-of-life babies" and menopausal passion, see Harry August, in Gross, ed., pp. 96-99, and Kinsey (1953), pp. 421-22. Hypochondria of the menopause is too well known to need detailed citations, but for a good popular résumé of the topic see Marguerite Clark, *Medicine Today* (N. Y.: Funk and Wagnall, 1960), pp. 269, 272-73. On involutional psychosis, see Newton Bigelow, in Arieti, ed., I, 540.

P. 190: Ackerman, pp. 168-69.

Pp. 193-94; Picture of the anxious, overprotective mother is from Arieti, in Arieti, ed., I, 469; Deutsch, II, 306; and many others; the theoretical basis of this formulation is to be found in Freud, *Totem and Taboo,* p. 845. (Modern Library ed. of *Basic Writings of Sigmund Freud*). On the harmfulness of concealed rejection, see Ackerman, pp. 37-38; Menninger (1942), pp. 223-24; and Arieti, ed., I, 122, 469, 472.

P. 197: For the shift toward work, see Children's Bureau Publication No. 382-1960; Scofield; and sources for chapter xi below.

CHAPTER NINE • MAN'S BEST FRIEND

Pp. 199-200: Dakota details from J. Mirsky, in Mead, ed. (1937); Homeric men from Finley; and other primitive details from Richards, Sumner, and Briffault.

Pp. 200-201: Periclean, Christian, troubadour, aristocratic, and bourgeois views of women are all given in greater detail in Hunt (1959), *passim.*

P. 202: Parsons, p. 227; Burgess (1939), p. 171; and Burgess (1953), pp. 216-66. Univ. of Mich. study: Blood (1960), p. 150 and Appendix.

P. 205: For rate of remarriage, see Bernard (1956), p. 65.

P. 206n: Sexual conduct of divorcees is from Gebhard, p. 143. Locke, Table 15.

P. 207: The angry woman is quoted from Rainwater (1960), p. 87.

P. 211: W. H. Whyte (1951), and W. H. Whyte (1951a). On the common-law doctrine and its demise, see Hunt (1960), and Hunt (1959), pp. 209-10.

Pp. 212-15: The downward course of companionship and communication is discussed in Blood (1960), chapter vi and pp. 263-66; Deitcher, *passim;* and Feldman.

Pp. 215-16: Direct communication from the Am. Inst. of Public Opinion, concerning a Gallup poll of 1952; and Agnes Meyer, in Gross, ed., pp. 149-50.

Pp. 217-18: Kluckhohn (1953) argues that husband-wife specialization can be harmful today. The case of the surgeon was presented in *Ladies' Home Journal,* May, 1960.

Pp. 218-19: On the decline and later upturn of marital friendship, see Deitcher, *passim;* Feldman; Blood (1960), pp. 263-66.

P. 220: Foote, pp. 26-27; Useem (1960); and Bernard (1956). The chance of divorce after ten years of marriage is computed by Jacobson, p. 145.

P. 221: W. H. Whyte (1951). Uncommunicativeness of the upper-echelon executive is reported by Blood (1960), p. 168.

P. 223: Blood (n.d.), "Effects of the Wife's Employment"; Blood (1960), pp. 164-65; Foote; and Gurin, pp. 210-11.

CHAPTER TEN • BELOVED ENEMY

P. 227: Council of Macon incident is from Gregory of Tours *History of the Franks* viii, 20. For the hope that women would be sexless in heaven, see Westermarck (1939), pp. 338-39.

Pp. 227-28: On the Marquesans, see Danielsson, pp. 187-88; on the Arapesh, Mead (1940).

P. 229: Sirjamaki, p. 77.

P. 230: For an authoritative popular exposition of the two-instinct theory, see Menninger (1942), chap. i, and pp. 295-96. On sublimation, *ibid.,* pp. 128-33.

P. 232: On symbolic meaning of politeness, see Gregory Zilboorg, in *Psychiatry,* VII (1944), 257-96.

P. 233: On different social status of husband and wife, see Bell, in N. Bell, ed., p. 11; Winch (1952), pp. 104-6; and Parsons, pp. 223-24.

P. 234: Deutsch, I, 192-93.

P. 235: For the wish to be a man, see "The Fortune Survey," and Brown, p. 234.

P. 237: W. H. Whyte (1951).

Pp. 237-38: Myrdal's original suggestion on woman as a marginal man is in *An American Dilemma* (N. Y.: Harper & Brothers, 1944), pp. 1073-78. Discussions of the concept are in Klein, pp. 171-72, and Hacker, *passim*. Blake's experiments with the isolation booths (p. 238n.) were described by him in a mimeographed report to the CEW dated 1953 and titled "Psychological Aspects of Conformity Behavior."

P. 239: Thomas' statement is quoted in Klein, p. 155.

Pp. 240-41: For a popular résumé of clinical findings on quarrels about money, see Hunt (1955).

Pp. 242-43: On frigidity as an expression of independence, see Terman (1938), p. 375, and C. Landis (1940), p. 190. The frigid woman is quoted from Hollis, p. 64. The use of various ailments to express hostility is dealt with by Mowrer, in Becker, ed., p. 387; D. Henderson and G. Cumberlege, *A Textbook of Psychiatry* (London: Oxford Univ. Press, 1956), pp. 88-93, 153; and Kimball Young, *Personality and Problems of Adjustment* (N. Y.: Appleton-Century-Crofts, 1951), p. 655.

P. 245: Data on family decision-making are from Blood (1960), pp. 22-23, 67.

Pp. 246-47: The importance of games and recreation is discussed by Menninger (1942), chap. vii, and Goode, pp. 92-95.

P. 248: The psychology of work is very clearly set forth by Menninger (1942), chap. vi. Lucy Kavaler, *The Private World of High Society* (N. Y.: David McKay Company Inc., 1960), chap. iii.

Pp. 250-51: Data on club membership are from *Enc. Brit. Book of the Year, 1961*. On volunteers, widely varying figures are given by National Manpower Council (1957), pp. 47-48; Donald Bell, "The Theory of Mass Society," *Commentary*, July, 1956; and others. I have used fresh estimates of volunteers and their average hours, made for me by knowledgeable research personnel of a major volunteer agency which declines to be named.

CHAPTER ELEVEN • THE MORE-OR-LESS CAREER WIFE

Pp. 252-53: Dr. Mudd's statement is from an interview with the author. Statistics on women workers are from the Women's Bureau via direct communication, and Bulletin 275 and Leaflet DC-62-271. Distinctions between labor and work are explicated by Hannah Arendt in *The Human Condition* (Chicago: Univ. of Chicago Press, 1958), chaps. iii, iv. On psychological functions of work, see Menninger (1942), chap. vi.

Pp. 254-55: *Ladies' Home Journal*, Nov., 1958, pp. 60, 154. Cattell's study is cited in F. H. Lund, *Emotions of Men* (N. Y.: Whittlesey House, 1930), p. 213.

P. 256: *Kibbutz* women are described in Spiro (1956) and Spiro (1958). On war workers' health, see Zapoleon, p. 15. Some of the clichés about emotional defects of women workers are given in Komarovsky, pp. 202-6, and in National Manpower Council (1957), p. 95.

P. 257: Pamela Hansford Johnson, in *The N. Y. Times Book Review*, Dec. 31, 1961, pp. 1, 22.

P. 258: The number of girls in financial studies is from CEW Newsletter, Oct.,

1959, and a direct communication from American Council on Education. Data on women in financial careers are from Women's Bureau Bulletin 279, and a direct communication from the New York Stock Exchange.

P. 259: Statistics on women in technical professions are from Women's Bureau Bulletins 253 and 275.

Pp. 259-60: Cussler, pp. 24-25, 65-66, 74-76. W. F. Whyte (1949).

P. 261: Woodhull quote from Paulina W. Davis, *History of the National Woman's Rights Movement* (N. Y.: Journeymen Printers' Co-op Assn., 1871), p. 118. Much the same language can be found in other feminist speeches and writings down to World War I.

Pp. 262-63: On the disappearing type of careerist, Eli Ginzberg, "The Changing Pattern of Women's Work," in *Am. J. Orthopsychiatry*, XXVIII (1958), p. 318. The new attitude toward careers is attested by many investigators; typical findings are in Komarovsky, pp. 45, 95-96; Douvan, in David, ed., pp. 24-25; and National Manpower Council (1957), pp. 310-11. On changing patterns of female employment, see Women's Bureau Bulletins 218, 253, 275, and Leaflet DC-62-271. Statistics on women college faculty members are from Bureau of the Census *Stat. Abst., 1961* plus a direct communication from the Office of Education (drawing upon advance data to be published in PC [1]-D, Summary, Detailed Characteristics, of the 1960 Census for the United States). Women's share of total take-home pay can be derived from figures in Women's Bureau Bulletin 275, p. 58. The quota system in graduate schools is mentioned in Hamill.

P. 264: For evidence as to the brevity of female careers, I drew upon "Facts About Nursing" (American Nursing Ass'n.); "Careers in Nursing" (Nat'l League for Nursing); "Sex Role and the Career Orientation of Beginning Teachers," *Harvard Educ. Rev.*, Fall, 1959; a direct communication for the Air Transport Association; and various articles in business magazines (of which see esp. *Business Week*, Oct. 7, 1961, pp. 92-99). On absenteeism, see National Manpower Council (1957), pp. 94, 230; Myrdal, pp. 74, 105; and D. Bell (1956).

P. 265: The bimodal curve of woman's work-life is from Women's Bureau Bulletin 275, and National Manpower Council (1957), p. 307.

Pp. 267-68: Sanders, "A Proposition for Women," *Harper's*, Sept., 1960. The Vassar woman is quoted by Sarah Blanding in an article in *Futures for College Women in New York*, Oct., 1960 (N. Y.: Alumnae Advisory Board).

P. 269: Typical neo-traditionalist statements of this sort appear all through White, Lundberg, Deutsch, Robinson, Wylie, and many others.

P. 270: De Mille, pp. 213, 230.

Pp. 270-71: Komarovsky, in *Ladies' Home Journal*, Nov., 1958, p. 156; Baber, pp. 392-95; Kirkpatrick, p. 416. Data on working mothers are from Children's Bureau Publication No. 382-1960; Hartley (1959a); and the Women's Bureau via direct communication and Bulletin 275. National Manpower Council (1958), p. 124. Buck, p. 79.

P. 272: *Ladies' Home Journal*, Nov., 1958, pp. 60, 154. Univ. of Mich. study cited by D. Bell (1956).

Pp. 273-74: Hoffman cited in Stolz, pp. 770-71. Nye, in *Marriage and Family Living*, Nov., 1952, pp. 327-32. Detroit study cited in Children's Bureau Publication No. 382-1960; for similar findings elsewhere, see Stolz, pp. 754-77, and Maccoby, in N. Bell, ed. (1960), p. 524. On the *kibbutzim*, Maccoby, *loc. cit.*, p. 533. Stolz, *passim;* quote is from p. 779. Bender is quoted by Elizabeth Pope in "Is a Working Mother a Threat to the Home?" *McCall's*, July 1955. Herzog, Children's Bureau Publication No. 382-1960, p. 18.

Pp. 274-75: The hotel cashier is requoted from Hunt (1961).

P. 276: On the complexity of decisions and job allocation in the two-career household, see Komarovsky, pp. 173-79, 184-99.

P. 277: K. B. Davis (1929), p. 43; Locke, pp. 289-93; Blood (1960), p. 101; Komarovsky, p. 188.

Pp. 277-79: Case of the "Pritchards" is adapted (with a change of name) from a joint interview published in the alumnae magazine of a leading Eastern girls' college.

CONCLUSION

P. 284: Stouffer's finding, and the theory of reference group behavior, are in Merton.

Pp. 285-87: Useem, via direct communication. Mead (1955), p. 183. On the relative happiness of married women and single ones, see Gurin, pp. xix, 232, and on the happiness of the complex life generally, see Rose (1955), and Locke, pp. 85, 145, 255. The quarreling and marital breakdown rate of lower-class marriages are indicated in many places in Blood (1960), Rainwater (1959) and (1960), Goode, and Koos.

P. 289: The ease with which daughters of working mothers envision a complex role-pattern for themselves is indicated in Hartley (1959a) and (1960). Change in the proportion of spinster schoolteachers is from *Women in Gainful Occupations, 1870-1920* (Census Monograph IX, 1929), Table 57, and *The Status of the American Public-School Teachers* (Nat'l Educ. Ass'n., 1957), Table 7.

P. 290: On the greater employability, or drive toward work, of married college graduates than drop-outs, see Women's Bureau Bulletin 275, p. 96.

P. 291: The maternity leave question is discussed in *Management Record*, July-Aug., 1959, pp. 232, 260; some of my details come from the American Management Ass'n., by direct communication. Riesman first suggested the four-hour day in *The Lonely Crowd* (1950); Montagu (1953) and others have expanded on the idea since then.

P. 292: Retaining programs given by public schools and industry are cited in Women's Bureau Bulletin 248.

BIBLIOGRAPHY

This is a partial list of sources consulted. It includes primarily works referred to in the Notes on Sources, plus a few additional titles by the same authors or by authors referred to in the text.

ACKERMAN, NATHAN W. *The Psychodynamics of Family Life.* New York: Basic Books, Inc., 1958.

American Handbook of Psychiatry; see Arieti, Silvano, ed.

ANDREAS (ANDREAS CAPELLANUS, or ANDREW THE CHAPLAIN). *The Art of Courtly Love,* trans. by John J. Parry. New York: Columbia University Press, 1941.

ARIETI, SILVANO, ed. *American Handbook of Psychiatry.* New York: Basic Books, Inc., 1959.

BABER, RAY E. *Marriage and the Family.* New York: McGraw-Hill Book Co., Inc., 1953.

BARTLETT, LYNN R. "Problems and Satisfactions of Women Active in Volunteer Work." Unpublished dissertation, Teachers College, Columbia University, 1959.

BEARD, MARY R. *Woman as Force in History.* New York: The Macmillan Company, 1946.

BECKER, HOWARD, and HILL, REUBEN, eds. *Family, Marriage, and Parenthood.* Boston: D. C. Heath & Co., 1955.

BEIGEL, HUGO G. "Romantic Love," *Amer. Sociol. Rev.,* XVI (1951), 326-34.

BELL, DANIEL (1956). "The Great Back-to-Work Movement," *Fortune,* July, 1956.

BELL, NORMAN W. (1960), and VOGEL, EZRA F., eds. *A Modern Introduction to the Family.* Glencoe, Ill.: The Free Press, 1960.

BELL, ROBERT (1959), and BLUMBERG, LEONARD. "Courtship Intimacy and Religious Background," *Marriage and Family Living,* XXI (1959), 356-66.

BELL, ROBERT (1960), and BLUMBERG, LEONARD. "Courtship Stages and Intimacy Attitudes," *The Family Life Coordinator,* March, 1960.

BERNARD (1956), JESSIE. *Remarriage: A study of Marriage.* New York: The Dryden Press, 1956.

BERNARD (1957), JESSIE. *Social Problems at Midcentury.* New York: The Dryden Press, 1957. See esp. chap. xv, "Status and Role Problems of Modern Woman: Family and Worker Roles."

BERNARD (1958), JESSIE, BUCHANAN, HELEN E., and SMITH, WILLIAM M., JR., eds. *Dating, Mating, and Marriage: A Documentary-Case Approach.* Cleveland: Howard Allen, Inc., 1958.

BERNAYS, DORIS F. *A Wife Is Many Women.* New York: Crown Publishers [1956].

BERRY, JANE B. (1955). "Life Plans of Freshman and Sophomore Women." Unpublished dissertation, Teachers College, Columbia University, as abstracted in *Jour. Natl. Assn. Women Deans and Counselors,* Jan., 1955.

BERRY, PAUL C., (1958). "An Exploration of the Interrelationships Among Some Non-Intellectual Predictors of Achievement in Problem Solving." Technical Report 4, Contract Nonr 609(20), Office of Naval Research. New Haven: Yale University Press, Dec., 1958.

BLOOD (1955), ROBERT O. "A Retest of Waller's Rating Complex," *Marriage and Family Living,* XVII (1955), 41-47.

BLOOD (1956), ROBERT O. "Uniformities and Diversities in Campus Dating Preference," *Marriage and Family Living,* XVIII (1956), 37-44.

BLOOD (1960), ROBERT O., and WOLFE, DONALD M. *Husbands and Wives: The Dynamics of Married Living.* Glencoe, Ill.: The Free Press, 1960.

BLOOD (n.d.), ROBERT O. "The Effects of the Wife's Employment on the Husband-Wife Relationship." Unpublished chapter to appear in a forthcoming book on the family, edited by F. Ivan Nye and Lois Hoffman.

BONAPARTE, MARIE. *Female Sexuality.* New York: International Universities Press, Inc., 1953.

BRAGDON, ELIZABETH, ed. *Women Today.* Indianapolis: Bobbs-Merrill, [1953].

BRIFFAULT, ROBERT. *The Mothers.* New York: The Macmillan Company, 1927.

BROWN, DANIEL G. "Sex-Role Development in a Changing Culture," *Psychological Bull.,* LV (1958), 232-42.

Bryn Mawr College, Dept. of Social Economy. "Women During the War and After." Philadelphia: Curtis Publishing Co., 1945.

BUCK, PEARL S. *Of Men and Women.* New York: The John Day Company, 1941.

BUNTING, MARY L. "A Huge Waste: Educated Womanpower," *The New York Times Magazine,* May 7, 1961.

BURCKHARDT, JACOB. *The Civilization of the Renaissance in Italy.* Harper Torchbook ed. (trans. of 15th ed. of German original); New York: Harper & Brothers, 1958.

Bureau of the Census. *Statistical Abstract of the United States, 1961.*

————. *Historical Statistics of the United States from Colonial Times to 1957.*

BURGESS (1939), ERNEST, and COTTRELL, LEONARD K. *Predicting Success or Failure in Marriage.* New York: Prentice-Hall, Inc., 1939.

BURGESS (1953), ERNEST, and WALLIN, PAUL, with SHULTZ, GLADYS DENNY. *Courtship, Engagement, and Marriage.* Philadelphia: J. B. Lippincott Company, 1953, 1954.

BURGESS (1953a), ERNEST, and LOCKE, HARVEY J. *The Family: From Institution to Companionship.* New York, etc.: American Book Company, 1953.

CALHOUN, ARTHUR W. *A Social History of the American Family.* Cleveland: Arthur H. Clark Co., 1918.

CAPLAN (1957), GERALD. "Psychological Aspects of Maternity Care," *Amer. Jour. Public Health,* XLVII (1957), 25-31.

CAPLAN (n.d.), GERALD. "Emotional Implications of Pregnancy." Mimeographed paper, n.d., Harvard School of Public Health.

CAPRIO, FRANK S. *The Sexually Adequate Female*. New York: The Citadel Press, 1960.

CARCOPINO, JEROME. *Daily Life in Ancient Rome*. New Haven: Yale University Press, 1940.

CASTIGLIONE, COUNT BALDESAR. *The Book of the Courtier*. New York: Charles Scribner's Sons, 1903.

CEW and CEW Newsletter; *see* Commission on the Education of Women.

Children's Bureau. Publication No. 382-1960: *Children of Working Mothers*, by Elizabeth Herzog.

CLARK, ALICE. *Working Life of Women in the Seventeenth Century*. New York: E. P. Dutton & Co., 1919.

Commission on the Education of Women (an office of the American Council on Education). Newsletter entitled "The Education of Women: Information and Research Notes." Issued irregularly at Washington, D.C., by the American Council on Education, from 1958 to 1961. The Commission has since been discontinued, and its files transferred to Radcliffe College.

COBB, STANLEY. *Emotions and Clinical Medicine*. New York: W. W. Norton & Co., 1950.

COULTON, G. G. *Medieval Panorama*. New York: Meridian Books, 1955.

CUSSLER, MARGARET. *The Woman Executive*. New York: Harcourt, Brace & Company, 1958.

DANIELSSON, BENGT. *Love in the South Seas*. New York: Reynal & Co., 1956.

DAVID (1959), OPAL, ed. *The Education of Women: Signs for the Future*. Washington, D.C.: Amer. Council on Education, 1959.

DAVID (1960), OPAL. "A Little Discontent Becomes You," *Wellesley Alumnae Magazine*, Jan., 1960.

DAVIS, KATHARINE B. (1929). *Factors in the Sex Life of 2200 Women*. New York: Harper & Brothers, 1929.

DAVIS, KINGSLEY (1950). "Statistical Perspective on Marriage and Divorce," *Annals of the Amer. Acad. of Polit. and Social Science*, Nov., 1950.

DAVIS, MAXINE (1956). *The Sexual Responsibility of Woman*. New York: Permabooks, 1959.

DE BEAUVOIR, SIMONE. *The Second Sex*. New York: Alfred A. Knopf, 1953.

DEITCHER, SAMUEL. "Development of Interspousal Verbal Communication of College-Educated Couples." Unpublished Ph.D. dissertation, Cornell University, 1959.

DE MILLE, AGNES. *And Promenade Home*. Boston: Little, Brown and Co., 1958.

DEUTSCH, HELENE. *The Psychology of Women*. New York: Grune & Stratton, 1944-1945.

DICKINSON, R. L., and BEAM, L. *A Thousand Marriages*. Baltimore: Wilkins & Wilkins Co., 1931.

DIETRICH, MARLENE. "How to Be Loved," *Ladies' Home Journal*, Jan., 1954.

DONALDSON, JAMES. *The Woman: Her Positions and Influence in Ancient Greece and Rome and Among the Early Christians*. New York: Longmans, Green and Co., 1907.

DOUVAN, ELIZABETH. "Adolescent Girls: Their Attitudes Toward Education," in David (1959) (q.v.).

EHRMANN, WINSTON. *Premarital Dating Behavior*. New York: Bantam Books, 1960.

EISENSTEIN, VICTOR W., ed. *Neurotic Interaction in Marriage*. New York: Basic Books, Inc., 1956.

ELLIS, HAVELOCK. *Studies in the Psychology of Sex*. Phila.: F. A. Davis, 1901-1928. All volume and page references in the Notes are to this set, rather than to later reprinting of the material.

ERIKSON, ERIK. *Childhood and Society*. New York: W. W. Norton & Co., 1950.

FARNHAM; *see* Lundberg.

FELDMAN, HAROLD. "Development of the Husband-Wife Relationship." Paper presented at the Aug., 1960, meeting of the Natl. Council on Family Relations.

FIELDING, WALDO L., M.D., and BENJAMIN, LOIS. *The Childbirth Challenge*. New York: Viking Press, 1962.

FINLEY, MOSES. *The World of Odysseus*. New York: Viking Press, 1954.

FISHBEIN, MORRIS, M.D., and KENNEDY, RUBY JO REEVES, PH.D., eds. *Modern Marriage and Family Living*. New York: Oxford Univ. Press, 1957.

FOOTE, NELSON. "Matching of Husband and Wife in Phases of Development," Third World Congress of Sociology, *Transactions*, IV. London: Internatl. Sociol. Assn., 1956.

FORD, CLELLAN S., and BEACH, FRANK A. *Patterns of Sexual Behavior*. New York: Harper & Brothers and Paul B. Hoeber, 1951.

"The Fortune Survey: Women in America," *Fortune*, Aug.-Sept., 1946.

FREEDMAN, MERVIN B. (1956). "The Passage Through College," in Sanford (1956).

FREEDMAN, MERVIN B. (1961). "Studies of College Alumni," in SANFORD, NEVITT, ed., *The American College*. New York: John Wiley and Sons, 1961.

FREEDMAN, R. (1959), *et al. Family Planning, Sterility, and Population Growth*. New York: McGraw-Hill Book Co., Inc., 1959.

FREUD (1927), SIGMUND. "Some Psychological Consequences of Anatomical Distinction between the Sexes," *Internatl. Jour. of Psycho-Analysis*, VIII (1927), 133-142.

FREUD (1933), SIGMUND. "The Psychology of Women," in *New Introductory Lectures on Psycho-Analysis*. New York: W. W. Norton & Co., 1933.

FRIEDAN, BETTY. "If One Generation Can Ever Tell Another," *Smith Alumnae Quarterly*, Winter, 1961.

GEBHARD, PAUL H., *et al. Pregnancy, Birth and Abortion*. New York: Harper & Brothers and Paul B. Hoeber, 1958. This is the third report by the Institute for Sex Research, founded by Alfred C. Kinsey.

GESELL (1946), ARNOLD L., *et al. The Child from Five to Ten*. New York: Harper & Brothers, 1946.

GESELL (1950), ARNOLD L., *et al. Infant and Child in the Culture of Today*. New York: Harper & Brothers, [1950].

GESELL (1956), ARNOLD L., *et al. Youth: the Years from Ten to Sixteen*. New York: Harper & Brothers, 1956.

GLASS, BENTLEY. *Genes and the Man*. New York: Columbia Univ. Press, 1943.

GLICK, PAUL C. *American Families*. New York: John Wiley and Sons, [1957]. A Bureau of the Census Monograph.

GLUECK, SHELDON and ELEANOR. "Working Mothers and Delinquency," *Mental Hygiene*, XLI (1957), 327-52.

GOODE, WILLIAM J. *After Divorce*. Glencoe, Ill.: The Free Press, 1956.

GORDON, RICHARD E., M.D., *et al. The Split-Level Trap*. New York: Bernard Geis Associates, 1960.

GORER, GEOFFREY. *The American People.* New York: W. W. Norton & Co., 1948.

GROSS, IRMA H., ed. *Potentialities of Women in the Middle Years.* East Lansing: Michigan State Univ. Press, 1956.

GURIN, GERALD, *et al. Americans View Their Mental Health.* New York: Basic Books, Inc., 1960.

GUTTMACHER, ALAN F. *Pregnancy and Birth.* New York: New American Library, 1956.

HACKER, HELEN. "Women as a Minority Group," *Social Forces,* XXX (1951-52), 60-69.

HAMILL, KATHARINE. "Women as Bosses," *Fortune,* June, 1956.

HAMILTON, G. V., and MACGOWAN, KENNETH. *What is Wrong With Marriage?* New York: A. and C. Boni, 1929.

HARTLEY (1959), RUTH E. "Sex-Role Pressures and the Socialization of the Male Child," *Psych. Reports,* V (1959), 457-68.

HARTLEY (1959a), RUTH E. "Some Implications of Current Changes in Sex-Role Patterns," *Merrill-Palmer Quarterly,* VI (1959-60), 153-64.

HARTLEY (1960), RUTH E. "Children's Concepts of Male and Female Roles," *Merrill-Palmer Quarterly,* VI (1959-60), 83-91.

HERMAN, ROBERT. "The Going-Steady Complex: A Re-examination," *Marriage and Family Living,* XVII (1955), 36-40.

HILL, REUBEN. "Plans for Strengthening Family Life," in Becker (q.v.).

HILLIARD (1957), MARION, M.D. *A Woman Doctor Looks at Love and Life,* Garden City, N.Y.: Doubleday & Co., 1957.

HILLIARD (1960), MARION. "Too Tired to Love?" *Reader's Digest,* April, 1960.

HOLLIS, FLORENCE. *Women in Marital Conflict.* New York: Family Service Assn. of Amer., 1949.

HUNT (1955), MORTON M. "Why They Fight About Money," *Cosmopolitan,* December, 1955.

HUNT (1959), MORTON M. *The Natural History of Love.* New York: Alfred A. Knopf, 1959.

HUNT (1959a), MORTON M. "How Husbands Really Feel About Pregnancy," *Redbook,* Nov., 1959.

HUNT (1960), MORTON M. "And Now—It's the Feminentity," *The New York Times Magazine,* July 31, 1960.

HUNT (1961), MORTON M. "How 10,000 Young Mothers Feel About Their Marriages, Their Children, Themselves," *Redbook,* Sept., 1961.

HUXLEY, JULIAN. *New Bottles for New Wine.* New York: Harper & Brothers, 1957.

JACOBSON, PAUL H. *American Marriage and Divorce.* New York: Rinehart & Co., 1959.

JAHODA, MARIE, and HAVEL, JOAN. "Psychological Problems of Women in Different Social Roles," *The Educational Record,* Oct., 1955.

JOHNSON, NORA. "Sex and the College Girl," *The Atlantic Monthly,* Nov., 1959.

KARDINER (1939), ABRAM. *The Individual and His Society.* New York: Columbia Univ. Press, 1939.

KARDINER (1954), ABRAM. *Sex and Morality.* New York: Bobbs-Merrill Co., 1954.

KELLY, AMY. *Eleanor of Aquitaine and the Four Kings.* Cambridge: Harvard Univ. Press, 1950.

KELSO, RUTH. *Doctrine for the Lady of the Renaissance.* Urbana: Univ. of Illinois Press, 1956.

KINSEY (1948), ALFRED C., *et al. Sexual Behavior in the Human Male.* Phila.: W. B. Saunders Co., 1948.

KINSEY (1953), ALFRED C., *et al. Sexual Behavior in the Human Female.* Phila.: W. B. Saunders Co., 1953.

KIRKPATRICK, CLIFFORD. *The Family as Process and Institution.* New York: The Ronald Press, 1955.

KLEIN, VIOLA. *The Feminine Character.* London: Kegan Paul, Trench, Trubner & Co., 1946.

KLUCKHOHN (1951), FLORENCE R. "America's Women," in MOWRER, O. H., ed. *Psychological Patterns.* Chicago: The Delphian Society, 1951.

KLUCKHOHN (1953), FLORENCE R. "The American Woman's Role." Unpub. paper presented at 1953 conference of the CEW (q.v.).

KLUCKHOHN (1953a), FLORENCE R. "American Women and American Values," in BRYSON, L., ed., *Facing the Future's Risks.* New York: Harper & Brothers, 1953.

KOLB, WILLIAM L. "Sociologically Established Family Norms and Democratic Values," *Social Forces,* XXVI (1947-48), 451-56.

KOMAROVSKY, MIRRA. *Women in the Modern World.* Boston: Little, Brown and Co., 1953.

KOOS, EARL LOMON. *Families in Trouble.* New York: Columbia Univ. Press, 1946.

LA BARRE, WESTON. *The Human Animal.* Chicago: Univ. of Chicago Press, 1954.

LANDIS, CARNEY (1940). *Sex in Development.* New York: Paul B. Hoeber, Inc., 1940.

LANDIS, JUDSON T. (1953), and LANDIS, MARY G. *Building a Successful Marriage.* New York: Prentice-Hall, Inc., 1953.

LANVAL, MARC. *An Inquiry into the Intimate Lives of Women.* New York: Cadillac Pub. Co., 1950.

LEOPOLD, ALICE K. "The Legal Status of Women," in *The Book of the States, 1960-61,* publ. by The Council of State Governments.

LERNER, MAX. *America as a Civilization.* New York: Simon and Schuster, 1957.

LINDBERGH, ANNE MORROW. *Gift from the Sea.* New York: New American Library, 1957.

LINDNER, ROBERT. "Adultery—Kinds and Consequences," in ELLIS, ALBERT, ed., *Sex Life of the American Woman and the Kinsey Report.* New York: Greenberg, 1954.

LOCKE, HARVEY J. *Predicting Adjustment in Marriage.* New York: Henry Holt & Co., 1951.

LOWRIE, SAMUEL HARMAN. "Dating Theories and Student Responses," *Amer. Sociol. Rev.,* XVI (1951), 334-40.

LUNDBERG, FERDINAND, and FARNHAM, MARYNIA F., M.D. *Modern Woman: The Lost Sex.* New York: The Universal Library, Grosset & Dunlap, n.d. [orig. published by Harper & Brothers, 1947].

MACCOBY, ELEABOR E. "Effects upon Children of Their Mothers' Outside Employment," in N. Bell (1960) (q.v.).

MADIGAN, FRANCIS C. "Are Sex Mortality Differentials Biologically Caused?" *The Milbank Memorial Fund Quarterly,* XXXV (April, 1957).

MAGOUN, F. ALEXANDER. *Love and Marriage.* New York: Harper & Brothers, 1948.

MANNIN, ETHEL. *Women and the Revolution.* London: Secker & Warburg, 1938.

MATTHEWS, ESTHER. "The Marriage-Career Conflict in the Career Development of Girls and Young Women." Unpub. Ph.D. dissertation, Graduate School of Education, Harvard Univ., 1960.

MAULDE LA CLAVIÈRE, M. A. R. DE. *The Women of the Renaissance*. New York: G. P. Putnam's Sons, 1900.

MCNEMAR, QUINN. *The Revision of the Stanford-Binet Scale*. Boston: Houghton Mifflin Company, 1942.

MEAD (1937), MARGARET, ed. *Cooperation and Competition among Primitive Peoples*. New York: McGraw-Hill Book Co., Inc., 1937.

MEAD (1940), MARGARET. "The Mountain Arapesh: II. *"Anthropological Papers of the Amer. Museum of Nat. Hist.*, XXXVII (1940).

MEAD (1950), MARGARET. *Sex and Temperament in Three Primitive Societies*. New York: New American Library, 1950.

MEAD (1955), MARGARET. *Male and Female*. New York: New American Library, 1955.

MENNINGER (1938), KARL. *Man Against Himself*. New York: Harcourt, Brace and Company, 1938.

MENNINGER (1942), KARL. *Love Against Hate*. New York: Harcourt, Brace and Company, 1942.

MERTON, ROBERT K., and KITT, ALICE S. "Contributions to the Theory of Reference Group Behavior," in MERTON and LAZARSFELD, PAUL, eds., *Continuities in Social Research: Studies in the Scope and Method of "The American Soldier."* Glencoe, Ill: The Free Press, 1950.

MILTON, G. ALEXANDER. "Five Studies of the Relation Between Sex-Role Identification and Achievement in Problem-Solving." Tech. Rept. 3, Contract Nonr 609 (20), Office of Naval Research. New Haven: Yale University, Dec., 1958.

MONTAGU (1953), M. F. ASHLEY. *The Natural Superiority of Women*. New York: The Macmillan Company, 1953.

MONTAGU (1953a), M. F. ASHLEY, ed. *The Meaning of Love*. New York: Julian Press, Inc., 1953.

MONTAGU (1955), M. F. ASHLEY. *The Direction of Human Development*. New York: Harper & Brothers, 1955.

MORGAN, CLIFFORD T., *et al. Introduction to Psychology*. New York: McGraw-Hill Book Co., Inc., 1956.

MOTZ, ANNABELLE B. "Conceptions of Marital Roles by Status Groups," *Marriage and Family Living*, XII (1950), p. 136 f.

MOWRER, HARRIET. "Getting Along in Marriage," in Becker (q.v.).

MOWRER, HARRIET. "Discords in Marriage," in Becker (q.v.).

MUDD (1957), EMILY, and KRICH, ARON, eds. *Man and Wife*. New York: W. W. Norton & Co., 1957.

MUDD (1958), EMILY, *et al.*, eds. *Marriage Counseling: A Casebook*. New York: Association Press, 1958.

MYRDAL, ALVA, and KLEIN, VIOLA. *Women's Two Roles: Home and Work*. London: Routledge & Kegan Paul, 1956.

National Manpower Council (1957). *Womanpower*. New York: Columbia Univ. Press, 1957.

National Manpower Council (1958). *Work in the Lives of Married Women*. New York: Columbia Univ. Press, 1958.

NEIMAN, LIONEL J. "The Influence of Peer Groups upon Attitudes toward the Feminine Role," *Social Problems*, II (1954-55), 104-111.

NEWTON, NILES. *Maternal Emotions*. New York: Harper & Brothers and Paul B. Hoeber, 1955.

NIMKOFF, MEYER F. *Marriage and the Family*. Boston: Houghton Mifflin Co., 1947.

NYSWANDER, MARIE; *see* ROBINSON, MARIE N.

OGBURN, WILLIAM F., and NIMKOFF, MEYER F. *Technology and the Changing Family*. Boston: Houghton Mifflin Co., 1955.

PAINTER, SIDNEY. *French Chivalry*. Baltimore: Johns Hopkins Press, 1940.

PARSONS, TALCOTT. *Essays in Sociological Theory, Pure and Applied*. Glencoe, Ill.: The Free Press, 1949.

POLLAK, OTTO. *The Criminality of Women*. Phila.: Univ. of Pennsylvania Press, 1950.

RAINWATER (1959), LEE, *et al. Workingman's Wife*. New York: Oceana Publications, 1959.

RAINWATER (1960), LEE. *And the Poor Get Children*. Chicago: Quadrangle Books, 1960.

REIK, THEODOR. *Of Love and Lust*. New York: Grove Press, Inc., 1959.

RICHARDS, AUDREY J. *Bemba Marriage and Present Economic Conditions*. The Rhodes-Livingstone Papers, No. 4; The Rhodes-Livingstone Institute: Livingstone, N. Rhodesia, 1940.

REISMAN (1956), DAVID. "Some Continuities and Discontinuities in the Education of Women." Reprint of June, 1956, lecture at Bennington College; Bennington College, Vt.: n.d.

REISMAN (1958), DAVID. "Permissiveness and Sex Roles," *Human Development Bulletin, 1958*, Committee on Human Development, Univ. of Chicago.

ROBINSON, MARIE N[YSWANDER], M.D. *The Power of Sexual Surrender*. Garden City, N. Y.: Doubleday & Company, 1959.

ROFF, CATHERINE. "The Self-Concept in Adolescent Girls," Unpub. Ph.D. dissertation, Boston University Graduate School, 1959.

ROSE (1951), ARNOLD M. "The Adequacy of Women's Expectations for Adult Roles," *Social Forces*, XXX (1951-52), 69-77.

ROSE (1955), ARNOLD M. "Factors Associated with the Life Satisfaction of Middle-Class, Middle-Aged Persons," *Marriage and Family Living*, XVII (1955), 15-19.

SANFORD (1956), NEVITT, ed. "Personality Development during the College Years": entire issue of *Jour. of Social Forces*, XII, (1956), No. 4. A series of reports on the Vassar studies.

SANFORD (1957), NEVITT. "The Uncertain Senior," *Jour. of the Natl. Assn. of Women Deans and Counselors*, XXI (Oct., 1957).

SANFORD (1958), NEVITT. "Changing Sex Roles, Socialization, and Education," *Human Development Bulletin, 1958*. Committee on Human Development, Univ. of Chicago.

SCHEINFELD (1944), AMRAM. *Women and Men*. New York: Harcourt, Brace & Company, 1944.

SCHEINFELD (1958), AMRAM. "The Mortality of Men and Women," *Scientific American*, Feb., 1958.

SCOFIELD, NANETTE E. "Some Changing Roles of Women in Suburbia," *Transactions of the N.Y. Acad. of Science*, Series II, Vol. XXII (April, 1960), 450-57.

SIRJAMAKI, JOHN. *The American Family in the Twentieth Century*. Cambridge: Harvard Univ. Press, 1953.

SMITH, W. M., JR. "Rating and Dating: A Re-Study," *Marriage and Family Living*, XIV (1952), 312-17.

SMUTS, ROBERT W. *Women and Work in America*. New York: Columbia Univ. Press, 1959.

SPIRO (1956), MELFORD E. *Kibbutz: Venture in Utopia*. Cambridge: Harvard Univ. Press, 1956.

SPIRO (1958), MELFORD E. *Children of the Kibbutz.* Cambridge: Harvard Univ. Press, 1958.

SPOCK, BENJAMIN. *The Commonsense Book of Baby and Child Care.* New York: Pocket Books, 1957.

SPRENGER, JACOB, and KRAMER, HENRY. *Malleus Maleficarum.* [London]: John Rodker, 1928.

STEKEL, WILHELM. *Frigidity in Women.* New York: Boni & Liveright, 1926.

STOLZ, LOIS MEEK. "Effects of Maternal Employment on Children: Evidence from Research," *Child Development*, XXXI (1960), 749-82.

STONE (1952), ABRAHAM, and STONE, HANNAH. *A Modern Marriage Manual.* New York: Simon and Schuster, 1952.

STONE (1953), ABRAHAM, and LEVINE, LENA. "Dynamics of the Marital Relationship," *Mental Hygiene*, Oct., 1953.

STONE (1954), ABRAHAM. "The Case Against Marital Infidelity," *Reader's Digest*, May, 1954.

STRECKER (1946), EDWARD A. *Their Mothers' Sons.* Phila.: J. B. Lippincott Co., 1946.

STRECKER (1956), EDWARD A., and LATHBURY, VINCENT T. *Their Mothers' Daughters*, Phila.: J. B. Lippincott Co., 1956.

SUMNER, WILLIAM GRAHAM, and KELLER, A. G. *The Science of Society.* New Haven: Yale Univ. Press, 1927.

TERMAN (1936), LEWIS M., and MILES, CATHERINE C. *Sex and Personality: Studies in Masculinity and Femininity.* New York: McGraw-Hill Book Co., Inc., 1936.

TERMAN (1938), LEWIS M., *et al. Psychological Factors in Marital Happiness.* New York: McGraw-Hill Book Co., Inc., 1938.

TERMAN (1951), LEWIS M. "Correlates of Orgasm Adequacy in a Group of 556 Wives," *Jour. of Psychol.* XXXII (1951), 115-72.

THOMPSON, CLARA. "Role of Women in This Culture," *Psychiatry*, IV (1941), 1-8.

United States Department of Commerce, Bureau of the Census; *see* Bureau of the Census.

United States Department of Health, Education and Welfare, Children's Bureau; *see* Children's Bureau.

United States Department of Labor, Women's Bureau; *see* Women's Bureau.

USEEM (1960), RUTH HILL. "Changing Cultural Concepts in Women's Lives," *Jour. Natl. Assn. of Women Deans and Counselors*, Oct., 1960.

USEEM (1961), RUTH HILL. "Who Needs Women?" *Jour. Natl. Assn. of Women Deans and Counselors*, June, 1961.

VATSYAYANA. *Kama-Sutra of Vatsyayana.* Calcutta: Medical Book Company, 1943.

VON MERING, FAYE H. "Professional and Non-Professional Women as Mothers," *Jour. Social Psychol.*, XLII (1955), 21-34.

WADDINGTON, C. H. *Introduction to Modern Genetics.* London: G. Allen & Unwin, 1950.

WALLER (1937), WILLARD. "The Rating and Dating Complex," *Amer. Sociol. Rev.*, II (1937), 727-34.

WALLER (1938), WILLARD. *The Family: A Dynamic Interpretation.* New York: The Dryden Press, 1938.

WESTERMARCK (1908), EDWARD. *The Origin and Development of the Moral Ideas.* London: Macmillan & Co., 1908.

WESTERMARCK (1939), EDWARD. *Christianity and Morals.* London: Paul, Trench, Trubner, 1939.

WHITE, LYNN. *Educating Our Daughters*. New York: Harper & Brothers, 1950.

WHYTE, WILLIAM F. (1949). "The Social Structure of the Restaurant," *Amer. Jour. Sociol.*, LIV (1949), 302-8.

WHYTE, WILLIAM H., JR. (1951). "The Wives of Management," *Fortune*, Oct., 1951.

WHYTE, WILLIAM H., JR. (1951a). "The Corporation and the Wife," *Fortune*, Nov., 1951.

WILLIAMS, ROBIN M., JR. "Progress Report: Social and Cultural Factors Affecting Role-Conflict and Adjustment among American Women: A Pilot Investigation." Mimeo. paper, dated Jan., 1956, at Cornell University, from the author's files.

WILSON, PAULINE PARK. *College Women Who Express Futility*. New York: Bur. of Publications, Teachers College, Columbia Univ., 1950.

WINCH (1952), ROBERT F. *The Modern Family*. New York: Henry Holt & Co., 1952.

WINCH (1958), ROBERT F. *Mate-Selection*. New York: Harper & Brothers, 1958.

WINTER, ELMER. *A Woman's Guide to Earning a Good Living*. New York: Simon and Schuster, 1961.

WINTHROP, JOHN. *Winthrop's Journal "History of New England" 1630-1649*, ed. by J. K. Hosmer. New York: Charles Scribner's Sons, 1908.

WOLFLE, DAEL. *America's Resources of Specialized Talent*. New York: Harper & Brothers, 1954.

Women's Bureau. Bulletin 157: *The Legal Status of Women in the U.S.A.* (1956 revision).

———. Bulletin 218: *Women's Occupations Through Seven Decades* (1951).

———. Bulletin 248: *"Older" Women as Office Workers* (1953).

———. Bulletin 250: *State Hour Laws for Women* (1953).

———. Bulletin 253: *Changes in Women's Occupations, 1940-1950* (1954).

———. Bulletin 268: *First Jobs of College Women* (1959).

———. Bulletin 270: *Careers for Women in the Physical Sciences* (1959).

———. Bulletin 273: *Part-Time Employment for Women* (1961).

———. Bulletin 274: *Training Opportunities for Women and Girls* (1960).

———. Bulletin 275: *1960 Handbook on Women Workers* (1960).

———. Bulletin 276: *Today's Woman in Tomorrow's World* (1960).

———. Bulletin 279: *Careers for Women as Life Underwriters* (1961).

———. Leaflet 31: "From College to Work" (1959).

———. Leaflet DC-62-271: "Background Facts on Women Workers" (Dec., 1961).

WYLIE, PHILIP. *Generation of Vipers*. New York: Pocket Books, Inc., 1960.

ZAPOLEON, MARGUERITE. *Occupational Planning for Women*. New York: Harper & Brothers, 1961.

Diseases, male-female susceptibility, 30-31

Divinity students, 41

Divorce, 6, 125, 129; adultery and, 129; average time of, 220; early marriage and, 289; education and, 106; frigidity and, 113, 113 n; greater freedom for, 139; lower classes, 287; marriage-age relationship, 80 n; in middle age, 219; rate in America, 139-40; remarriage: rate, 205-6, reason for, 206, 206n; sexual permissiveness and, 132; women's refusals of mate, 105

Divorcees: companionship and, 213; promiscuity, 206, 206 n; recreations, 247; sex enjoyment, 115 n

Doctors, women, 6-7, 25, 149; in Russia, 6

Domesticity: birth rate and, 166; emphasis on, 150; frustrations of, 246, 292; part-time, 153; reason for revival, 150; woman's historical preoccupation with, 150 (*see also* Housekeeping)

Double standard, 71; absence of, 121

Douglas College, 268

Duke University, 184

Dunbar, Flanders, 244

Dunn, Alan, 34

Ecclesiastes, 11

Educated classes: divorce, 287; infidelity in, 97

Education: change in, 289-90; college, for women, 148-49, 153, 267; contraception and, 112 n; domesticity and, 246; female adultery, 118-19; female quotas, 263; graduate, 291; housekeeping and, 146; intercourse and, 111-12; M-F scale in, 41-42; motherhood and, 185; outside interests, 223; personal cost of, 61 (*see* College girl); postgraduate, for split career, 268; sex understanding and, 105-6

Ego gratification, need for, 138

Egyptians, goddesses, 20

Ehrmann, Winston, 78, 81

Elizabeth I, Queen, 228

Ellis, Havelock, 111, 112, 139

Emancipation: domesticity and, 246;

woman's partial withdrawal from, 150

Employment (*see* Careerists *and* Working wives)

Engagement, 85-86; college girls, 85; intercourse and, 88; and marital adjustment, 85

England: Age of Reason, 19-20; college education for women, 149; life expectancy, infants, 31 n; Merry Monarch, 118; Restoration, 39; Victorian, 70

Envy, 234

Epicurus, 18

Esteem, 98

Eternal feminine, the, 11-13

Eugene Gilbert Co., 155

Europe: the affair, 127-28; marriage, 128; mistress-lover situation, 91; romantic love and marriage, 93 n; women, 149

Eve, 17

Executives, women, 259-60

Exhibitionism, 52

Existentialists, 293

Fadiman, Clifton, 160

Family: history of, 157-58; larger, advocates of, 168; relationships, 63-64

Family Service Association of America, 240

Farnham, Marynia, 7, 105, 163

Fatigue, motherhood and, 179-80

Faulkner, William, 232

"Favors," granting of, 81 n, 82 n

Female: ailments, emotions and, 243-44; built-in conflict in character, 51; fertility, 47; intellectualism (*see under* Intellectualism); -male differences, 45-46; marriage, reasons for, 97; masochism, 43-44, 108; mentality, 34-38; passion ranges, 103 n; passivity, 28-29, 77; sexual aggressiveness, 107 ff.

Female nature, 21; economy and, 15-16; multi-concepts of, 21; "natural deficiency," 16-20

Feminine character, myth of, 24-46

Femininity: backward search for, 146-150; definition, changing, 258-59; determinants, 42-43; Freud on, 27;

ABOUT THE AUTHOR

Morton Hunt was born in Philadelphia in 1920. He graduated from Temple University in 1941 with honors, and won a graduate fellowship to the University of Pennsylvania. Work for his Master's degree was interrupted by four years of wartime duty, of which two were spent as a combat pilot in the U.S. Air Force.

Returning to civilian life, Mr. Hunt joined the staff of *Look* magazine; then, in 1947, he moved to *Science Illustrated* as associate editor and feature writer. He has been a free-lance writer since 1949, and his work has appeared in such magazines as *The Saturday Evening Post, The Reader's Digest, Fortune, Harper's Magazine*. He also regularly contributes "Profiles" to *The New Yorker*. His range of subject matter has been extraordinarily wide, but he writes most often on the behavioral sciences, particularly psychology and sociology.

Mr. Hunt is married to Lois Hunt, the opera, television, and stage singer. The Hunts have a seven-year-old son, Jeffrey, and live in New York City.